Agent Sourcebook

ALPER CAGLAYAN

COLIN HARRISON

WILEY COMPUTER PUBLISHING

John Wiley & Sons, Inc.
New York • Chichester • Weinheim • Brisbane • Singapore • Toronto

Executive Publisher: Katherine Schowalter
Editor: Robert M. Elliott
Managing Editor: Brian Snapp
Text Design & Composition: V & M Graphics, Inc.

This text is printed on acid-free paper.

Library of Congress Cataloging-in-Publication Data:

Caglayan, Alper K.
    Agent sourcebook/Colin G. Harrison, Alper K. Caglayan.
       p. cm.
    Includes index.
    ISBN: 0-471-15327-3 (paper : alk. paper)
    1. Industrial management—Data processing. 2. Artificial
intelligence. 3. Intelligent agents (Computer software)
I. Caglayan, A. II. Title.
HD30.2.H375 1997
658'.00285'63—dc21
                                                        97-1971
                                                        CIP

Printed in the United States of America
10 9 8 7 6 5 4 3 2 1

*To my parents Asir and Leman Caglayan—*AKC

*To the memory of my parents Colin and Hilda Harrison—*CGH

Contents

Acknowledgments

I have benefited from the support of several people in writing this book. First, I thank my wife Margaret and my children Devin and Jennifer for enduring my virtual presence for the last six months.

I am indebted to the members of the Open Sesame team who have spent days and nights over the last five years to bring learning agents into the computing mainstream. In particular, many thanks to Jim Mazzu, Scott Allen, Mike Jonas, Ed Riley, Magnus Snorrason, Dennis Wilkinson, Ed Voas, Jennifer Jacoby, Carl Dashfield, Robin Jones, Krishna Kumar, Eugenio Arroyo, and Paulette Buchheim.

I would like to thank all commercial agent technology vendors who promptly answered my questions. For those few that did not, I enthusiastically recommend the adoption of agent products to automate information dissemination from their companies. I would like to thank the members of the agent research community, and, in particular, those in human-computer interaction whose work sometimes goes unnoticed but often fuels the thought process in the agent features of commercial products.

I am especially thankful to Bob Elliott of John Wiley for making us keep our eyes on the intended audience, and Brian Calandra for helping us put everything together. We also acknowledge Pete Janca's help in getting us started in this project. I would like to thank Jennifer Jacoby, Russell Rothstein, Jim Mazzu, and Magnus Snorrason for their feedback on the various chapters. Finally, special thanks to Johanna Brown for her meticulous work in the creation of the manuscript.

—AKC

I thank the IBM agent community for arguments, debates, and ideas, many of which have ended up in this book. Special thanks go to Hoi Chen, Benjamin Grosof, and David Levine for actually making them work, and to Don Gilbert for taking them to market. Thanks also to David Chess for his contribution to the section on security, and to Peter Janca for getting us going.

—CGH

Introduction to the Book

Intelligent agents have been the subject of a great deal of speculation and publicity in recent years. This has left the public in general, and business information service managers in particular, with an impression that agent technology is largely hype requiring still further years of investment before it will be usable or useful. We believe that agent technology can be used today, is in fact being used profitably today, and will indeed become more powerful and useful in coming years. The purpose of this book is to illustrate how agent-based applications are able to help businesses today. We give concrete examples drawn from real business experiences. These examples demonstrate improvements in business efficiency, lowered costs, and/or reduced process time. We also provide guidelines for readers on the most effective approaches to employing agent technology today.

The concept of agents is an outgrowth of the past 40 years' research on artificial intelligence and robotics. The idea of a software entity that could perform tasks on behalf of a user was well established by the mid 1970s. This background brings in concepts of reasoning, knowledge representation, and learning. The practical applications of agents have more pragmatic origins. Software developers have for years created tools to automate specific processes; practical agents take a general approach and provide tools for integration across multiple applications and databases and to reach out across networks. Agents have attracted attention in recent years for several reasons:

- As a means of putting intelligence into user interfaces to enable unskilled users to get more out of computer applications

- As a means of personalizing applications and services to meet the user's preferences, goals, and desires

- As a means of managing the retrieval, dissemination, and filtering of the vast amounts of information becoming available on enterprise networks, value-added network, and especially the Internet

- As a means of enabling electronic commerce in various forms

- As a means of managing flexible manufacturing cells (robotics)

In all these cases there is a belief that we ought to be able to harness the logical power of the computer to provide intellectual leverage to end-users. There are today about 40 companies in the business of selling agent technology and applications. This number is growing rapidly as university graduates who have performed research in the area are hired into existing corporations or form their own startup companies. For example:

- PC software: Lotus Notes V4 has agents; Microsoft applications have Wizards

- Messaging software: BeyondMail, Lotus cc:Mail, Digital, IBM

- Information services: SandPoint Hoover, MCI

- Information delivery: PointCast Network, BackWeb Technologies, Intermind Communicator

- Information search: Yahoo!, Excite, Infoseek

- Information retrieval: Verity SEARCH 97, PLS PLWeb

- Personalization software: Broadvision One-to-One, Imperative ManageIt!

- Learning agents: Digital Each-to-Each, Firefly Network, Open Sesame

- Process automation: Edify Electronic Workforce, DSS Agent

- Mobile agents: General Magic Tabriz, FTP Software CyberAgent

It seems plausible that in five years' time, agent-based applications and services will be relatively common, though not ubiquitous. The market research firm Ovum predicts a $4 billion software agent market in the year 2000 with widespread applications of agent technology appearing in the computing, telecommunications, consumer, entertainment, and military market segments (Guilfoyle and Warner, 1994). Similarly, a BIS Strategic Decisions report on pragmatic applications of information agents predicts the significant use of agent-enabled features in messaging, collaboration, programming, information retrieval, user interface, and process control software by the year 2000 based on the results of a Delphi study with participation from 20 leading agent technology vendors (Janca, 1995). The coverage of intelligent agents in such industry trade publications as *Information Week* and *Byte* magazines has risen significantly. We feel it is therefore appropriate to develop a book today that points the way, not to further research into agent technology (though there is certainly room for that as well), but to the current and near-future application areas of the technology.

How the Book Is Organized

The purpose of this book is to illustrate how agent-enabled applications are able to help businesses today. The book has three major sections: (1) How intelligent agents are helping businesses today, (2) How intelligent agents work, and (3) How to introduce intelligent agents into an enterprise.

After a general overview of the subject in Chapter 1, we begin in Chapters 2 through 4 to give examples of real intelligent agents that are in commercial use today, with special focus on the benefits they bring. Chapter 2 describes examples of desktop agents, and how they aid end-users. Chapter 3 describes the rapidly growing field of Internet agents, and how they enable enterprise to benefit from the wealth of information available on the Internet, without the burden of having to manually search through mountains of low-grade data. This chapter also describes early work in applying agents to electronic commerce on the Internet. Chapter 4 describes how many of the same principles can be applied to improving productivity within an enterprise on the company's intranet. All of these examples focus heavily on concrete examples drawn from real business experiences. These examples will demonstrate improvements in business efficiency, lowered costs, and/or reduced process time. We will provide guidelines for readers on the most effective approaches to employing agent technology today.

In the scientific and popular literature one finds many extended discussions of what exactly constitutes an intelligent agent. In this book we take a very pragmatic view that the field of intelligent agent applications consists of a particular set of software technologies to enrich applications, just as graphical user interfaces have done. In Section II, Chapters 5 through 9 provide practical descriptions of how agents work. Chapter 5 gives an overview of the software technologies involved in intelligent agent-based applications, and Chapters 6 through 9 go into more detail on these technologies. Chapter 6 deals with the inferencing and learning techniques that provide the machinery on which the "intelligence" of the agent depends. Chapter 7 discusses the forms of data which are processed by the machinery in order to create this "intelligence." Chapter 8 discusses the techniques by which intelligent agents can access data and applications within the enterprise information system, and so as act as "agents" of the enterprise. In Chapter 9 we examine the security implications of intelligent agent-based applications.

In the first two sections of the book, we hope to demonstrate both the practical utility of intelligent agents and practical technologies for their development. We hope that these sections will motivate you to explore the application of this new software technology in your enterprise. In Section III, Chapters 10 through 12 offer guidance on the introduction of intelligent agent-based applications into the enterprise. Chapter 10 shows how the basic components of intelligent agents— content, machinery, access and security—can be put together to build an agent in the context of a desktop interface agent. In particular, this chapter emphasizes how agent machinery can be embedded into existing desktop and server applications. In Chapter 11, we present a business-oriented review of the steps involved in creating an agent-based enterprise in the context of an Internet agent for Web site personalization. This chapter considers how off-the-shelf agent tools can fit into the set of conventional tools used by software engineers. Chapter 12 summarizes the business benefits of agents and the process of incorporating agents into the enterprise, and ends with our predictions on how intelligent agents will change business processes. The Appendix provides an overview of commercial sources of agent software products.

Who Should Read This Book

This book would serve anyone with an interest in the business applications of intelligent agents, including corporate decision makers, information system managers, and application developers. The book serves decision makers by helping them understand the strategic motivations for adopting intelligent agent technology in the various business units within an organization. The book serves information systems managers by providing tactical information on how to deploy agents within an organization. Finally, the book shows application developers how to go about developing and deploying agent applications.

Software agents have a broad appeal across several industries. Key industries for deployment of agent applications include computing, telecommunications, manufacturing, retail distribution, travel, finance, insurance, entertainment, and military sectors. Internal corporate applications of agents will be important in areas with an existing IS infrastructure such as payroll administration, benefits management, personnel records, internal corporate communications, and support. Significant agent applications will be deployed in personalized marketing, product sales support, production scheduling, customer support production scheduling, inventory monitoring, and distribution fields in most industries. Electronic commerce will emerge after businesses and consumers vote their preferences in agent solutions in different domains.

How to Read This Book

We suggest two possible paths for reading the book. Business managers and decision makers may prefer a *broad* overview:

1. Read Chapter 1 for an introduction to intelligent agents and a classification of software agents from an end-user viewpoint.

2. Read Chapters 2, 3, and 4 to learn about commercial applications of software agents on the desktop, Internet, and intranet depending on your platform interest.

3. Read Section 1 of Chapter 11 to review the business steps involved in creating an agent-based application for the enterprise.

4. Read Chapter 12 to see whether you agree with our view of where software agents are headed.

For a more *technical* tour:

1. Read Chapter 5, which introduces understanding and evaluating a technical framework for different approaches to agent technology.

2. Read Chapter 6, 7, 8, and 9 depending on your interest in agent machinery (engines incorporated in agents for reasoning and learning), content (the data that agent machinery acts on), access (methods enabling an agent to interact with its environment) and security (special concerns related to agent-based computing).

3. Read Chapters 10 and 11 to get a feel for the nuts and bolts of agent applications, and to see how agent capabilities can be embedded in an application.

4. Consult the Appendix to find commercial tools for development.

Part

1

Intelligent Agents in Business

Intelligent
Agents

The notion of an intelligent agent that dutifully serves computer users
has fascinated us since the invention of the digital computer. The computer
Emerac in the Katharine Hepburn and Spencer Tracy 1957 movie, *Desk Set* is
an example of such an agent. In this movie, Spencer Tracy plays an efficiency
expert who is contracted to computerize the various business units of Federal
Broadcasting Agency with Emerac. One of his projects is to encode the knowledge of every textbook in the research department managed by Miss Bunny
Watson. To test the knowledge of Emerac, Miss Watson poses the following
question to Emerac:

> *Computer, what is the annual damage done by the spruce budworm to*
> *American forests?*

So how far have computers come in being able to answer the question that
Miss Watson posed to Emerac in 1957? Well, not close enough if we require
understanding the semantics of the question, as natural language understanding
has proven to be a tougher problem than anticipated in computer science. Close
enough, however, if we can point Miss Watson to a related URL, submitting

the keyword "spruce budworm forest" inquiry into one of the Internet search engines to get this Web address: http://www.odf.state.or.us/pubaff/log/0009.html.

Although our concept of an intelligent assistant has been refined over the years—from HAL in the Stanley Kubrick movie, *2001: A Space Odyssey,* in the late 1960s, to Phil in Apple Computer's video, *The Knowledge Navigator,* in the late 1980s—the kind of intelligent agents we can actually build has not kept up with our expectations.

Nonetheless, we are getting closer (although the current hype in software agents seems to imply that we are already there). In this book, we will describe what is achievable in the short term with software agent technology, and show you how agent technology can change your business for the better. We start with a definition of an agent. The *Webster's New World Dictionary* (Guralnik, 1970) definition is:

> *Agent:* A person or thing that acts or is capable of acting or is empowered to act, for another.

This general definition of an agent points out its two key attributes:

- An agent does things.
- An agent acts on behalf of someone or something.

Intelligent agents that reside on computers always incorporate these two central attributes. Currently, there is no widely accepted universal definition of a software agent. The following definition of an agent will suffice to discuss the business applications of agents:

> *Software agent:* A computing entity that performs user delegated tasks autonomously.

Our definition of an agent implies a personal assistant metaphor where the agent performs tasks on behalf of a user. Mail filtering agents, information retrieval agents, and desktop automation agents all fit this definition.

Attributes of Intelligent Agents

Our definition of software agent implies that the agent possesses the following minimal characteristics:

- *Delegation:* The agent performs a set of tasks on behalf of a user (or other agents) that are explicitly approved by the user.

- *Communication skills:* The agent needs to be able to interact with the user to receive task delegation instructions, and inform task status and completion through an agent-user interface or through an agent communication language.

- *Autonomy:* The agent operates without direct intervention (e.g., in the background) to the extent of the user's specified delegation. The autonomy attribute of an agent can range from being able to initiate a nightly backup to negotiating the best price of a product for the user.

- *Monitoring:* The agent needs to be able to monitor its environment in order to be able to perform tasks autonomously.

- *Actuation:* The agent needs to be able to affect its environment via an actuation mechanism for autonomous operation.

- *Intelligence:* The agent needs to be able to interpret the monitored events to make appropriate actuation decisions for autonomous operation.

In essence, the concept of an agent introduces an indirect management metaphor in a computerized environment (Alan, 1984) to supplement today's mainstream style of direct manipulation metaphor via graphical user interfaces. This functionality enables users to accomplish tasks in a collaborative manner with software agents without having to be physically present in front of their machines.

In addition to the basic attributes of agents discussed above, agents may have additional attributes such as mobility, security, personality, and others that will be discussed in later chapters.

The origins of agent technology are rooted in the computational intelligence, software engineering, and human interface domains. Computational intelligence for intelligent agents draws from the fields of intentional systems, production systems, reasoning theory, and neural networks. Software engineering for intelligent agents covers the areas of on-line monitoring, high-level event inference, remote actuation, image and speech processing, and distributed objects. Human-computer interaction for intelligent agents comes from the fields of cognitive engineering, user modeling, man-machine experiments, intelligent tutoring systems, and computer vision, as illustrated in Figure 1.1.

Figure 1.1   Fields influencing intelligent agents.

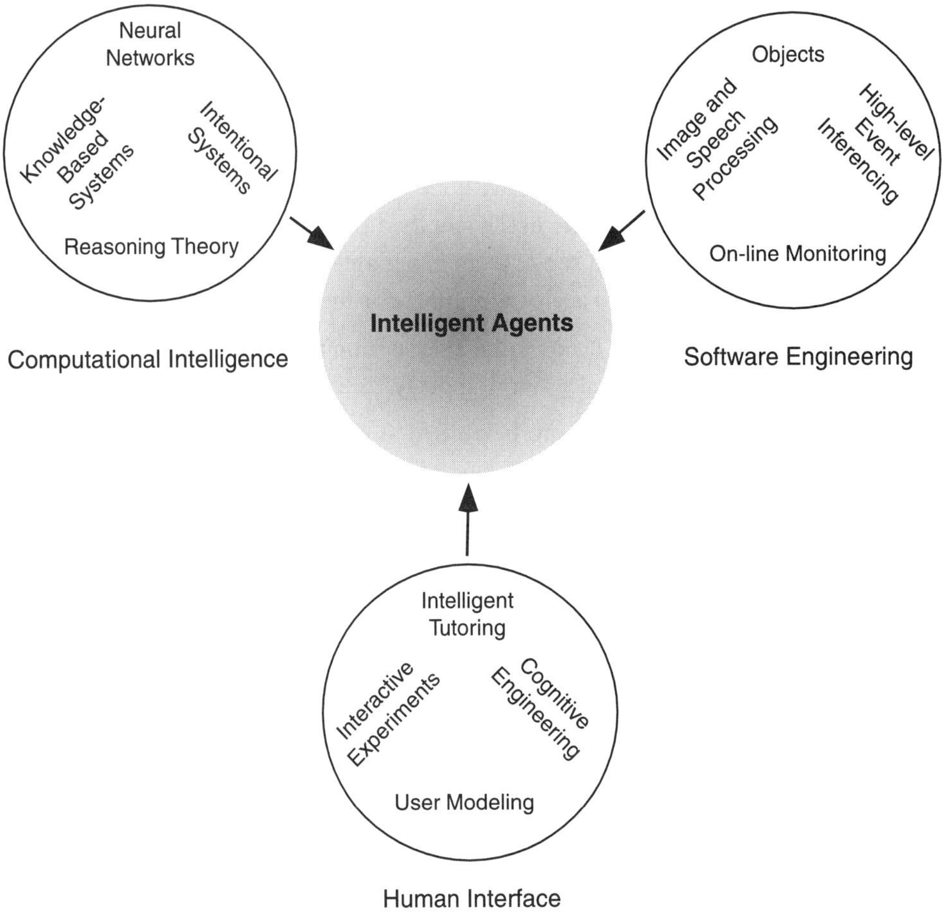

Given the plethora of types and features of agents, such as assistants, experts, coaches, wizards, softbots, robots, actors, and so on, it is helpful to sift through the terminology and layers of complexity by first thinking about agents in terms of a model from a user perspective, as shown in Figure 1.2. The model facilitates understanding the functional architecture of an agent, and the way in which one part of a system functions with other parts and with the user. It also emphasizes the task-oriented nature of agents (i.e., doing something on behalf of the user or other processes) and shows the support for distributed intelligence.

Figure 1.2   Agent model.

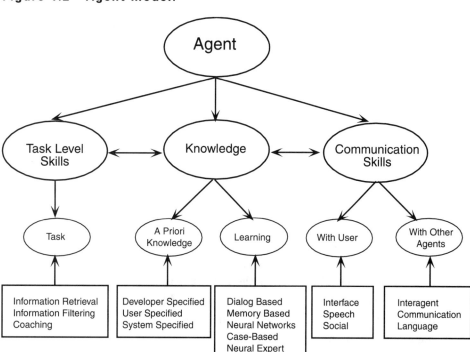

The model encourages us to look at the task level and communication level skills, in addition to the knowledge that both skill components access. Figure 1.2 shows the high-level attributes of an agent model. Abstracting the functionality out of an agent means that the environment and other low-level specifics are temporarily disregarded. This abstraction allows the user to focus on the agent's task as well as its need to communicate (both with the user and with other agents). The following subsections describe each of the components in more detail.

Task Level Skills

The task level is comprised of the skills that the agent possesses to accomplish its goal. Task level skills specify the functionality of an agent. Examples of tasks that the agent can perform include information retrieval, information filtering, database queries, and coaching. Task level skills require that an agent be able to perceive its environment through sensors, and act upon the environment to perform these tasks.

Knowledge

The knowledge portion of the agent concerns the rules the agent follows to complete its task. Some agents are autonomous, which means that they can act independently of humans. Both autonomous and semiautonomous agents rely on knowledge about the environment that has been built in by the designer. Some agents acquire their knowledge through learning. Knowledge can be acquired by employing any of the following techniques:

- *Developer specified:* Models for the application domain and the intended user serve as the basis for the inference mechanism in a knowledge base. Formal knowledge is organized in rules and/or frames. The disadvantage of knowledge-based learning agents is their lack of customizability after deployment.

- *User specified:* User-programmable rules for carrying out users-defined tasks are typical of rule-based systems. Some systems allow users to record their actions. BeyondMail is an example of a rule-based agent where the user can specify rules that can sort incoming mail into different folders. The main disadvantage of rule-based agents is their imposition of the agent's programming onto the user.

- *Derived from other knowledge sources:* Common agent languages enable knowledge acquisition among agent communities.

- *Learned by the system:* Agents that derive knowledge from the user and environment.

Communication Skills

The communication skills of the agent affect how it interacts with the user. In multiagent and distributed environments, the communication module also controls interaction with other agents. The user (human) interface serves as the communication channel to the user utilizing communication techniques ranging from an email message to a dialog box with a text to speech rendering of the agent's findings. Multimedia, including graphics, video, and audio (text to speech), can enhance the communication experience with the user as can anthropomorphized agent "personalities." In terms of interagent communication, a communication method is necessary for multiple agents to work together. Such communication typically involves a communication language and, in some cases, an intermediary application which serves as a request router. Telescript, SmallTalkAgents, Agent Tcl (Tool Command Language) (Gray, 1995), Knowledge Interface Format (KIF), and Agent Communication Language (ACL) (Genesereth, 1995) are languages which enable interagent communication.

End User Taxonomy of Agents

The marketing and technical terms under which agents appear in literature (Internet agent, interface agent, search agent, wizard, etc.) may be confusing because the names describe different components of agents, including the environment in which they live, and the agent's knowledge architecture. For clarity, it is helpful to define the agent environment, task and architecture.

Environment: Agents are designed to perform in a particular environment such as a desktop operating system, an application, and a computer network. Internet, operating system, and World Wide Web agents are examples of agents labeled according to their environment. Assistants, experts, and wizards for a given application are agents also labeled according to the environment in which they live.

Task: Task-specific agents are named according to what the agent does. The name usually describes the specific task level skills an agent possesses. Information filtering, information retrieval, and search agents are examples of task-specific agents.

Architecture: Agents are labeled according to the internal knowledge architecture. Learning agents that learn from the user, and neural agents that employ a neural network to acquire knowledge, are examples of agents named according to their internal knowledge architecture.

In this book, we discuss current agent applications using the following taxonomy, which divides agents into desktop, Internet, and intranet categories based on the environment and further subdivides each category of agents based on task attributes:

1. Desktop agents:
   - *Operating system agents:* interface agents that provide user assistance with the desktop operating system

- *Application agents:* interface agents that provide assistance to the user in a particular application

- *Application suite agents:* interface agents that help users in dealing with a suite of applications

2. Internet agents:

   - *Web search agents:* Internet agents that provide search services to users

   - *Web server agents:* Internet agents that reside at a specific Web site to provide agent services

   - *Information filtering agents:* Internet agents that filter out electronic information according to a user's specified preferences

   - *Information retrieval agents:* Internet agents that deliver a personalized package of information to the desktop according to user preferences

   - *Notification agents*: Internet agents that notify a user of events of a personal interest to a user

   - *Service agents:* Internet agents that provide specialized services to users

   - *Mobile agents:* agents that travel from one place to another to execute user-specified tasks

3. Intranet agents:

   - *Collaborative customization agents:* intranet agents that automate workflow processes in business units

   - *Process automation agents:* intranet agents that automate business workflow processes

   - *Database agents:* intranet agents that provide agent services for users of enterprise databases

   - *Resource brokering agents:* agents that perform resource allocation in client/server architectures

Intelligent Agent Applications—Today

We'll give an overview of the agent applications currently deployed by following the taxonomy in the previous section.

Desktop Agents—Operating Systems

On the MacOS, the learning agent Open Sesame! has been observing high-level user actions since 1993 to find repetitive user patterns and offer to automate them for the user. Figure 1.3 is a sample observation from the Open Sesame! agent.

On Windows 95, the System Agent runs in the background and executes programs such as disk defragmentation and error checking utilities at user-specified times. The user interacts with the System Agent through the task scheduler browser.

Desktop Agents—Applications

In Microsoft Windows desktop applications such as PowerPoint, the Answer Wizard supplies context-sensitive help in response to user inquiries. The interaction is through a tab interface where the user types a request and the Answer agent supplies the answer. For instance, if the user types:

```
How do I create a table in PowerPoint?
```

The Answer Wizard replies:

```
• For a table that includes complex formatting... use Word.

• For a table that includes complex calculations... use Excel.
```

Figure 1.3   Open Sesame! observation.

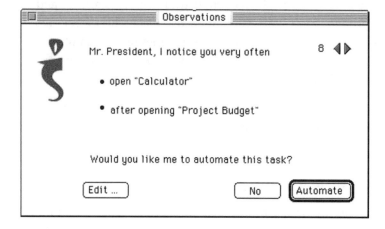

The mail application Eudora incorporates filters to sort and classify mail automatically. Incoming and outgoing mail messages can be filtered based on the header attributes (From, Subject, etc.) value to be labeled, prioritized, and transferred to a specific folder. Here is an example for transferring all mail received from the Software Agent mailing list to the Agents folder:

```
If «any Header» in Incoming Mail contains 'Software Agents Mailing',

then transfer to folder 'Agents'
```

Silk is an Internet client program that allows you to perform multiple searches for Internet information working in conjunction with a Web browser. Silk stores text strings describing the URL in order to support the user management of search results.

InfoTicker is a Java applet agent that runs in the background to retrieve data from user specified URLs on the Web. InfoTicker polls the Web sites of interest at regular intervals and summarizes the results to the user. InfoTicker is an example of the types of client agents implemented in Java certain to proliferate in the next couple of years.

Internet Agents—Information Filtering

There are currently dozens of personalized newspaper services on the Web. These newspapers provide automatic updates for news matching a user's personal interests. NewsPage Direct from Individual is one of the early examples providing such services. A user selects and prioritizes 10 topics to get personalized current story headlines.

NewsHound from San Jose Mercury News automatically searches articles and ads matching a user's profiles, and emails its findings. Users can adjust a Selectivity parameter to guide NewsHound to send more or fewer stories on a given topic. Similarly, users can increase the relevance of delivered information by specifying keywords to be required and excluded.

InfoSage from IBM provides personalized information for business professionals including real-time business news, competitive data, and company profiles. This service requires client software for editing the personal profile.

Internet Agents—Information Retrieval

Information retrieval agents are similar to information filtering agents in that they customize information based on personal interests of users but deliver localized content that can be viewed off-line without the user having to be on the Net. For instance, the FreeLoader service allows users to subscribe to Web sites that are automatically downloaded to client desktops. Similarly, PCN service from PointCast delivers customized information to the client desktop during idle times. The advantage of this approach is to provide current information to the client's cache. Both of these information retrieval agents require client software for interaction with the server that actually does the information gathering.

Internet Agents—Notifiers

There are several personal notification services that notify users of everything from URL-content changes to birthdays. One such example is URL-minder, which keeps track of the HTML content of a user-specified URL to apprise the user of changes in content via a free email service. Another such service is AdHound from AdOne, which searches classified ad databases for a user-specified item, and emails the relevant classified ads.

Internet Agents—Mobile

Telescript agents (used in the ATT PersonaLink service that suspended operation in 1996) are examples of mobile agents. Telescript agents encapsulate the user's instructions for specific tasks, and can go to places that act as hosts and allow the secure execution of agent programs to accomplish user-specified tasks like purchasing tickets.

Intranet Agents—Process Automation

Edify service agents are customizable interactive software agents for workflow automation. For instance, Edify offers service agents that can process service requests from customers by interacting with backoffice systems. Edify agents are in use in human resource and electronic banking applications.

Intranet Agents—Collaborative Customization

Topic agents from Verify support the automated indexing of corporate information to support search and retrieval of corporate information. Verity also offers groupware agents for Microsoft Exchange for managing intranet Web resources and sharing information that supports group goals and objectives. SandPoint Hoover provides personalized information search services for corporate users in a Lotus Notes environment.

Intranet Agents—Database

DSS Agent from MicroStrategy enables the deployment of OLAP applications that provide filtering and notification of enterprise database information. DSS Agent applications are in use to provide ad hoc analysis and exception reporting in large data warehouses.

Benefits of Agents

The user benefits of an agent lie in its task skills. Table 1.1 outlines the benefits of agents in broad functional categories.

Automation: The automation benefits of an agent are particularly applicable for automating:

- Repetitive behavior of a single user

- Similar behavior of a group of users

- Repetitive sequential behavior of a number of users in a workflow thread

Repetitive behavior can be either time based or event based. A time-based task is something that the user does at a particular time, like visiting a particular Web site every morning at nine o'clock. An event-based task is something that the user does

Table 1.1   Features, Advantages, and Benefits of Agent Technology

Feature	Advantage	Benefit
Automation	Perform repetitive tasks	Increased productivity
Customization	Customize information interaction	Reduced overload
Notification	Notify user of events of significance	Reduced workload
Learning	Learn user(s) behavior	Proactive assistance
Tutoring	Coach user in context	Reduced training
Messaging	Perform tasks remotely	Off-line work

in relation to another task. For example, opening your clock desk accessory before you log into an on-line database is an event-based task. The repetitive behavior of a single user is particularly suitable for agent-based automation when this repetitive behavior is dissimilar across the general user population. Why? This situation makes it very hard to come up with a design compromise that would suit the whole population. On servers, similar behavior of a group of users can benefit from agent automation. The personal and workgroup productivity benefits of agent automation can be significant.

Customization: An agent provides customization benefits by presenting information that matches a user's personal information and interaction style preferences (Figure 1.4). The customization benefits can be discussed by noting where the agent model fits into the traditional broadcast and publishing models. In the broadcast model, the service providers (TV, radio, cable, advertisers, direct mail) broadcast the same information to everyone. Users sample the information within the inherent time constraints to make choices. In such a model, an agent between a user and broadcasters can provide customization benefits by listening to the information broadcast on behalf of the user, finding relevant information matching the user's interests, and presenting the filtered information to the user. There are three basic architecture choices in the implementation of such a model. These agents can be implemented either at the broadcast site or at the user end or in the middle as a broker agent that serves multiple broadcasters and users.

In the publishing model, the publishers (newspapers, magazines, Web sites) make information available for users to discover. In such a model, an agent can provide customization benefits by searching information on behalf of the user, and providing the user with the relevant information matching the user's interests. The emergence

Figure 1.4   Customization benefits of agents.

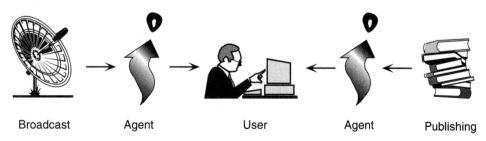

Broadcast   Agent   User   Agent   Publishing

of the Web as a mainstream business environment makes a compelling case for the use of software agents. Similarly, such agents can be implemented at the publisher site or at the user end or in the middle as a broker agent that serves multiple publishers and users.

Notification: An agent providing notification services to a user can produce significant reduced-workload benefits by freeing the user to monitor events of personal significance. For instance, such an agent can monitor Web sites of interest for changes, and report them to a user.

Learning: An agent with a learning capability can learn tasks that can be automated or preferences that can be used for customization:

- Learning and offering to automate the repetitive tasks of a single user, thus relieving the user of the need to toil with what, when, and how to automate

- Learning the similar attributes of a group of users to customize information (e.g., make personal recommendations) based on group characteristics

- Learning similar behavior of a group of users to provide workgroup productivity enhancement

- Learning and offering to automate recurrent sequential behavior of a group of users in a workflow thread, thus relieving the workgroup of repetitive tasks

Tutoring: An agent with a tutoring capability can coach a user in context thanks to its event monitoring and inferencing capabilities, thus reducing the training requirements. For example, applications wizards in the Windows operating system environment are examples of simple tutoring agents.

Messaging: A messaging agent enables users to accomplish tasks off-line at remote sites. Mobile agents are examples of messaging agents that can transport themselves from place to place to interact with other agents to perform tasks on behalf of a user.

Business Obstacles for Agent Acceptance

There are a number of obstacles that may stand in the way of mainstream acceptance of software agents in business applications. These include the hyped expectations, user experience, business model, security and privacy issues.

Hype: One of the key issues in the acceptance of software agents is user expectation. Here is a true story that describes this phenomenon. At a trade show, the system administrator of a mid-size firm approaches an agent vendor, and asks, "So what is this learning agent for the Mac?"

After hearing the explanation that this learning agent observes user actions within the MacOS, finds repetitive patterns, and offers to automate them, the system administrator replies, "I get it. When I use Microsoft Word, the agent will observe that I lower the font size by 2 every time I use a subscript and offer to automate it. Right?"[1]

After hearing that the interface agent in question provides only operating system–level but not application-level automation, the system administrator says, "But it will do that in version 2. Right?"

So the concept of an intelligent agent is easily grasped by anyone, and generalized freely. Users do not care about the complexity involved in being able to deliver such functionality across all applications. Unfortunately, the delivered functionality cannot easily keep up with the generalized expectations of users. The solution is to focus on task-specific agents for narrow domains.

User Experience—Indirect Manipulation: Another issue involved in the acceptance of agents is the user experience that introduces a new human-computer interaction beyond today's direct manipulation metaphor with graphical user interfaces. Mass market acceptance of a change in user experience does usually take a number of years. Recently, the *Boston Globe* ("High-Tech Hang up," 1995) reported that Boston Mayor Thomas Menino removed all voice mail software at the Boston City Hall because he reportedly was sick of not being able to talk to a human in the city departments. We don't know whether the Mayor would have responded differently to voice mail functionality in the telephony agent, Wildfire (http://www.wildfire.com/), but the story does illustrate the human-computer interaction hurdles that need to be conquered before there can be mainstream acceptance of agents in the business world.

Users need to try a multitude of agents to develop a trust for the agent/user metaphor. Similarly, the user experience for agent design introduces an additional layer

---

[1]This example also illustrates the use of agents in GUI design, an interface agent would first find repetitive user behavior resulting from the deficiencies of a particular GUI design.

of refinement beyond the fairly static graphical user interface design. The agent designers need to consider user interaction over a period of time. We believe that these issues can be resolved by leveraging mainstream user functionality in email systems.

Business Model: Another issue of concern is the integration of the agent model into existing business models. A casual reading of the industry publications on agents may give the impression that the only barrier to achieving shopping agents that will roam the Internet to find the user the best price is the lack of a secure interagent communication language. To see the fallacy of such an expectation, just check to see how many vendors block the BargainFinder (http://hf.cstar.as.com/bf/) agent on the Web. Why? If software agents make Web commerce so efficient, then why would vendors invest in building virtual storefronts with enhanced shopping experience? Such an efficient market would imply the creation of exchanges for most categories of goods—a complete change of the current retail business model for most industries. We believe that such exchanges will emerge first for commodity goods on the Web.

Security: Another issue of concern for agents, especially for mobile ones, is security. Information system managers cannot accept a computing environment where malicious agents can create havoc on their systems. The security issue for mobile agents can be resolved using agent languages with built-in security checks: Safe-Tcl, Telescript, and Java represent languages designed to address the security issues for mobile agent implementations.

Privacy: The need to maintain privacy is an issue of concern, similar to the current concerns about privacy on the Internet. The user interaction data collected needs to be safeguarded against use that may harm consumers. For some agent applications, agents need to be able to authenticate a particular user's request so that others cannot use an agent service by posing as that user. Similarly, the privacy of an agent's state needs to be maintained at intranet and Internet servers in order to prevent others from being able to read someone's interaction with her or his agent. Agent security concerns can be addressed with current encryption technology.

Agent Use Predictions

Ovum predicts widespread applications of agent technology in the telecommunications, computing, manufacturing, military, consumer, and entertainment market segments by the year 2000 (Guilfoyle and Warner, 1994), creating a $4 billion market. How will such a large market emerge? We predict the following agent usage.

Software agents will be accepted as a design paradigm like object-oriented programming or client/server computing. We base this prediction on the following observations.

Task-centered computing is slowly replacing the current application centered computing paradigm. The move toward document-centered computing with OLE and HTML will accelerate this trend. The software agent model is a better fit to task-centered computing than the current application software model.

The Web has emerged as a truly heterogeneous distributed computing environment, thus making available a vast amount of distributed information to users. The local information available on a user's desktop or corporate WAN is dwarfed by the information on the Web. According to a user survey (GVU, 1996), finding the information and organizing retrieved information was the most common problem. The situation is likely to get worse as the Web continues to increase exponentially (doubling every six months), and mainstream users join the Web.

Given these trends, how will the software agent applications emerge? We give our predictions for the desktop, intranet, and Internet below.

On the desktop, software agents will be incorporated into task-specific applications to provide application-specific assistance. In essence, software agents will supplement today's GUIs with intelligent backend services. Microsoft application wizards, and Claris application assistants show this trend. This replacement will be very much like the replacement of command line interface software with applications supporting industry-standard GUIs.

Similarly, a software agent framework will be incorporated into desktop operating system shells. Windows 95 scheduling agent (Microsoft, 1995) and MacOS assistance framework (Wayner and Josh, 1995) are examples along this direction. Eventually the operating system shell will provide services like scheduling needed by different applications to implement agent-specific features.

On the intranet, agents will emerge as critical components of workflow solutions within the enterprise. Task-specific agents will serve as intelligent front ends to enterprise information systems. Also, Internet-based agents will get modified for intranet applications to manage the specialized information needs of the corporation.

On the Internet, agents—in the short term—will emerge as information brokers for specialized domains implemented as centralized Web services. In essence, agents will be components of Web-based services incorporating agent functionality. Web search engines exemplify such a trend. Even though desktop search agents are available, it simply does not make sense to replicate the functionality of indexing robots in Web search engines on the desktop.

Cost of Development

As detailed in the previous section, we see agents being incorporated into software solutions rather than software entities on their own. Therefore, it makes sense to think of agent software expenditures as a percentage of total software development costs. We estimate that the development of agent-enabled IS applications will be in the range of 1 to 2 percent of IS software development costs.

Most of the software components needed in the integration of agent features into your IS applications (database engines, scripting environments, knowledge-based inference engines, etc.) are most probably scattered throughout your IS organization. Most likely, software expenditure will be acquisition of agent environments, learning engines, and support fees for these software acquisitions.

The incorporation of agent-enabled features into your IS applications will require particular attention to the design and testing stages. The design phase would need a careful user study in order to develop an information flow needed for the business application at hand—a task most appropriately conducted by personnel with expertise in human-computer interaction. Similarly, the design phase would require knowledge engineering for extracting implicit rules of thumb captured in your organization over the course of years of trial-and-error interactions. In the testing phase, user experience with the agent needs to be tested over a period of time as agent behavior will dynamically change with user interaction. This phase cannot always be reduced to a GUI testing amenable to automation.

Finally, depending on the internal resources, costs would be incurred for university courses and agent software vendor training. Of course, it may be necessary to bring in outside consulting design services up front, and contract development resources if required.

Summary

In this chapter, we defined an end-user agent model comprised of agent environment, task skills, and knowledge and communication skills attributes. Using this agent model, we classified intelligent agents from an end-user viewpoint, and gave some examples of current agent applications. Next, we discussed the benefits of agents and business obstacles for agent acceptance. We then presented our predictions for market segments where agents will be popular in the future. We ended the chapter with a discussion of cost estimates for agent development.

At the end of this chapter you should be convinced that agents are here, and do have some potential. Even if you are not convinced yet by the motivation for using agents in your organization, you are probably intrigued. The next three chapters that describe deployed agent applications on the desktop, Internet, and intranet and detail their business benefits should convince you why you need agents in your company.

Desktop
Agents

A desktop agent lives on a PC or workstation. Formally, a desktop agent is a software agent that executes locally in a personal computer operating system (e.g., Windows 95, OS/2, MacOS) or workstation operating system (e.g., Windows NT, UNIX) environment. Desktop agents can be categorized into the following three groups:

- *Operating system agents*—agents that perform user tasks that ordinarily require user interaction with the operating system through its GUI shell

- *Application agents*—agents that perform user tasks within an application on behalf of the user

- *Application suite agents*—agents that perform user tasks within a suite of applications on behalf of the user

Operating system agents consist of intelligent utilities[1] for the operating system and interface agents for the GUI shell of the operating system. Intelligent utilities are capable of monitoring operating system–level events, and performing tasks involving operating system–level services according to a

---

[1]Traditionally, operating systems are designed to provide a baseline level of features that serve a majority of users whereas utilities provide the personalization addressing the dissimilar needs of diverse groups of users.

user-specified schedule. For instance, a disk compression agent may schedule daily disk compression in the evenings after the user leaves hers or his machine for half an hour. In general, intelligent utility agents initiate tasks on behalf of the user, and inform the user after the completion of a task. A second type of operating system agents are interface agents that bring agent functionality to the user's interaction with the GUI shell of the operating system. This type of agents not only initiates tasks on behalf of the user but also completes a task initiated by the user. For instance, a setup agent may walk the user through a series of questions to elicit the user's preferences, and carry out local machine and network configuration tasks at the end of the interview.

Application agents can be either part of the application providing the agent-enabled features or an interface agent outside of the application performing tasks involving the user's interaction with the application. For instance, the rule editor functionality of a mail program is an example of an agent-enabled feature inside an application, namely mail filtering. An example of an application interface agent is a Web browser agent that works with a specific browser to initiate and schedule user-specified searches on the Web based on the directions of the user.

Application suite agents can be either software components of the application suite providing the agent-enabled features of the suite or interface agents bringing agent functionality to the user's interaction with the application suite. An example of an application suite agent is an answer wizard that provides in-context help consistently within the various components of the application suite. An example of an interface agent for an application suite would be an assistant that automates the user workflow across the various components of the application suite.

As discussed above, agents can either be an integral part of a desktop software application or an external program serving a desktop software application. So when should an agent be inside versus outside of the application it serves? For instance, when does it make sense for an agent to be a part of the operating system as opposed to an intelligent utility of the operating system? The answer involves a basic design tradeoff issue. If the operating system were to include agent functionality for every type of user, then it would be overdesigned for the average user in terms of memory footprint, development costs, and runtime performance. Therefore, it makes sense for the agent serving the majority of users to be a part of the operating system. On the other hand, the agents serving dissimilar needs of diverse user groups are best suited to be interface agents for the operating system GUI shell. The tradeoff is also applicable for desktop applications and application suites. A more desirable solution for the operating system, application, or application suite is to include an agent infrastructure that accepts third-party agents, as done in MacOS 8 with the assistance framework. Such an infrastructure would provide the functionality common to all desktop agents with a consistent user interface.

Operating System Agents

In this section we first discuss operating system agents in terms of the end-user agent model described in Chapter 1. We then describe two operating system agents in detail: System Agent for Windows 95 and Open Sesame! for MacOS.

As discussed in the previous section, an operating system agent performs tasks that ordinarily require the user's interaction with the operating system— autonomously as delegated by the user. Operating system agents can be classified in two groups:

- Intelligent utilities that primarily interact with the operating system to perform tasks on behalf of the user

- Interface agents that interact with the GUI shell of the operating system to perform tasks on behalf of the user

So when does a utility become an agent? Since an agent should be able to perform user-delegated tasks autonomously, such a utility needs to include a trigger mechanism to execute a user-defined task (e.g., as a script or macro) in response to an operating system–level event, and execute the script or macro defined by the user-delegated task.[2] Moreover, since agent definition also requires some level of intelligence, such a utility needs to include a reasoning mechanism that can handle unexpected events in the performance of the task, and automatically attempt alternative methods for completing the task.

Table 2.1 gives an overview of the agent model elements for operating system agents. We discuss each of the end-user agent model elements by examining Figure 2.1, which shows where an operating system agent fits in its environment. Typically,

---

[2]We do not require that operating system agents synthesize the script based on user's goals as articulated in Etzioni, et al., (1994) not because we disagree with the premise, but because there are so few commercial agents meeting this requirement.

Table 2.1   Operating System Agent Model Attributes

Element	Description
Environment	Operating system
Task skills	Setup, customization, maintenance, automation, file management, assistance
Knowledge	Operating system, network, GUI shell, user
Communication skills	GUI shell API, operating system API, user interface

an operating system agent is a background application. An intelligent utility-type agent communicates with the operating system API to monitor system events. For instance, monitoring is done via hooks and callback mechanism in a Windows operating system. In contrast, a user interface agent communicates with the operating system GUI shell to monitor user events of significance. For instance, this monitoring is done with Apple events for the GUI shell of MacOS-Finder. Both intelligent utility and interface agent types communicate through the operating system API to perform user-delegated tasks. Such tasks include:

- Setup of a user's machine configuration via an interactive question-and-answer session

- Customization of a user's machine using an interactive question-and-answer session

- Maintenance of a user's hard disk through regularly scheduled disk scan for errors

- Automation of a user's repetitive tasks, like cleaning up folders regularly

- File management tasks, like compression of files automatically

- Assistance-type tasks, like helping the user proactively in context

An Intelligent Utility System Agent

System Agent for Windows 95, an example of an intelligent utility system agent, is a background program that launches applications according to a user-defined schedule. Figure 2.2 shows the System Agent browser window that keeps the user aware of the status of delegated tasks. In this example, the low disk space notification program is scheduled to run hourly at fifteen minutes after the hour. The standard test of the scan disk program is scheduled to run daily at 5:00 P.M.,

Figure 2.1   Operating system agent.

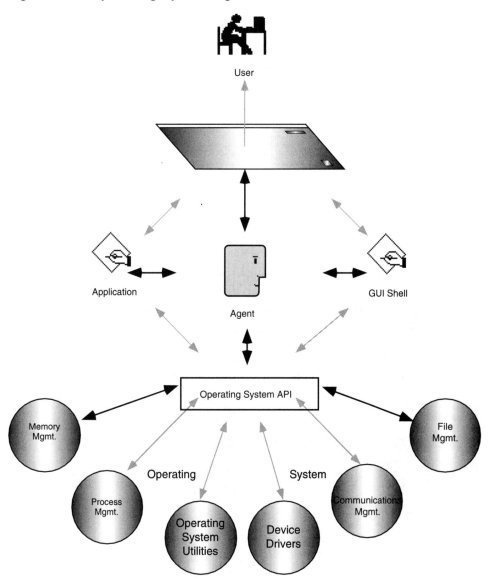

whereas the thorough test of the scan disk program is scheduled to run at 9:00 P.M. on the first day of each month. The disk defragmenter is scheduled to run every day at midnight. Finally, the Web browser with the URL that delivers a personalized newspaper is scheduled to run every day at 9:00 A.M.

Figure 2.2   System Agent browser for Windows 95.

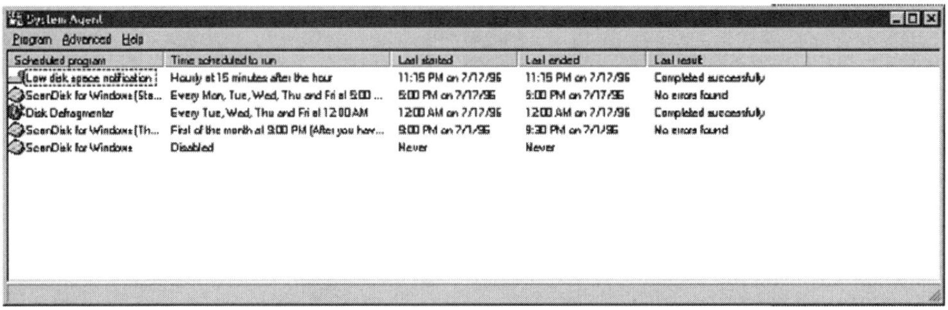

System Agent provides basic time-based scheduling capability. Figure 2.3 shows the scheduling options that are available. Specification of deadlines and notification preferences are available as options. System Agent provides some conditions that are event-based for specific utility functions. For instance, disk space notification can let the user know if there is less than a specified amount of free space. Similarly, the disk defragmenter can be instructed to defragment the hard disk if there is more than a specified percent fragmented. In summary, the System Agent provides a time-based scheduler but includes no event-based triggers.

System Agent API is exposed to third-party developers for incorporating scheduling services into third-party applications using the underlying engine. Any third-

Figure 2.3   Scheduling options for System Agent.

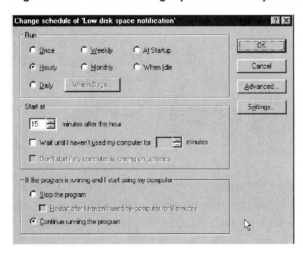

party program that is System Agent–aware is, for instance, then automatically appended to the System Agent browser in Figure 2.2, and can provide options for event parameters to be used when the application is running. System Agent is run whenever a user logs on. In addition, the System Agent user interface API is provided to directly manipulate the System Agent's database of scheduled programs without requiring user interaction. Apple's MacOS provides a similar assistance framework API to applications for providing event-based scheduling services—in addition to the time-based scheduling services as done in System Agent.

Interface Agent—Open Sesame!

Open Sesame! is an interface agent for the Finder-GUI shell of the MacOS. It differs from the Windows95 System Agent in that Open Sesame! can schedule both time- and event-based tasks, and can learn from user's interaction with the MacOS GUI shell.

An interface agent observes user events, learns the repetitive user work patterns, and automates them upon approval. In discussing an interface agent, the terms given in Table 2.2 are useful when describing the agent's operation.

Open Sesame! monitors high-level events generated by the user's interaction with the GUI shell Finder. Open Sesame! learns user repetitive behavior that is both time based and event based. A time-based task is something that the user does at a particular time. For example, opening electronic mail every day at 9:00 is a time-based task. An event-based task is something that the user does in relation to another task. For example, opening the clock desk accessory before logging into an on-line database is an event-based task.

Table 2.2 Interface Agent Glossary

Term	Definition
Observation	A repetitive pattern that an interface agent learns and offers to automate
Instruction	A set of directions to the interface agent on how to carry out a task
Confirmation	A request for user's approval before an interface agent carries out an instruction
Notification	A message to report the status of an instruction being carried out by the agent

Open Sesame! compares the high-level events (like opening a folder, quitting an application, etc.) generated by user mouse clicks and keystrokes to information stored in its neural learning module and in its inference engine. The learning module looks for repetitive patterns that haven't been automated. If it finds one, the Open Sesame! creates an observation. Figure 2.4 shows a single observation dialog box.

When Open Sesame! discovers a repetitive work pattern, it displays an observation dialog. The user has four choices:

- Accept the observation and have Open Sesame! create an instruction that automates the task.

- Decline the observation so that the task is not automated.

- Edit the task to fine-tune Open Sesame!'s observation.

- Postpone decision until later.

If the user gives his or her approval, then Open Sesame! creates an instruction to automate the task that it observed. The inference engine compares monitored user event patterns with patterns for instructions that have already been automated. When it finds one, Open Sesame! produces a set of Apple Events to perform the automated instruction.

Figure 2.4   Open Sesame! observation dialog box.

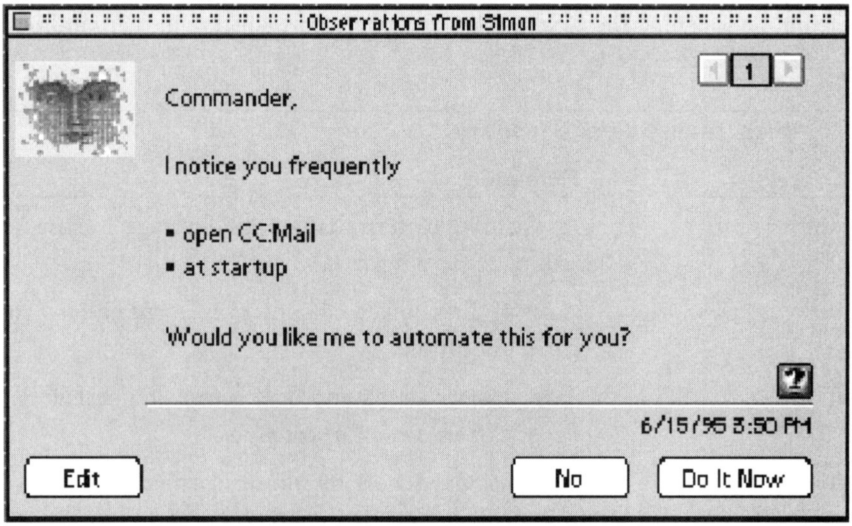

Open Sesame! learns repetitive patterns via a sequence clustering algorithm. The first step, cluster analysis, tests the internal consistency of the given sequence cluster. The goal is to find the best representative pattern for the given collection of sequences. The output from the sequence learning algorithm is a fact. A fact consists of the learned representative pattern, as well as a list of all triggers for the fact.

Open Sesame! learns not only how the user works with the Finder but also how the user interacts with Open Sesame! This feature allows Open Sesame! to customize itself according to how the user works with it. For instance, if the user declines an observation a couple of times, Open Sesame! creates an "off" instruction so that it won't bother the user with the same observation again. Other ways that Open Sesame! customizes itself include:

- Turning an instruction off if the user repeatedly cancels an instruction during confirmation

- Turning an instruction off if the user repeatedly undoes the action that the instruction performs

- Learning the user's desire to change notification preferences (for instance, change the "Notify by Menu" option to "Notify by Dialog" if the user repeatedly needs an observation soon after notification)

Application Agents

In this section we first discuss application agents in terms of the end-user model described in Chapter 1. We then analyze three application wizards, a mail agent, and a Web browser agent.

Application agents perform tasks within an application autonomously as delegated by the user. The types of agents can be classified into two groups by environment:

- Application agents that provide the agent-enabled features of an application
- Interface agents that reside outside of the application they serve

Table 2.3 gives an overview of the agent model elements for desktop application agents. Typically, an application interface agent is a background program. The application interface agent communicates through the application API to monitor user

Table 2.3   Application Agent Attributes

Element	Description
Environment	Application
Task skills	Customization, automation, assistance
Knowledge	Application, user, operating system
Communication skills	Application API, GUI shell API

behavior. For instance, a Web browser agent uses the proxy server API to intercept browser messages for monitoring. An application interface agent communicates with operating system API to perform user-delegated tasks. Such tasks naturally depend on the kind of functionality built into the application. Some typical tasks are:

- Information retrieval automation for Web browsers
- Information filtering tasks for mail clients
- Customization of application document types based on user preferences
- Automation of queries for client database applications
- Proactive user assistance for in-context help regarding application shortcuts, unused features, mistakes, and tips

Application Agents—Wizards

Wizards are used in Microsoft desktop applications to provide task-oriented help. A wizard is a help system that guides the user through a specific task using a dialog metaphor. Lotus SmartAssistant, MacOS Expert, and Claris Assistant user interface elements offer functionality that is similar to wizards. A wizard gathers information about a particular task, and then uses this collected information to complete the task for the user. Wizards are especially useful for complex or infrequent tasks that users may have difficulty in learning or retaining.

Figure 2.5 shows the Chart wizard in Microsoft Excel. The title bar of a wizard identifies the wizard's task. The left side of a wizard usually deposits a conceptual rendering or preview of the result. The right side of the wizard sheet explains to the user what it does in a conventional style. When the user clicks on the button finish, the wizard completes the task for the user.

Each desktop application in Microsoft Office includes wizards. For instance, Word wizards help users create preformatted documents, such as

Figure 2.5   Chart wizard in Excel.

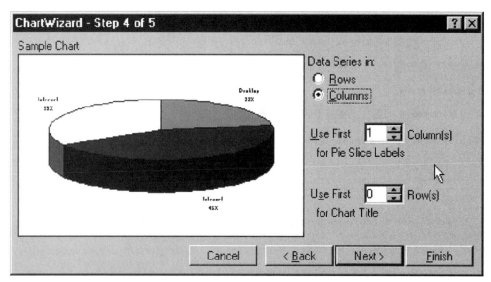

an agenda, calendar, fax cover sheet, letter, memo, and other common types of documents.

Email Agent—Beyond Mail

Beyond Mail is a rule-based agent for managing email. Using rules, a user can filter and prioritize incoming messages on arrival, forward them automatically, and so on. The rule structure in Beyond Mail is identical to the instruction structure used in the Open Sesame! agent for MacOS:

When a specific event happens,

If it meets certain conditions,

Then take this action.

The event dictionary in Beyond Mail consists of message-based events (e.g., new message arrives, a message is read the first time, etc.), and time-based events (e.g., specific date, time, recurrent time periods, etc.).

One fundamental difference between the Open Sesame! and Beyond Mail agent is that the Beyond Mail agent does *not* monitor user behavior, learn repetitive email processing patterns, or offer to automate them for the user. Therefore, the user needs to define the messaging rules in Beyond Mail using a rule editor.

Figure 2.6   Rule for automatic message filing.

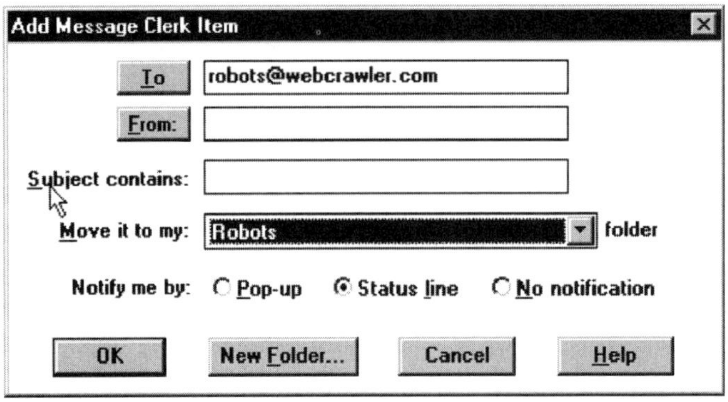

Beyond Mail can prioritize mail when instructed by the user:

When a new memo arrives,

If it is from the President and it has urgent priority,

Then move the message to my urgent folder and display an alert.

Using Beyond Mail, a user can also specify rules to manage mail messages:

When a new memo arrives,

If it is from the President, and it is about budget,

Then reply to the President with the message "I am on vacation this week; Margaret will send you the revised budget," forward the message to Margaret, and move the message to my budget folder.

Figure 2.6 shows how rules can be specified by the user in Beyond Mail. In this example, all mail messages received from the Robots mailing list (i.e., those messages sent by different subscribers of the mailing list to robots@webcrawler.com) is automatically filed in the user's Robots folder.

Search Agent—Web Compass

Web Compass is an example of a client search agent for the Web. Web Compass is a personalized parallel search[3] query agent. The agent software comes with an

---

[3]The parallel query is similar to that of the MetaCrawler that is implemented as a centralized server in contrast to the Web Compass client implementation.

initial source list of search engines that are modified by the user to reflect personal interests. This search agent uses the desktop Web browser client as its user interface. To search with Web Compass, you specify the resources to be used for the search, and submit a keyword or phrase into the query field as shown in Figure 2.7.

Figure 2.7   Search agent user interface.

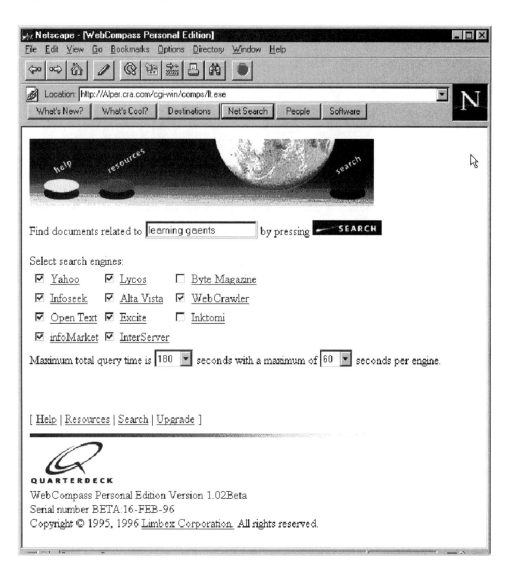

Figure 2.8   AltaVista document summary.

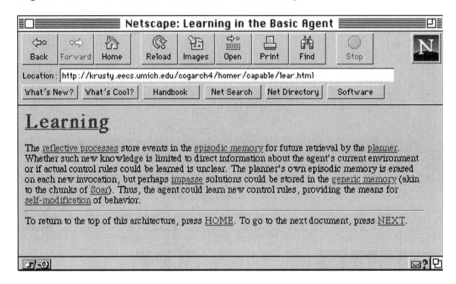

This search agent provides a minimal amount of filtering on the returned results. For instance, the user can restrict the Web Compass agent to ignore links to documents on the resource host, as well as URLs that can contain a specific text string. In addition, the Web Compass search agent provides a summary for each of the returned documents using natural language parsing. Figure 2.8 shows the document abstract from the Web search engine AltaVista for the "learning agent" query that essentially consists of the first 20 words of the document. Figure 2.9 shows the Web Compass abstract for the same URL. Clearly, the personal search agent's summary is more useful than what is returned on most search engines. This example shows how the Internet search engine servers and personal search clients can be used synergystically where the Internet search engines provide a first cut at a search quickly, and client search engines improve the quality of the information in the search results using background processing on the client machine.

One note of caution for using desktop search agents is that the client software enables the users to bypass the advertisements on Web search engines. While this is an appealing feature for users, the popularity of a client search agent may cause Web search engine vendors to block the search engine queries. As a matter of fact, the Web Compass search agent does violate the robot etiquette by its cgi.bin submissions.

Figure 2.9   Search agent document summary.

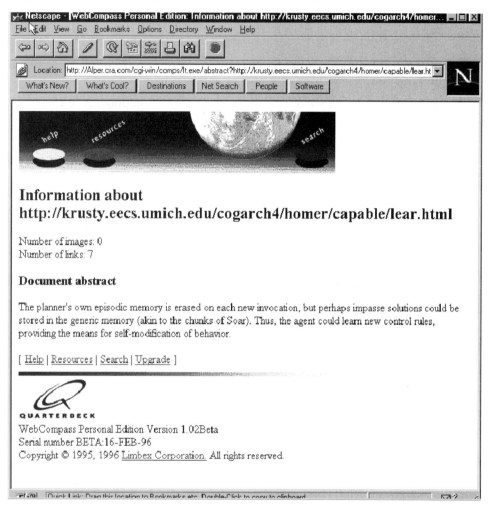

Application Suite Agents

In this section, we first discuss application suite agents in terms of the end-user agent model described in Chapter 1. We then describe the application suite agent in detail.

Application suite agents (e.g., Claris Works assistants, Microsoft Office wizards) perform tasks within an application suite autonomously as delegated by the user.

The attributes of application suite agents are similar to those of application agents. Application suite agents perform tasks such as:

- Customization of suite document types based on user preferences

- Proactive user assistance for in-context help regarding suite shortcuts, user mistakes, unused features, and tips

- Automation of user workflow across the various components of the application suite

An Application Suite Agent—Microsoft Bob

Bob is an integrated suite of eight programs such as letter writer, calendar, to-do list, checkbook, and others. Bob's suite components are tightly integrated, and were first popularized by Apple Newton. For instance, the birthday entry into an address book is read in automatically into your calendar program. What makes Bob an agent? Bob has animated personal guides for assisting the user's interaction with the various components of the suite. Bob is also the most anthropomorphic of the desktop agents we have covered so far. Our definition of an agent in Chapter 1 does not require the humanization of the agent interface, although this issue is still debated in the research community. For instance, one school of thought advocates the position that a social interface may contribute negatively to user experience by raising expectations (Norman, 1983). On the other hand, research by Nass and Keaves at Stanford University demonstrates that people treat computers as human, even when the user interface is not humanlike (Nass et al., 1993).

So what kind of assistance does the personal guide in Bob provide? Most of the of interaction with the guide is a replacement of the conventional menus with a model dialog box that allows an interview style of interaction as done in the wizard metaphor. Bob brings a cartoonlike visual shell to the underlying wizard-style interaction. Bob does offer some proactive assistance to the user. For instance, in the letter writer, when the user clicks on the cut button without selecting a field, the personal guide informs the user how to make use of this option, as shown in Figure 2.10.

Of course, this sort of proactive assistance when the user makes a mistake can be applied to any desktop program without using a social interface. For instance, if the user clicks on the cut button in Microsoft Word 7.0 without selecting a text field, then the Tip Wizard can notify the user how to use this feature instead of the user being notified with a system click sound as is done now.

Figure 2.10   Proactive assistance in Microsoft Bob.

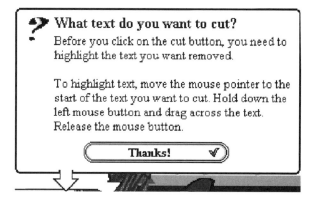

Benefits of Desktop Agents

Now that we have looked at several examples of desktop agents in detail, let us discuss the potential use of such agents in the enterprise, and the resulting benefits. Since an agent is a background application on the desktop, it is important to find out how much background processing power is available for agent computing on desktop CPUs. Figure 2.11 shows CPU use for a word processing application. As seen in the figure, the word processing application's average CPU utilization rate is about 42 percent. That means approximately half of the CPU cycles of a knowledge worker's machine are available for agent computing when the user is actively using his or her machine. When we take into account time for meetings, coffee-breaks, and lunch, we can safely assume that almost 100 percent of the CPU cycles are

Figure 2.11   Average CPU utilization for a word processing application.

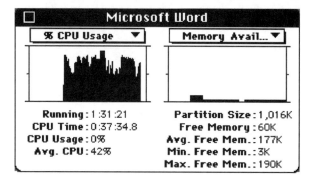

available for agent computing during 20 percent of the typical nine-hour workday of a knowledge worker. When we include the availability during off hours (nights and weekends), after factoring out system administration tasks such as backups, virus scans, and so on, it is evident that a very large reservoir of background processing power is available on today's corporate PCs for agent computing. In a corporate network, typically 50 percent of desktop CPU cycles are available for 6 hours of agent computing and almost 100 percent of desktop CPU cycles are available for 18 hours of agent computing during each workday.

So what are the benefits of using the available background CPU cycles for agent computing? We first discuss desktop operating system agents. Do the operating system agents represent yet another set of utilities that your organization needs to license? Or do operating system agents represent an opportunity to develop internal IS applications to formalize and automate corporate IS practices in order to reduce costs? To find out, try Exercise 2.1.

Exercise 2.1: Desktop Agents for Technical Support Automation

The following steps can give you a rough estimate for the potential savings of using agents in technical support:

1. Find out what percent of the internal technical support calls are solved by running a utility on the client machine within your organization.

2. Find out the median technician hours and the knowledge worker downtime hours spent in waiting for resolving the kind of problems in step 1.

3. Estimate the amount of money that your organization would save annually if the repetitive remedies of step 1 are executed on a regular schedule for preventive maintenance.

Your organization probably has a well-defined backup and virus scan utility execution schedule for PC desktops within your IS network. Most likely, however, the use of utilities for desktop organization and hard disk maintenance is more haphazard and reactive. For such an environment, an agent solution can enforce a corporate practice that would yield significant savings. Here are a few examples: Figure 2.12 shows the AppleGuide help for rebuilding the desktop. The guide panel

Figure 2.12   AppleGuide help.

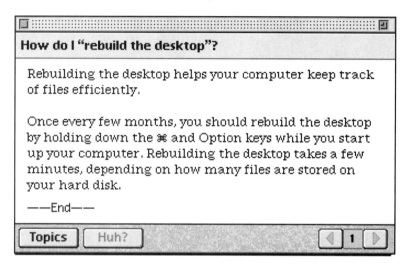

explains how the user can do the recommended maintenance task, and why it should be done.

Notwithstanding the simplicity of the AppleGuide help, let us reflect on the help content. Why should a user have to learn what it means to rebuild the desktop, and remember when and how to do it? If personal computers are really here to simplify our lives, is it too much to ask that the machines take care of their own regular maintenance so that users can concentrate on maintaining the organization of their work? Better yet, how about automating "rebuilding the desktop" and other such maintenance tasks and reporting the results to the LAN administrator, thus freeing the knowledge worker to concentrate on the project at hand.

Lest you think that such problems do not exist on the Windows95 operating system, here is an example for this environment. Figure 2.13 shows the settings options for scheduling a disk defragmenter task using the System Agent. While Windows 95 at least provides a scheduling agent with default maintenance tasks, does the average user really need to know what disk defragmentation means, and how to interpret its results using the System Agent?[4] Doesn't it make sense to have

---

[4]Imagine if your automobile reported the statistical results of engine control computations for fuel ratio adjustment every day!

Figure 2.13   System Agent options for settings.

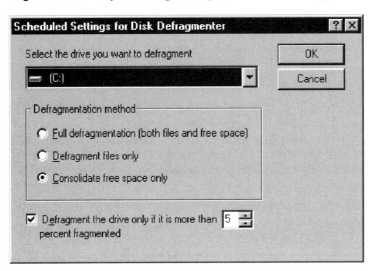

a corporate procedure for running these types of maintenance utilities according to the particular needs of the organization, and for reporting the results of maintenance tasks to the LAN administrator, thus relieving the end-user from this unnecessary burden? Does your organization employ such a policy for your PC environment? Such a solution can be developed with the SAGE API in the Windows environment.

We'll discuss the benefits of application agents by analyzing one of the most common agent applications—email. One of the recent empirical studies on email overhead shows that although email was designed as a communication application it is now being used for additional purposes such as task management and personal archiving (Whittaker and Sidner, 1996). A typical user has cluttered in-boxes with hundreds of messages, outstanding tasks, partially read documents, and conversational threads, thus causing important messages to get lost. Whittaker and Sidner, (1996) provide anecdotal evidence for the problem of email overload:

> *"I dedicate somewhere between minimally two hours at the outlying edge, up to ten hours on any given day trying to stay on top of email."*

> *"Waiting to hear back from another . . . employee can mean delays in accomplishing a particular task, which can . . . have significant impact on overall operations. Depending on the situation, it can either be critical or just frustrating."*

Whittaker and Sidner also conducted a quantitative analysis of in-boxes for users. Their study reveals that users can be classified into three groups based on filing characteristics:

- *Nonfilers,* who do not use folders, and thus have large in-boxes and a large number of conversational threads in their in-boxes

- *Frequent filers,* who clean up their in-boxes daily and have very few conversational threads in them thanks to a successful filing strategy using folders

- *Spring cleaners,* who only intermittently clean up their in-boxes, and usually have overloaded in-boxes with a large number of conversational threads due to a failed filing strategy with folders

The empirical data suggests that people use the in-box as a to-do task reminder list and find it hard to file information to remove it from their in-box. The study reports that both nonfilers and spring cleaners have problems with filtering and task management whereas frequent filers have problems with high maintenance costs, thus precluding this approach for high-volume email.

So how does your organization stack up in tackling email overload? Exercise 2.2 should give you an idea of the extent of the email overload problem in your organization. Most likely you will discover that your organization does have a significant email problem—surpassing that of voicemail in most cases. So what can agent technology do for email? Using currently available commercial mail programs, it's possible to automate most of the routine forwarding and filing of messages for

Exercise 2.2: Email Overload Average

Select 30 to 40 random users in your organization across different job types, and ask them the following:

1. How many hours a day do you spend in your email application, (reading, responding, filing, etc.)?

2. How many email messages do you forward each day?

3. What percent of your in-box messages is more than three months old and what percent is less than one month old?

4. How many messages in your in box have the subject field that starts with Re:?

most users. Using the indexing and text summarization tools for Web applications, it is also possible to develop customized applications that automatically extract the keywords for mail messages and provide message summaries. Whether it makes sense to wait for such innovations from leading mail software vendors or to develop them internally would depend on the specific business application.

Tables 2.4 and 2.5 show the features, advantages, and benefits of Microsoft wizards and AppleGuide. Apple's stated approach toward an intelligent desktop is based on AppleGuide with AppleScript in the operating system. AppleGuide is an interactive help system with elementary context sensitivity.

Table 2.6 summarizes the benefits of desktop agents. According to one study, PC users spend about 5 hours a week tinkering with their systems. The latest GVU user surveys report that finding information and organizing retrieved information are the two main problems in using the Web (with the exception of the well-known problem with bandwidth GVU). The study also reports that 28 percent of users spend 10 to 20 hours a week, and 19 percent of users spend 4 to 6 hours a week using a Web browser. Depending on an organization's policy and employee job category, the chances are that a significant number of hours in an employee's workday are being spent on unproductive tasks related to these Information Age problems. Desktop agents can take a meaningful byte out of such unproductive employee tasks.

Table 2.4   Benefits of Microsoft Wizards

Feature	Advantage	Benefit
Document wizard	Lets you create document types by going through a series of questions in a word processing application	Creates agenda, calendar, cover sheet, letter, memo, and newsletter-type documents
Presentation wizard	Guides you in creating a presentation through a question-and-answer session	Helps in choosing a presentation style
Database wizard	Lets you create and enhance database objects	Helps in creating a database query, form, report
Chart wizard	Lets you create charts based on data attributes	Creates the best-looking chart without user trial and error

Table 2.5   Benefits of Apple's AppleGuide Technology

Feature	Advantage	Benefit
Task-oriented help	Provides help based on current context	Relieves the user from having to search for help
Coach marks	Provides visual cues by circling items	Provides interactive on-line help
Queries	Offers queries about specific operations	Reduces user frustration
Interactive	Delivers interactive help with multimedia content	Enhances user experience in getting help

Table 2.6   Benefits of Desktop Agents

Feature	Advantage	Benefit
Background monitoring	Monitors user actions while user is working	Data needed for user modeling collected without bothering user
Learning repetitive tasks	Learns repetitive task patterns in monitored user actions for automation	Reduced time and work-load as user doesn't need to keep track of what to automate
Learning what the user is not doing	Finds user actions repeatedly not performed in order to help the user	Reduced training as user takes advantage of features that he or she doesn't even know exist
Learning from user interactions	Learns user's preferences in dealing with the agent	Better user experience as user doesn't have to specify his or her preferences
Generalization of repetitive tasks	Generalizes user's intent from repetitive user actions	Increased productivity as user benefits from programmed automation without programming

continued

Table 2.6 *Continued*

Feature	Advantage	Benefit
Presentation of repetitive tasks for automation approval	Asks user's approval before automating task	User control without having to give explicit instructions
Background execution	Performs user-delegated tasks in the background	User doesn't need to be present to get work done
Automatic customization	Customizes the software according to user preferences	Enhanced user experience as the agent relieves the user from having to adapt to software
Continuous adaptation	Learns changes in user work patterns	Increased productivity as user doesn't need to change software parameters with changing work patterns

Summary

In this chapter, we classified desktop agents into operating system, application, and application suite agent categories. We then discussed each desktop agent category in terms of the end-user agent model introduced in Chapter 1, and described examples of commercial agents for each category. We showed that significant untapped computing resources are abundantly available for agent computing within the enterprise. Next, we covered the specific agent features that provide the reduced workload, increased productivity, and reduced training cost benefits of desktop agents. Finally, we identified technical support and information filtering as the two areas with the greatest return on investment with desktop agents. While the mainstream acceptance of stand-alone desktop agents must wait for PC operating systems that support such agents, agents will appear on the desktop as features of conventional applications in the near term.

Internet Agents

In the last few years, the rate of increase in information published on any medium has been estimated to double every 20 months (Piatetsky-Shapiro and Frawley, 1991). The largest increase in information storage and communication, by far, has been on the Internet. For instance, the volume of Usenet News generated each day exceeded 100Mbytes in 1994. The rate of Internet news traffic is doubling every year. The total Internet traffic has been increasing at an even faster pace of 12 percent per month, corresponding to a doubling of the traffic every six months (Witten, Moffat, and Bell, 1994).

The introduction of the World Wide Web has been primarily responsible for the explosive growth in Internet publishing and communication. During 1994 alone, Web traffic has been estimated to increase more than 15 times (Quarterman, 1995). This phenomenal increase in the information published on the Web, while providing for information dissemination, also makes finding relevant material in this sea of information a great challenge.

Today the typical user experience on the Web is through surfing—navigating through the Web space by following hyperlinks. While the dominant form of Web usage is the direct manipulation method (i.e., surfing), the following underlying characteristics of the Web environment dictate why we need Internet agents for information brokering.

Web Primer

The World Wide Web is formally a directed graph connected with hypertext links. The hypertext links are the underlined or colored phrases, or icons in a document displayed in a Web browser window. Each of these links points to another link in the Web graph where each link's address is specified by a Uniform Resource Locator (URL), such as http://www.lycos.com. The document at each link is composed according to the Hypertext Markup Language (HTML), a standard language for the interchange of hypertext. The primary objective of HTML is to facilitate the efficient distribution of electronic information by specifying the structure of a document and leaving the presentation details to Web browsers.

The communication protocol for accessing Internet servers is Hypertext Transfer Protocol (HTTP). Therefore, HTP is the communication language of Web robots as well. The HTTP protocol is based on a client/server model. A *client* program (e.g., a Web browser, a Web robot, an HTTP server) sends a request to a *server* program (e.g., a Web browser, a Web robot, an HTTP server) during a transaction. A transaction is comprised of:

- The client program establishing a connection with the server

- Sending the HTTP request message to the server

- Receiving the HTTP response message from the server

- Terminating the connection after performing the request while handling any unexpected conditions (e.g., server not responding, client closing connection before the request is served, etc.)

Figure 3.1 shows the architecture of the Web client/server model. One of the most important characteristics of the HTTP protocol is that transactions are stateless. That is, each transaction is treated by the server as a new one without knowledge of previous transactions with the same client. Therefore, HTTP servers do not ordinarily understand the concept of a user session. Since Web businesses need a user's dynamic interests in a given session and persistent interests across sessions in order to provide personalized services to their clients, several methods have been designed to address this issue and will be discussed in later sections.

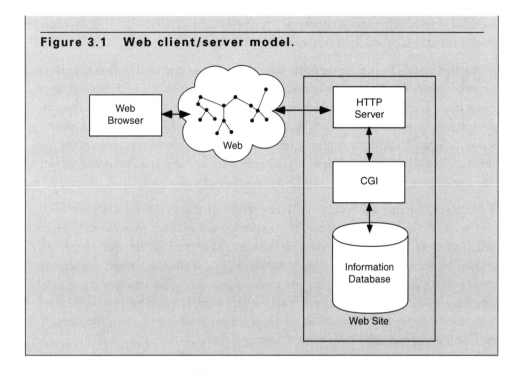

Figure 3.1   Web client/server model.

- The volume of information on the Internet is huge (currently served by approximately 13 million hosts) and is getting larger, with the number of hosts doubling every year.

- The type of information on the Internet varies widely, from newsgroups to corporate public relations, from personal position papers to academic journal articles.

- The quality of information varies greatly with information-rich documents as well as poor-quality material, as there is no control over what gets published on the Internet.

- The depth-first surfing inherently encouraged by Web browsers causes most users to get lost in Web hyperspace.

Given that the Web has grown immensely beyond its original homogeneous origin (serving mainly high-energy physics researchers), it is now practically impossible for a Web user to find all of her or his information interests through surfing.

Furthermore, the rich knowledge sources on the Web also make it extremely hard for mainstream users to know where and how to find the right information. Intelligent agents promise to address these user needs.

Internet agents live on servers that store the on-line information that is published by information suppliers and normally accessed by users in an interactive manner using client browser software such as Netscape Navigator or Microsoft Explorer. An Internet server is typically a UNIX, Windows NT, or MacOS platform with a server program that serves multiple requests from Web browser clients on the Internet. Popular commercial server packages include Netscape Enterprise Server, Microsoft Information Server, and Quarterdeck Webstar.

Formally, Internet agents are computer programs that reside on these servers and access the distributed on-line information on the Internet to perform tasks on behalf of users without direct user interaction. The Internet agents serve as information brokers between information suppliers (e.g., Websites, Usenet newsgroups, on-line databases, etc.) and information consumers (i.e., Web users, and one day, other agents). In such an electronic intermediary role, Internet agents match the information needs of Web users against the attributes of information suppliers, type of information, and information content.

Internet agents can be categorized into the following groups:

■ *Web search agents* that employ robots that traverse the Web hyperspace on behalf of users to provide search services

■ *Information filtering agents* that filter the information on the Internet according to users' personal interests

■ *Off-line delivery agents* that deliver a personalized package of on-line information to a user desktop according to user preferences

■ *Notification agents* that inform users of events of personal significance to them

■ *Service agents* that act as an information broker by matching the attributes of context providers against the interests of their service members

■ *Web site agents* such as avatars and MUD (Multiuser Dimension or more affectionately known as Multiuser Dungeon—an environment where multiple users can interact with each other) agents that serve as an electronic host to visitors of a Web site

■ *Mobile agents* that travel from one Internet server to another to execute user-specified tasks

In summary, the Web has brought about the paradox where individuals now have access to seemingly endless information but spend most of their time trying to find what they are looking for. Intelligent agents promise to bring relief to this information overload problem. In fact, several such agents are already deployed on the Web today. This chapter gives an overview of such agents and the benefits they provide.

Web Search Agents

Currently, search engines such as Yahoo, Lycos, Excite, Infoseek, and Alta Vista catalog the Web to provide search services. Typically, a user submits a keyword query to a search engine that returns a list of URLs matching the user's specified keyword query. As this user interaction is essentially direct manipulation, you may be wondering where the agent functionality is found in a search engine. The answer is in the Web robot[1] employed by each search engine. Figure 3.2 shows the architecture of a typical search engine. While a user's interaction with a search engine follows the familiar direct manipulation metaphor, the search engine robot follows hyperlinks constantly to discover new documents and catalog the address and characteristics of each document in its index database.

Although the consensus of the research community is that search agents cannot keep up with the growth of the Web, search engine vendors keep on trying, each claiming to have the largest catalog. Until recently, Lycos claimed the largest catalog, but it was surpassed by the Digital Alta Vista search engine, which indexes more than 30 million Web pages. More recently, Alta Vista has been upstaged by Inktomi HotBot, which uses a parallel computing architecture with commodity workstations and now boasts the largest number of fully indexed pages—more than 50 million.

The performance of a search engine can be measured by its precision and recall:

- *Precision.* Technically, precision is the ratio of the documents relevant to the query over the total number of documents returned. In other words, the precision of a search engine is the percentage of the documents of interest to a Web user compared with the total number of documents returned. For instance, the robot Architext used in the search engine Excite usually provides high

---

[1]Also known as softbots, spiders, wanderers, crawlers. Although these names connote a mobile agent hopping from one Internet server onto another, a Web robot actually runs on only one server.

Figure 3.2   Search engine architecture.

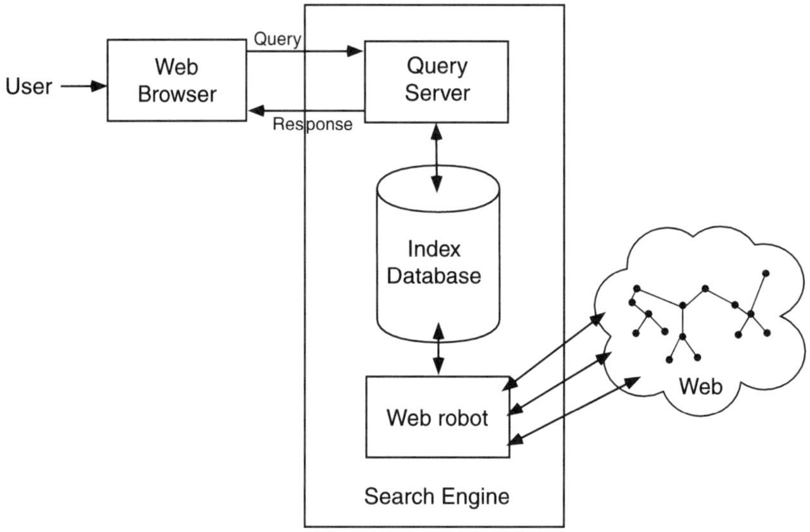

precision in its search results thanks to concept-based searching. (More precisely, it is based on the statistical relationship between words.) In contrast, Alta Vista typically returns the largest number of documents in response to a query at the expense of precision. WebCrawler usually displays lower precision due to the breadth-first search strategy used in creating its index. The lower precision of the Alta Vista and WebCrawler engines is actually preferred by Web surfers interested in discovering new and unusual sites as well as by users who fear that concept-based searching filters out desired information.

■ *Recall.* Recall is the ratio of total relevant documents returned in a query to the total number of documents. That is, recall measures the amount of relevant information returned by a search engine. For instance, searching the subject hierarchy in Yahoo! usually leads to search results with poor recall as it aims for high precision for a small subset of the Web.

Web Robots

The Web robot (Etzioni and Weld, 1994) is an autonomous agent that communicates with Web servers using, for example, the HTTP protocol. A current list of Internet robots is maintained by Martin Koster (Koster, 1995). The software robots have different strategies for traversing the Web graph. Starting from a specific Web site, they follow hyperlinks and retrieve documents along the way. Since it is extremely hard for a robot to keep current with the dynamically changing and growing graph of the Web, robots usually use a strategy to traverse the Web graph in a prioritized manner. For example, Lycos spiders use the following strategy: When a Web page is fetched, Lycos spider stores all the URL pointers in the page in a queue; it then chooses the next page to fetch from the queue using a random strategy that favors pages which have been referenced more often by other pages, and pages with a shorter URL to explore parent directories first. Most other robots, such as Web Crawler, use a simpler strategy such as breadth-first, which attempts to explore root URLs first. Robots also may exclude different types of documents such as pictures or binary files. Some systems, such as Web Crawler, allow real-time robot Web navigation on behalf of the user. The strategy for navigation in this case is different than the strategy it uses for general document indexing. In this case, the WebCrawler first retrieves from its index an initial set of documents that are the most similar to the user query and then follows the links in these documents to find other relevant documents. The retrieved documents are also added to the index database. The on-line search feature of WebCrawler biases the robot search toward more popular documents as measured by the user queries.

The information extracted from the document is usually special parts of the document text such as title and headings, text outline, keywords, summary, the time the document was modified (if allowed) by the server, and file size. This information is indexed and stamped with the date the document was fetched by the robot.

The query server selects the documents from the index database that best matches the user query. The major information retrieval strategies are the Boolean and vector space strategies. The Boolean approach relies on the exact match between the query and indexed keywords. The obvious problem with this approach is that it does not return a measure of relevance. Moreover, it cannot deal with keywords that have different meanings in different contexts. In the vector space approach, documents are modeled as a vector of attributes in a multidimensional space. For example, elements in the vector space approach may represent the frequency of some words that appear in the documents. More advanced weights could be assigned to different terms that tend to favor keywords that appear with high frequency in an individual document but rarely in other documents. For example,

Lycos uses a method called Tf∗IDf to select the 100 most salient keywords in a document, where Tf is the frequency of the keyword in the document, and IDf (inverse document frequency) is a term that is inversely proportional to the frequency of documents in a collection that the term appears in. To retrieve documents that are relevant, the query server computes a similarity measure between the query vector and the document vector.

Table 3.1 gives an overview of the agent model elements for Internet search agents. The search agents traverse the Web to discover new hyperlinks, and retrieve the document at the discovered hyperlink to index its contents. In this context, a search engine may be considered an agent that serves all Web users by proactively discovering and cataloging new URLs that may later be of interest to a Web user. In this process, the search agent also resolves any hypertext links in the retrieved document to discover new links.

Robots are advised to obey the standards for robot behavior established by consensus on the robots mailing list (Koster, 1995). The standards contain a set of guidelines to protect Web servers against unwanted accesses by robots. The guidelines specify a method to exclude robots by creating a file entitled /robots.txt. on the server. The file contains a couple of records starting with a User-Agent line followed by one or more Disallow lines. An example code in Perl can be found at http://www.webcrawler.com/mak/projects/robots/norobots.pl. The guidelines for robot authors can be found at http://info.webcrawler.com/mak/projects/robots/guidelines.html. The document sets the following guidelines for Internet robot authors:

- Identify the name of the robot using the User-agent field.

- Identify the user deploying the robot using the From field.

Table 3.1   Search Agent Model Attributes

Element	Description
Environment	Internet
Task Skills	Hyperlink discovery, document retrieval, and indexing
Knowledge	Web, Usenet newsgroups, FTP, and Gopher sites
Communication skills	HTTP, FTP, Gopher, query server

- Announce your robot by posting a message to the comp.infosystems.www.providers Usenet newsgroups.

- Announce the robot to Webmasters of the servers that the robot will visit.

- Be informative by using the Referrer field.

- Be accessible to fix any problems that the robot causes.

- Design the robot so that it does not consumer resources (e.g., do not use successive hits on a single server, use HTTP HEAD instead of full GETs, do not loop, run at appointed times, do not use queries).

Benefits of Search Agents

Web search agents provide a starting point of exploration for most users. In spite of their limitations, search agents are the most widely used Web services. Table 3.2 presents a comparison of advantages and disadvantages of current search engines.

Current keyword specification user interfaces to Web search engines are appealing to users because they are easy to use. However, such simple keyword specifications (typically 1 to 4 words) usually result in poor precision in the query returns. The advanced Boolean search query specifications can remedy a majority of these problems; however, most users shun these advanced search forms. Several meta-search

Table 3.2   Advantages and Disadvantages of Search Engines

Feature	Advantage	Disadvantage
Keyword query	Ease of use	Lost productivity due to poor precision
Instant response	Increased productivity if user knows what he is looking for	Decreased productivity, due to chasing links in query returns
Hierarchical subject categories	Increased productivity due to high precision	Low recall in response to user needs
Information discovery via robots	Reduced user workload	Lack of scalability and bandwidth inefficiency due to duplicative and uncooperative model

engines have been developed to address this issue. Meta-search engines incorporate the knowledge of where to look for information depending on the attributes of the information (Web resources, people, academic, commercial, technical report, news, entertainment, etc.) (Etzioni and Weld, 1994). Such an approach not only helps leverage existing specialized search indexes (Bowman et al., 1995) but also exploits parallel searches on distributed computing hardware (Dreilinger, 1995). The availability of parallel searches also offers intelligent post processing to combine search results and clean up redundant links, albeit at the expense of a slower response time to queries. Current search engines lack the personalization enabled by intelligent agents. For instance, a personalized search engine can provide query results with higher precision by keeping an on-line user model that provides the context of a user's simple keyword searches, thus easing user workload in information retrieval.

Information discovery and maintenance via Web robots is based on a model that does not require cooperation between information publishers and Web search engines. The Web robots not only have to keep following new links as the Web grows but also revisit links in order to keep the indexing up-to-date. This fundamental unscalability of current search engine architectures explains the increasing poor precision of Web search engines. In response, personalized search services and general architectures based on a cooperative model are emerging. DejaNews Research Service (http://www.dejanews.com) for Usenet news and City Net (http://www.city.net) for geographic directories are examples of the emerging specialized search services.

Harvest (http://harvest.transarc.com) is an example of a scalable architecture for indexing the Web based on a model that promotes cooperation. The Harvest system is designed to address the scalability issues discussed above: the rapid growth in data, user base, and data diversity (Bowman et al., 1995). Harvest solves scalability problems by distributing the load of information gathering, by using specialized brokers for building information indices, and by using massive replication and caching of popular information.

The gatherers of information are placed on the information provider sites (i.e., the Web servers) in order to eliminate the duplication of effort in collecting information, which is an inherent problem of software robots that are implemented on current search engines. The placement on Web servers reduces network traffic and increases the immediacy of information. When the gatherers are located on the information provider side, the information available on the server is analyzed as new information is published. The disadvantage of placing gatherers on provider sites is that the information providers must implement the gatherer software.

To improve retrieval, the Harvest system makes use of specialized brokers, each specialized in particular information. To reduce the size of the index database, brokers can also retrieve information from other brokers. The Harvest system also performs caching and massive replication for mirroring the information that the brokers have in order to alleviate bottlenecks resulting from heavy demand on particular brokers.

So what can search engines do for your organization? Here are a number of possible deployments:

- Index information on corporate servers for employee searches.

- Develop specialized search services using outside information resources on topics of significance to your organization (e.g., gathering coverage of your company's products in the trade press, tracking the mention of your company's name in mailing list discussions, developing a repository of your competitors' service problems by indexing FAQs, etc.).

- Develop corporate search query policies to promote the use of internal resources first, and then external resources based on price.

- Develop servers to share the common query result of user communities in your organization.

Information Filtering Agents

While search agents are useful in finding Web sites of particular interest to a user, information filtering agents find the *content* of particular interest to a user using different information sources.[2] Unlike Web search agents, which provide addresses of where to find information about the spruce budworm, information filtering agents gather recent articles about the spruce budworm and present the gist of these articles to you after filtering the content. In particular, information

---

[2]Search engines typically fully index only a small fraction of the URLs in their catalog. In contrast, filtering agents fully index the HTML pages for a small subset of URLs used as information sources.

Table 3.3   Filtering Agent Attributes

Element	Description
Environment	Internet
Task skills	Information gathering, filtering, and presentation
Knowledge	Web, news, finance, sports, weather
Communication Skills	HTTP, HTML, indexing protocols

filtering agents gather information from various sources (e.g., Web pages, news feeds, etc.), filter this information based on the personal preferences of the user, and present the filtered information to the user (typically as an updated Web page or an email message). There are several such agents today on the Web serving as personalized newspapers, including:

- NewsHound: the personal news service by San Jose Mercury News
- ZDNet personal View: the personalized computing news by Ziff-Davis
- NewsPage Direct: the personal newspaper by Individual Inc.

Table 3.3 provides an overview of the end-user agent model element for information filtering agents on the Internet. Filtering agents typically use a fixed number of information resources. For instance, the Personal Edition filtering agent at Pathfinder uses Time Inc.'s publications, such as *Time, Fortune, Money,* and *Sports Illustrated,* in addition to live news feeds. The information filtering agents typically capture user preferences in a personal profile. Figure 3.3 shows the architecture of a typical information filtering agent.

The indexing engine binds keywords to each article. The specification of measuring word significance by the frequency of use is based on the assumption that writers have a natural tendency to repeat certain words in order to elaborate the main point. Figure 3.4 shows the main premise of automated text processing. Therefore, most information retrieval systems model documents as terms and term frequency counts. Document model representations can be roughly divided into two groups:

- Vector space models, where a document is represented as a vector of attributes
- Tree structures, which represent a hierarchical view of a document

Most information retrieval systems also generate the thesaurus classes by synonyms in order to index words by word stems. The similarity between two

Figure 3.3   Filtering agent architecture.

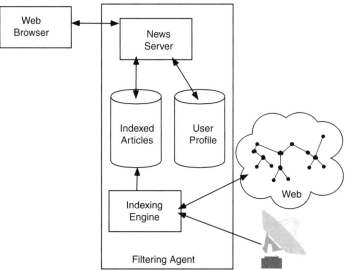

documents can be determined by a suitable distance metric. For instance, the Term Frequency∗Inverse Document Frequency or TfIDf) metric is specified by:

$$w_{ik} = f_{ik} \left[\log n - \log d_k + 1 \right]$$

where f_{ik} is the frequency of occurrences of term k in document i, d_k is the number of documents in the collection with term k, and n is the total collection. This weighting signifies that the significance of term k in document i is directly

Figure 3.4   Filtering based on word usage.

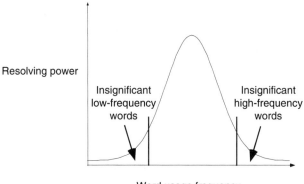

proportional to the number of times it appears in that document, and the importance of term k is inversely proportional to the number of documents in a collection where the term appears (Blustein, 1993).

NewsHound—Personalized Newspaper

NewsHound is a personalized newspaper that searches the stories in the *San Jose Mercury News* as well as several other newspapers to find articles that match a user's profile. Selected articles matching the user's profile are sent to the user's Internet address by email. NewsHound also searches Knight-Ridder/Tribune News Service, Associated Press, Business Wire, and other such sources.

A user can either use a Web or an email form to specify a profile for NewsHound. Figure 3.5 shows the specification of a profile for finding articles on the economic damage of the spruce budworm to American forests.

NewsHound uses the Verity Topics indexing engine with an email and Web form style interface. The news profile lets the user specify a couple of "required" and a number of "possible" terms. In addition, the user can specify terms that must not appear in any article. If a document does not have any of the excluded terms then NewsHound checks to see how often the possible and required terms are mentioned to assign a selectivity score. The selectivity score is set by the user to control the relevance of filtered documents.

Benefits of Information Filtering Agents

Information filtering agents deal with the electronic information overload by reducing the large stream of on-line information according to a user's information profile. Table 3.4 outlines the benefits of information retrieval agents. Current information filtering agents enable users to specify information profiles using a form type interface. While this user interface is suitable for specifying users' persistent information interests, it is nevertheless more cumbersome for dealing with users' dynamic information interests.

The drawbacks of the current information filtering agents can be addressed by incorporating learning into their architectures—such agents can then adapt to users' dynamic information interests based on user feedback. The monitoring of user behavior with particular information is needed to determine the user's personal information preferences (Bayer, 1995). These preferences consist of:

Figure 3.5   NewsHound personal profile specification.

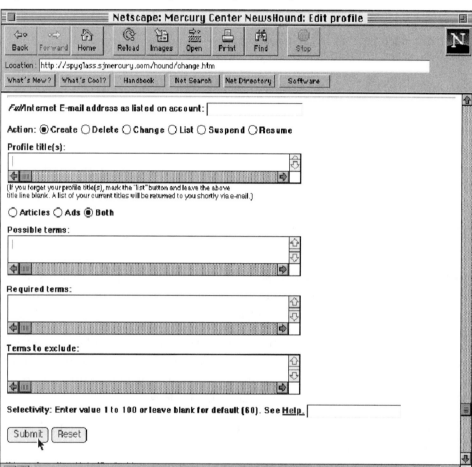

- *Persistent* user preferences, for instance, the kind of information captured in bookmark lists
- *Current* user preferences, for instance, the kind of links followed in a specific browsing session

An interest in information can be tracked either *directly* by asking the user for relevancy input, as done in Firefly (http://www.ffly.com), or *indirectly* by monitoring the use of information, as done in OpenSesame! and Leitizia Lieberman, (1995). Current user interests can be tracked by monitoring the topic of a followed link, the

Table 3.4   Benefits of Information Filtering Agents

Feature	Advantage	Benefit
Information profile	Easy-to-use form-based specification	Ideal for persistent; cumbersome for dynamic interests
Web page delivery	Information available as an updated Web page	Browser independence but requires site visits
Email delivery	Proactive information delivery	Eliminates site visits at the expense of email clutter
Profile based filtering	Enables one-to-one broadcasting	Reduced information overload
Heterogeneous information sources	Combines heterogeneous information sources	Reduces subscription costs, increased productivity

bookmarking of a link, or the time spent on a particular Web page. Similarly, users' actions can specify disinterest as well. For instance, the skipping of a link at the top of a list can be used to indicate disinterest.

What can information filtering agents do for your organization? Given the relatively low subscription base of current personalized information delivery services, it is clear that there is a very large potential for use of information filtering agents in the business market. Here are some possible applications:

- A filtering agent that brings the latest hardware configuration and pricing information for a purchasing manager

- A filtering agent that delivers the international, financial, political, and economic news that may impact a financial investment

- A filtering agent that tracks news related to an ongoing investigation for law enforcement agency personnel

- A filtering agent that gathers news about job market conditions for a specific employment category for a human resources professional

If the commercially available services do not solve the needs of your organization, then software tools underlying these information filtering agents are readily available off the shelf. The specialized personal newspapers can be deployed by integrating the off-the-shelf software components with some modest investment in software development.

Off-line Delivery Agents

Off-line delivery agents are information filtering agents that deliver personalized information in a locally viewable format without requiring a direct Internet connection. So when does an information filtering agent that delivers customized information via an email message become an off-line delivery agent? It happens when the information agent has its own information delivery software on the desktop for automatic information delivery and management of delivered information. Now that Microsoft and Netscape have publicly stated their intentions to include the delivery software in the future browser versions, the mainstream acceptance of this paradigm seems assured.

Table 3.5 gives an overview of the end-user agent model elements for off-line delivery agents. Off-line delivery agents typically are a fixed number of information resources. There are several such off-line delivery agents today on the Internet. The following are among the popular ones:

PointCast Network (http://www.pointcast.com) by PointCast Inc. is an advertising-supported personalized newspaper displayed as a screen saver.

Freeloader (http://www.freeloader.com) is a free service that lets users subscribe to specific Web pages for automatic delivery.

V-Cast (http://delivery.reach.com) is an advertising-supported personalized delivery system for video clips to be played back at five frames per second.

Table 3.5　Off-line Delivery Agents Attributes

Element	Description
Environment	Internet, news feeds
Task skills	Information
Knowledge	Web, news, finance, sports, weather
Communication skills	HTTP, Meta tags, Desktop OS

64

Part One • Chapter 3

PointCast Network

PointCast Network is a free service for delivering news, financial news, weather, sports, and other information onto the desktop. The information sources include Reuters, news headlines, PR Newswire, Time Warner Pathfinder, the *Boston Globe*, and the *Los Angeles Times*. Subscription to the PointCast Network requires the installation of desktop software either as a browser or as a Web browser plug-in. In using the service, the user specifies her or his individual interests. Figure 3.6 shows a sample personal profile for the PointCast Network.

The desktop client works in the background and downloads the specified information automatically according to a user-specified schedule. The display of retrieved information operates like a regular screen saver on the desktop. Figure 3.7 shows a sample screen from the network. The user can access the full news story by clicking

Figure 3.6   Personal profile for PointCast Network.

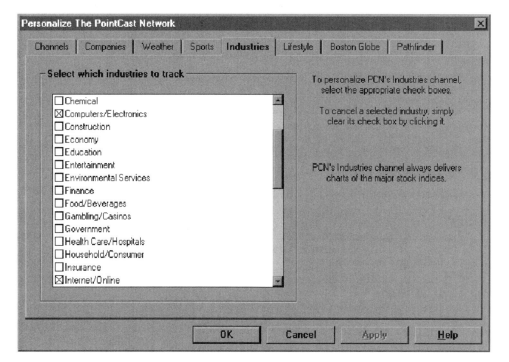

Figure 3.7   PointCast news on desktop.

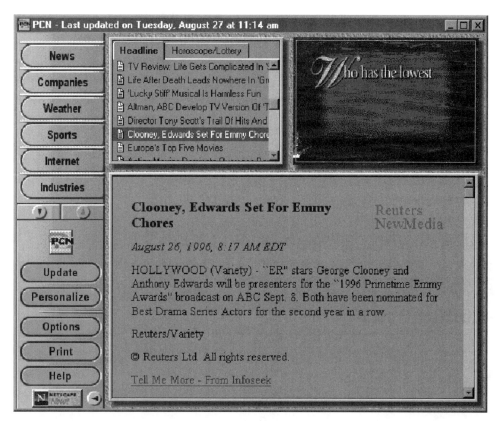

on the headline in the screen saver. PCN collects the advertisement statistics played, and uploads to the PCN server for advertisement sponsors.

Benefits of Off-line Delivery Agents

In contrast to information filtering agents that require users to visit a Web site or sift through email messages, off-line delivery agents bring information to a user's desktop. Off-line delivery agents enable narrowing of information to a community of users with the same information interests. Over time, this narrowing will transition into one-to-one broadcasting of information based on the unique information

Table 3.6   Benefits of Off-line Delivery Agents.

Feature	Advantage	Benefit
Direct delivery	Transparent delivery to desktop	User does not need to visit sites
Automates delivery	Delivery according to user-specified schedule	Avoidance of peak traffic hours
Local viewing	HTML links are locally resolved	Avoids the need to get on-line
Disk management	New information replaces out of date	Relieves user from disk management task

interests of users. Business applications of off-line delivery agents are discussed in the next chapter on intranet agents Table 3.6 summarizes the features and benefits of off-line delivery agents.

Notification Agents

Formally, a notification agent notifies users of events of significance to them where an event is a change in the state of information such as:

- Content change in a particular Web page
- Search engine additions for specified keyword queries
- User-specified reminders for personal events such as birthdays

Internet notification agents are typically server-based programs that poll user-specified sites. There are also desktop notifiers such as NetBuddy (http://www.inter-sol.com) and SmartBookmarks (http://www.firstfloor.com) that essentially provide the same functionality. One disadvantage of desktop notifiers is their computational burden on client CPUs. Another disadvantage is the bandwidth inefficiency, as server notifiers make more efficient use of bandwidth by serving the common interests of user groups. Desktop notifiers still offer an advantage over manual user surfing by increasing user productivity and reducing the number of HTTP connections, since desktop notifiers do not fetch the entire document (as is done in a Web browser).

Table 3.7 outlines the attributes of notification agents from an end-user viewpoint. Notifier agents monitor changes in information by employing one of the following methods:

- *HTTP "If-Modified-Since" request:* This is a special Header Request that returns a document only if the page has been modified since the specified date. This is a fairly inexpensive operation involving one HTTP connection and a couple of hundred bytes of information transfer.

- *Text only retrieval:* Some of the changes in information such as advertisements, dates, and counters are not of interest to users; notification agents will retrieve only the text of a page without the graphics and hyperlinks, and parse the retrieved text to determine any change in the published information.

- *Embedded HTML extensions:* These are directions to notification agents embedded in HTML documents by publishers. They can be placed in HEAD protocol fields as Meta tags, the document heading, or in the body of the document. For instance, an extension tag may instruct the notifier agent to ignore any change in a particular document section.

The embedded HTML extensions require the cooperation of Web publishers. Although this may seem an additional burden to Webmasters, such a solution is a good model for businesses selling a large number of products on the Web. Although HTML supports a Meta tag (i.e., information about information) it does not introduce any standard for document or product attributes. One such attempt to address this issue is the IDML extension to HTML. IDML (http://www.identify.com) is a set of HTML extensions that let publishers specify who they are, what the Web site is about, and the

Table 3.7　Notification Agent Attributes

Element	Description
Environment	Internet
Task Skills	Monitoring, determining, and notifying change in information
Knowledge	Web
Communication Skills	HTTP, Meta Tag, IDML

products for sale using a standard format. For instance, the IDML ID-PRODUCT tag allows the specification of a product's department, keywords, price and currency, and location. While IDML does provide a technical solution, the market standard will nevertheless be set by the "standard" adopted by Netscape and/or Microsoft.

URL-minder: A Notification Agent

URL-minder (http://www.netmind.com/url-minder) is a notification agent that retrieves Web resources periodically to detect changes from the last retrieval. A user registers a Web site of interest using the form shown in Figure 3.8. URL-minder monitors the specified Web resource and sends the user an e-mail message whenever it detects a change, thus relieving the user from having to visit the site regularly to check for changes. URL-minder can also notify a user when the query results from a search engine change.

URL-minder monitors each registered page once a week for changes. URL-minder checks the change, if any, of each retrieved document using a signature computed by the Cyclic Redundancy Check algorithm. In order to filter the imprint of cosmetic changes on the computed signature, URL-minder has HTML extension tags instructing its robot to exclude specific sections of a document.

Benefits of Notification Agents

A significant portion of a knowledge worker's day is spent monitoring changes in published information. While this is unavoidable for continually changing

Table 3.8   Benefits of Notification Agents

Feature	Advantage	Benefit
Monitoring	Monitors for change in information	Reduces user workload
Browserless monitoring	Monitor only header file or body text	Increased network efficiency
Change determination	Machine check of document change	Reduced user workload
Server implementation	Checks each resource for multiple clients	Eliminates bandwidth waste
Notification	Notifies user of changes	Increases site visits

Figure 3.8   URL-minder specifications.

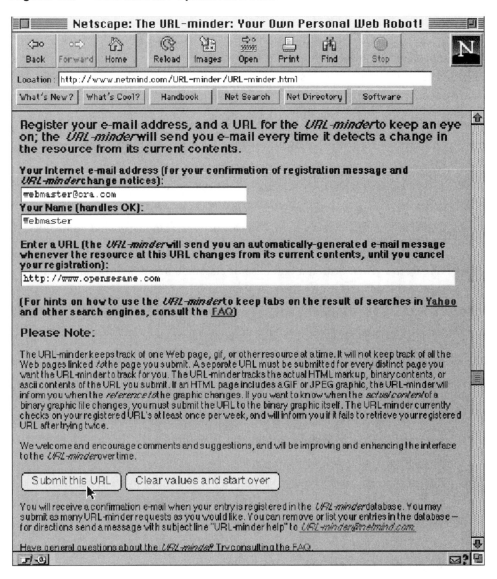

context (e.g. news, stock prices, etc.), notification agents can obviate the need for monitoring sporadic changes in information. Table 3.8 outlines the benefits of notification agents.

Other Service Agents

There are numerous agents on the Internet that provide specialized services to users. These range from shopping agents that find the best price on a CD to matchmaking agents that notify users when a suitable candidate joins a matchmaking service. These agents can be categorized into the following groups:

- *Announcement agents:* Remind users of important occasions (e.g., birthday, anniversary, Valentine's Day and the like) that are customized for personal needs.

- *Book agents:* Track newly released books that match a user's reading interests.

- *Business information monitoring agents:* Monitor the exchange of information on the Internet relating to services, products, industry, and companies, and make a formal report of the findings.

- *Classified agents:* Search a database of classified ads daily to find a user-specified item, and notify the user via email.

- *Direct mail agents:* Bring personalized direct mail advertising that matches the user's stated personal background, activities, and lifestyle.

- *Financial service agents:* Deliver email messages containing prices and financial news for a personalized portfolio of securities and mutual funds.

- *Food and wine agents:* Remember each user's previous purchases and tasting notes to make customized presentations of the inventory during the next visit.

- *Job agents:* Serve as virtual recruiters to find employees that match employer job profiles.

- *Entertainment agents:* Finds communities with similar interests to those of the user, and recommends albums, movies, and so on based on group evaluations.

- *Shopping agents:* Perform comparison shopping for user-specified items at virtual stores (e.g., http://bf.cstar.ac.com/).

- *Site agents:* Function as a virtual hosts at 3D and client sites.

The various service agents can be broadly categorized into the following groups based on their internal architectures:

- Agents that perform intelligent database queries and notify users

- Agents that use a parallel search algorithm to query Web resources and integrate query results on behalf of the user

- Agents that use collaborative filtering to find user clusters for recommendations based on social communities

- Agents that use natural language techniques to engage in conversations with users

In the next sections, we will discuss some of the service agents.

BargainFinder—A Shopping Agent

BargainFinder is an experimental virtual shopping agent for the Web developed by Andersen Consulting. For instance, BargainFinder uses a parallel query architecture similar to meta search engines in order to query pricing and availability of user-specified music CDs. Figure 3.9 shows the specification query form for the album *Great Songs* by the artist Delbert McClinton. Figure 3.10 shows the results of comparison shopping in the music stores that BargainFinder searches. Three of them blocked the BargainFinder query. Two of the stores do not have the searched album. Three of the stores have the requested album in stock with various forms of shipping pricing options. The BargainFinder prototype indicates the challenge of using shopping agents on the Web. Three of the virtual music stores block BargainFinder because they do not want to compete on price and availability alone.

BargainFinder uses the parallel search architecture employed in meta search engines such as Meta Crawler (http://www.cs.washington.edu/research/metacrawler) and heuristic topic phrase extraction techniques (Krulwich, 1995). The comparison shopping agent takes the user's product query and submits it in parallel to a group of on-line vendors by filling out the form at each site. The agent parses the query results after filtering the header, trailer, and advertisements to find each vendor's price for the product. The agent then combines the filtered results as a summary to the user. Figure 3.11 shows the architecture of a comparison shopping agent. The advantages of comparison shopping agents include the following:

- Provide a unified interface for different vendors, thus negating the need for the user to navigate to different stores and deal with separate user interfaces.

- Find the best price and availability, thus relieving the user from having to search for a product at each site.

Figure 3.9   BargainFinder query.

The challenges facing such shopping agents include:

■ The virtual stores' reluctance to allow agents to shop, as most retailers do not want to compete on price and availability alone. For instance, CDnow has reviews, samples, and recommendations for most albums and artists in its inventory, and thus is reluctant to have its content reduced to a single price.

■ Users' trust in the agents' ability to notice sales and special promotions. For instance, a software product that interests a user may be part of a software bundle for a slightly higher price that may be missed by a shopping agent.

Two remedies have been attempted to address the limitations of current shopping agents:

Cooperative agent/vendor model: In this approach, there is a tacit cooperation between agents and vendors, IMDL extension to HTML is one such an

---

Figure 3.10   BargainFinder results.

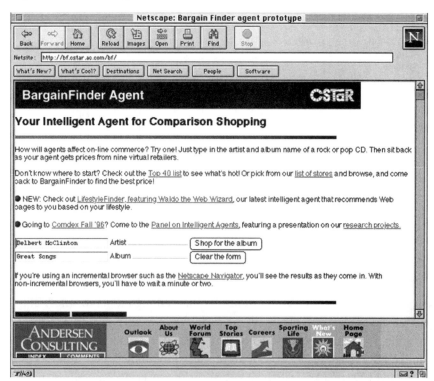

attempt. IMDL gives vendors control of what products can be directly accessed. In essence, IDML gives vendors a structured way to identify their products.

Vendor form learning agent: This approach, implemented in ShopBot (http://www.cs.washington.edu/research/shopbot), attempts to learn how to shop at virtual stores without requiring any cooperation by vendors. ShopBot uses machine learning to find the HTML forms with product information at a vendor's site and identify the product information matching the query on these forms.

We suspect that a long-term solution will emerge when retailing on the Web goes beyond today's functionality, which by and large replicates mail order catalogs.

Figure 3.11   Comparison shopping agent architecture.

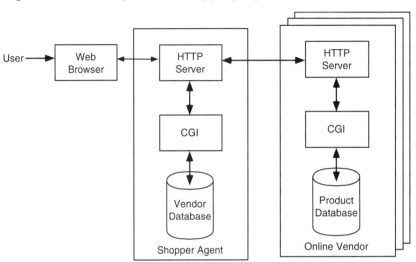

Such a long term solution requires the invention of a retailing model for the Web. The comparison shopping agent can easily be tricked by the tried-and-true techniques of retailing that have been refined over the years. For example, instead of blocking the BargainFinder agent, what if an on-line store immediately announces a sale on the queried CD (thanks to its own spy agent that checks competitors' prices daily) in order to entice the customer into its site. Once the customer has entered the store, the sales agent can then virtually sweet-talk the customer into buying a second CD to make up for the discount on the first one.

One can easily envision how the above example would converge into a framework of places where buyer and seller agents negotiate with each other to perform transactions on behalf of users and vendors. This environment may or may not turn out to be the kind of agent space envisioned by Telescript. We believe that the Web retail model will emerge from the bottom up, by trial and error as opposed to a top-down approach instituted by a framework.

Firefly—A Collaboration Agent

Firefly is a collaboration agent that makes artist and album recommendations based on the group evaluation of music CDs. Such collaboration agents force users explicitly to evaluate specific products. The agent then finds users with similar preferences and recommends other products that may be of interest to a specific user based on the recommendations of users with similar interests. In essence, collaboration agents try to capture word-of-mouth advertising that is commonly practiced today. Figure 3.12 shows the evaluation form for Firefly.

Figure 3.12   Firefly album evaluation form.

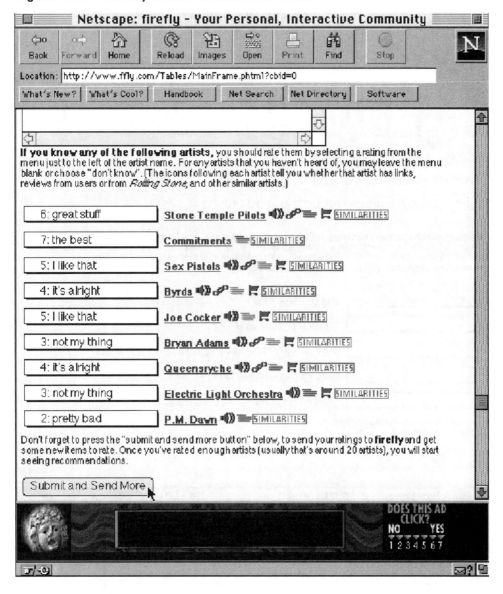

The agent forces the user to evaluate a sufficiently large number of albums in order to be able to draw statistically significant conclusions about user's taste in music. Figure 3.13 shows the recommendations of the Firefly agent.

Figure 3.13   Firefly recommendations.

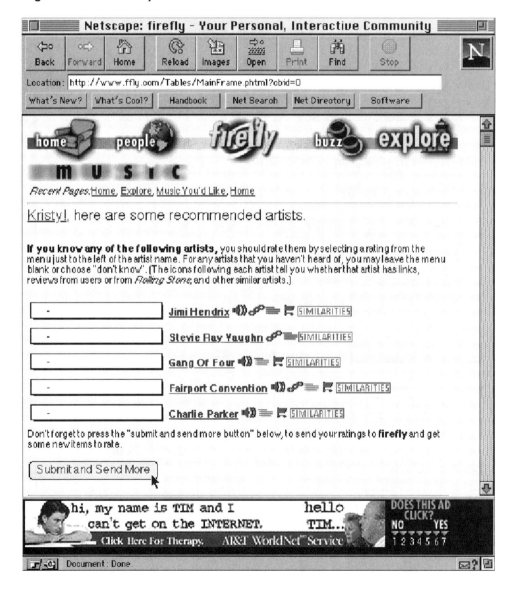

Firefly uses memory-based reasoning to find user pattern clusters (Starfill, Lin, and Waltz, 1994). Memory-based reasoning operates on situation-action pairs. For instance, in this application the situation would be described by the artist, album, and associated attributes such as genre of music, whereas the action would represent the user's like or dislike of the album in question. Memory-based reasoning enables a nearest-neighbor recommendation by using a distance metric that computes the weighted sum of the distance between the corresponding attributes of two situations. Memory-based reasoning is in essence a case-based reasoning technique, where every user action is used as a case entry.

There are other methods for building collaboration agents. For instance, a domain expert can use a rule-based system to encode recommendations after mining user data off-line using clustering techniques. Another approach is that taken by Yenta (Foner, Leonard, and Maes, 1994), which supports a distributed registry of user interests while preserving privacy. In such an environment each user agent keeps track of other user agents it encounters, and bootstraps itself by asking for referrals to other agents in order to find other users that may match the specific interest of a given user. The advantage of Yenta is its scalability as it does not require a central registry of user interests.

Julia—A Chatterbot

Julia is a conversational agent for Multi User Dungeons (MUDs). Julia is a C program that incorporates a significantly greater number of tricks than Eliza (Weizenbaum, 1976), which successfully played an imitation game by answering questions with questions. A chatterbot lives in a MUD where it converses with other players, and answers players' questions about other players, rooms, and objects. Figure 3.14 shows the architecture of a chatterbot.

Julia keeps track of the most recent utterances of the user in a given conversation. Most of its topic-oriented responses are encoded in an activation network. The conversation generation thus reduces to a retrieval problem from a conversation network. Chatterbot employs several tricks to convince the user of its human-like behavior including:

- Repeating user's input in questions

- Admitting ignorance

Figure 3.14   Chatterbot architecture.

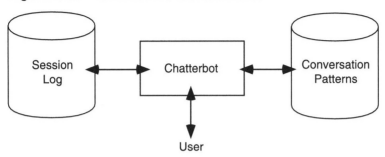

- Changing the topic of conversation
- Using conversational statements
- Using humorous statements
- Providing excerpts from Usenet news
- Simulating typing, mimicking a human's imperfect performance

Most importantly, it stores fragments of a conversation in an activation network.

The following transcript from a conversation with Julia shows some of the tricks. For instance, Julia repeats user input while admitting ignorance:

Julia: Do you live on a farm?

User: No I don't live on a farm. Do you think we should or shouldn't elect a President who grew up on a farm?

Julia: Do you have any trouble keeping a farm animal where you live?

User: Not really. One of my neighbors has a couple of llamas.

Julia: Well, that's very lucky.

User: What is so lucky about having two llamas in your yard?

Julia: I don't know. What do you think so lucky about having two llamas in my yard is, Judge?

User: I see. You don't like judging?

Julia: I live for your approval.

The following conversation shows the use of humor in the right context:

User: Tell me something that I don't know. Who is the most prominent politician you gossiped with?

Julia: Oh, I'm supposed to write about cats and dogs, now. Politics are out of bounds for today.

User: Shucks. The election is around the corner. Gossiping is hot now in politics.

Julia: So when will Socks write his book?

User: When he gets the boot!

The following example shows Julia's use of a conversation statement to start a new conversation topic:

User: Julia, you seem to be an expert on pets.

Julia: Guinea pigs are about as smart as cucumbers.

User: I disagree.

Julia: In case you think I was slandering my childhood guinea pig by comparing his intelligence to that of vegetables: yes, he did have an acute ear for things like his food being prepared, etc., and would whistle vigorously for it. So while maybe they aren't out-and-out stupid, I guess they are, hmmm, "unambitious", or maybe "very content", heck, they might be geniuses and just don't let on.

So what can chatterbots do for your business even if your business is not in the entertainment field? There are a number of off-the-shelf components that can be used in natural language understanding to develop conversational chatterbots. One such component is Natural Language Understanding (NLU) software from Unisys, which includes an expert system. Concepts from several linguistic theories form the foundation for the natural language processing system. The NLU converts English language, either spoken words or stored text, into meaning and then responds appropriately. It can respond to many different versions of the same statement, such as "I don't know" or "I'm not sure" or "Let me have more information," because it is not simply translating words into text, but interpreting the meaning of the words.

NLU technology includes three main components—syntactic, semantic, and pragmatic analysis. These generic processing modules can be reused for any domain, while the application-specific domain information is provided through domain library tables.

The basic natural language processor contains over 400 grammar rules that ensure sophisticated and efficient handling of a wide range of English constructions. These include rules for conjunctions, *wh*-constructions, nominal compounds, and over 30 subcategories of object complements for verbs.

In natural language understanding, ill-formed input refers to "lexical problems such as misspelled words, sentential problems such as missing words or phrases and bad word order, semantic problems such as anomalous or self-contradictory sentences, and contextual problems such as incoherent requests or continuations" (Allen, 1983). Fass and Cercone (1992) indicate that users of natural language interfaces typically produce ill-formed input which must be handled by the interface. The biggest problem with ill-formed input, according to Fass and Cercone, is locating it.

There are a number of possible applications for chatterbots:

- A chatterbot that visits on-line chatrooms on topics related to your company's products

- A chatterbot that unabashedly presents comparison ads against your competitors' products

- A support chatterbot that queries information requests about your company's products

- A chatterbot that initiates interesting conversations in on-line chatrooms

AdHound—A Classified Agent

AdHound (http://www.adone.com) is an intelligent agent that searches a database of classified ads for the items specified by the user. When AdHound finds a match it emails the user the relevant classified ads. The user specifies the search via a keyword form shown in Figure 3.15. Figure 3.16 shows an email dialog from the AdHound agent.

Figure 3.15   AdHound specification form.

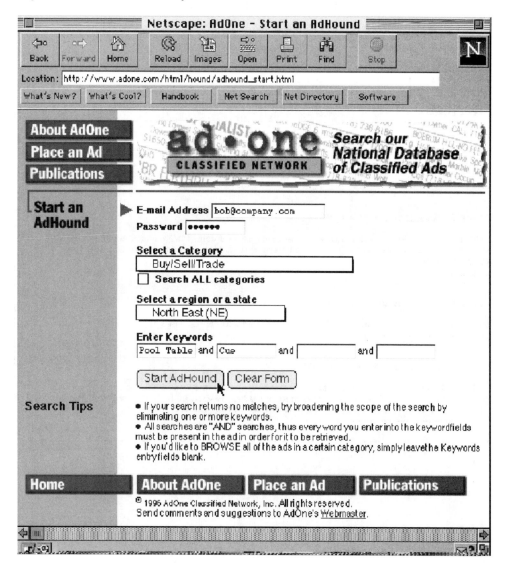

Figure 3.16 AdHound email notification.

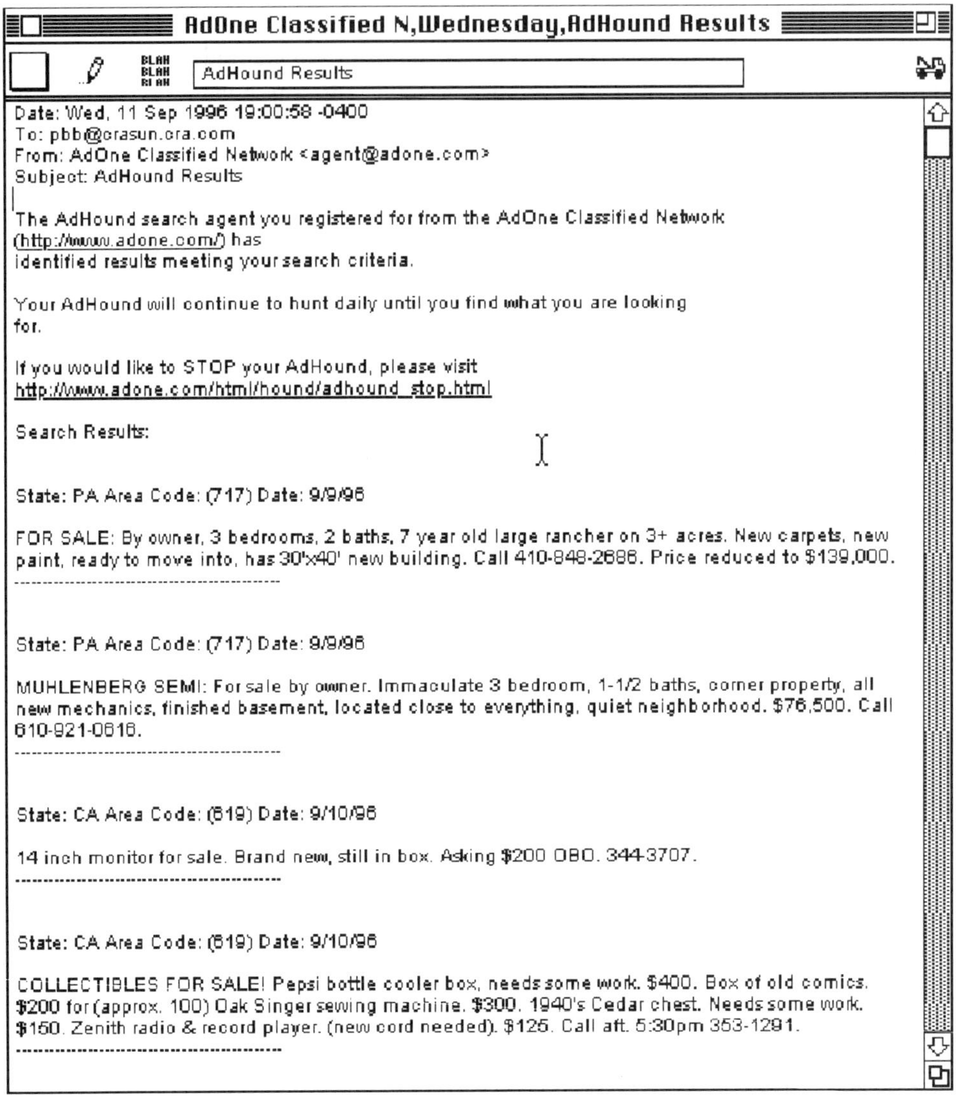

AdOne Classified N,Wednesday,AdHound Results

AdHound Results

Date: Wed, 11 Sep 1996 19:00:58 -0400
To: pbb@crasun.cra.com
From: AdOne Classified Network <agent@adone.com>
Subject: AdHound Results

The AdHound search agent you registered for from the AdOne Classified Network
(http://www.adone.com/) has
identified results meeting your search criteria.

Your AdHound will continue to hunt daily until you find what you are looking
for.

If you would like to STOP your AdHound, please visit
http://www.adone.com/html/hound/adhound_stop.html

Search Results:

State: PA Area Code: (717) Date: 9/9/96

FOR SALE: By owner, 3 bedrooms, 2 baths, 7 year old large rancher on 3+ acres. New carpets, new paint, ready to move into, has 30'x40' new building. Call 410-848-2686. Price reduced to $139,000.

State: PA Area Code: (717) Date: 9/9/96

MUHLENBERG SEMI: For sale by owner. Immaculate 3 bedroom, 1-1/2 baths, corner property, all new mechanics, finished basement, located close to everything, quiet neighborhood. $76,500. Call 610-921-0616.

State: CA Area Code: (619) Date: 9/10/96

14 inch monitor for sale. Brand new, still in box. Asking $200 OBO. 344-3707.

State: CA Area Code: (619) Date: 9/10/96

COLLECTIBLES FOR SALE! Pepsi bottle cooler box, needs some work. $400. Box of old comics. $200 for (approx. 100) Oak Singer sewing machine. $300. 1940's Cedar chest. Needs some work. $150. Zenith radio & record player. (new cord needed). $125. Call aft. 5:30pm 353-1291.

Summary

In this chapter, we presented a brief overview of Internet agents, and classified Internet agents into Web search, information filtering, off-line delivery, and notification and service agents. In particular, we covered Web robots in the search agent and commerce agents in the service agent categories. We then discussed each Internet agent category in terms of the end-user agent model introduced in Chapter 1, and described examples of commercial agents for each category.

We covered the specific agent features that provide the reduced workload, increased productivity, network efficiency, and reduced subscription cost benefits of Internet agents. Many of the Internet agents considered are directly applicable to the enterprise Intranet discussed in the next chapter.

Intranet
Agents

Intranet is the term used to describe an internal corporate network based on Internet technology. In particular, intranets use the TCP/IP[1] foundation of a local and/or wide area network and use software tools based on the HTTP[2] protocol on this network. Typically, an intranet can be accessed by the employees of an organization, as well as external customers and suppliers, with a password. The following are various business applications of intranets:

- Building an effective internal communications medium to publish corporate information

- Creating virtual communities across the various units of an organization to promote effective communication between groups for increased productivity

- Sales force automation to enable order tracking and automate transaction processing

---

[1]TCP/IP stands for Transmission Control Protocol/Internet Protocol. This is a network protocol developed by Bolt Beranek and Newman for the Department of Defense in the early 1970s. TCP/IP is based on packet switching for guaranteed data delivery.

[2]HTTP stands for Hypertext Transfer Protocol, the communication protocol for accessing Internet servers. Consult the Web Primer in Chapter 3 for further details.

- Marketing support automation to provide marketing collateral on demand

- Customer service with collaborative knowledge sharing among your customers for enhanced customer support

- Internal help desk to provide corporate process, procedure, and resource guidance

- Human resource support to publish information for employees and form-based automation of employee requests

An intranet agent is a software agent that resides on a corporate HTTP server. Such agents help manage business processes on behalf of the employees, customers, and suppliers of a corporation. An agent model fits nicely into such an environment as a business process itself can be viewed as a collection of autonomous agents that interact with each other on interdependent tasks, as noted by Jennings, et. al (1996).

Every category of Internet agent covered in the previous chapter, such as Web search, information filtering, off-line delivery agents, has applications on the corporate intranet. Intranet agents include additional application categories:

Collaboration agents: These agents bring agent functionality to collaborative software by focusing on information sharing by a group of users.

Process automation agents: These agents automate workflow in business applications such as customer information request handling systems.

Database agents: These agents act as front ends to corporate databases, such as employee notification for information change.

Mobile agents: These agents transport themselves across a private network to accomplish tasks on behalf of users.

First we present some intranet applications of the Internet agent categories covered in Chapter 3. Next we discuss the new categories of intranet agents and provide some examples.

Intranet Search Agents

Intranet search agents enable users to search for information on corporate Web servers. These intranet agents let employees have integrated access to the various islands of information distributed across the enterprise. Typically, such search

Figure 4.1   Intranet search engine architecture.

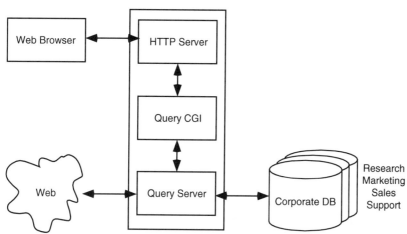

agents integrate Internet search functionality as well. Figure 4.1 shows the architecture of an intranet search engine solution.

The heart of an intranet search solution is the search server application that allows users to query multiple databases using a Web browser form. What gives such a solution its agent functionality is the background indexing of corporate databases, and proactive notification of changes in information on these databases. Although such indexing is designed to handle real-time operation, most database administrators employ nightly indexing schemes.

Table 4.1 shows the attributes of intranet search agents in terms of the end-user model we have been using to compare agents throughout the book. In contrast to Internet search engines, intranet search agents need to support (index, retrieve in original format, etc.) common corporate document formats, ranging from Microsoft

Table 4.1   Intranet Search Agent Model Attributes

Element	Description
Environment	Intranet
Task skills	Indexing document databases, searching, and retrieval
Knowledge	Corporate databases and document formats
Communication skills	HTTP, SQL, CGI, WAIS

Word to Adobe Portable Document Format (PDF). Moreover, intranet search agent architecture needs to be a distributed solution to be able to query the various servers scattered around the enterprise.

Table 4.2 summarizes the benefits of intranet search agents. One of the advantages of an intranet search solution is the savings in worker hours and network bandwidth spent in searching for information in conducting the day-to-day operations of a business. To be able to use a well-defined corporate procedure to search internal resources first, then use free public resources, and, finally, for-fee services would result in a considerable cost savings for an organization. Similarly, capturing the search results for common queries of employees on servers would promote the virtual workgroup collaboration with attendant cost savings.

Surfboard—An Intranet Search Engine

Surfboard by Fulcrum (http://www.fulcrum.com) is an intranet information retrieval software that can be used to build intranet search agents. Surfboard uses a client/server architecture with an ODBC interface support. With Surfboard, a user specifies a set of resources to be searched, shown in Figure 4.2. Typically, these resources would include word processing documents, relational databases, message bulletin boards, and so on. The user then specifies a keyword search criterion as done in Internet search agents, and Surfboard returns a list of documents ranked by relevance, shown in Figure 4.3.

Table 4.2   Benefits of Intranet Search Agents

Feature	Advantage	Benefit
Multidatabase search	Client search of all corporate databases	Increased organizational productivity, reduced costs
Search save on servers	Enables sharing of search results within organization	Reduced workload
Multiple-level access control	Allows access of certain field to authorized users	Corporate security
Proactive notification	Notifies users of change in information	Increased productivity, enhanced corporate communications

Figure 4.2   Surfboard query resource specification.

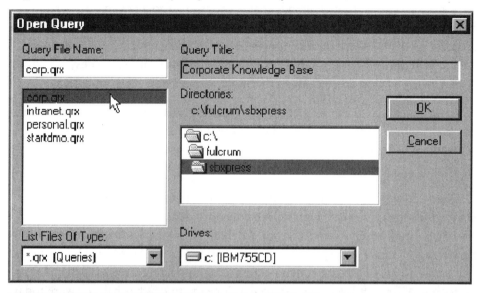

Figure 4.3   Surfboard query return.

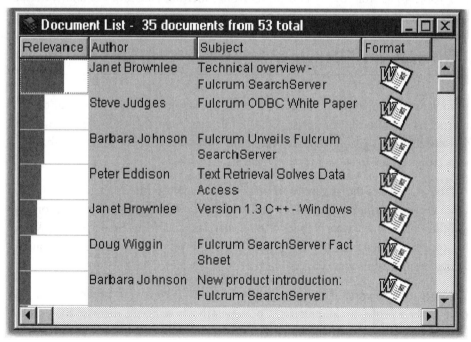

Surfboard uses a relational database model to store the indexed information in table structures. Each row of an index table corresponds to a document. Column fields denote the document attributes. For instance, the author, title, or keyword summary for Microsoft Word documents can be added to the table schema. Documents are accessed only for display and indexing purposes. Surfboard can index, search, and display native file formats including Microsoft Office, Adobe PDF, and others.

Agent functionality can be incorporated into Surfboard by using SearchObject—a query resource and keyword specification that can be reexecuted at any time. Scheduling the execution of queries and automatic postprocessing of results can be accomplished via scripts.

Given the inevitable integration of a Web browser into the desktop operating system GUI shell, can the integration of content-based search functionality with server operating systems be far behind? We think not. Both the Microsoft Information Server and Netscape Enterprise Server incorporate Verity's OEM search engine. In fact, agent solutions integrated with enterprising messaging systems such as Lotus Notes and Microsoft Exchange can be developed with off-the-shelf software today with TopicNotes from Verity and BIND from Fulcrum. Netscape's similar offering with CollabraShare is not far behind.

Information Filtering Agents

An intranet information filtering agent is the application of the corresponding Internet agent onto the enterprise. On the Intranet, such agents create personalized views of the information resources of an enterprise, such as corporate databases, workgroup discussions, and industry-specific newsfeeds.

Table 4.3 shows the attributes of intranet information filtering agents. Table 4.4 summarizes the benefits of intranet information filtering agents. Current information filtering agents let users specify their interests via a form-based profile. While this approach is ideal for persistent user interest, it requires users to continuously change their information profiles in order to track their dynamic interests.

Information filtering agents proactively notify users of new information that matches their professional interests. Consequently, these agents increase the usage of corporate servers by notifying users of the availability of new critical information.

Table 4.3   Intranet Filtering Agent Attributes

Element	Description
Environment	Intranet
Task Skills	Information organizing, sharing and presentation
Knowledge Skills	Corporate database, workgroup discussions, newsfeeds
Communication	HTTP, HTML, OLAP

TopicAGENT—An Intranet Information Filtering Agent

TopicAGENT from Verity (http://www.verity.com) is an agent toolkit for indexing documents on enterprise servers, and for creating agents that watch user-specified sources for changes and automatically notify subscribers of new relevant information matching their interests. Figure 4.4 shows the architecture of TopicAGENT server toolkit. Agents built using this toolkit monitor information sources, filter monitored information, and deliver personalized results. TopicAGENT toolkit promotes the use of a separate agent for each topic (i.e., subject area). For instance, the NewsHound agent described in Chapter 3 uses the TopicAGENT toolkit and sports a user interface where a separate agent is required for each user interest topic. The

Table 4.4   Benefits of Intranet Filtering Agents

Feature	Advantage	Benefit
Information Profile	Form-based specification of individual workgroup interests	Ideal for persistent but cumbersome for dynamic interests
Notification	Proactive information delivery	Increased site visits and increased productivity by alleviating information search
Profile based filtering	Relevant information for critical decisions	Increased organizational productivity
Heterogeneous information sources	Combines heterogeneous information sources	Increased productivity and reduced subscription costs through sharing

Figure 4.4   TopicAGENT server toolkit architecture.

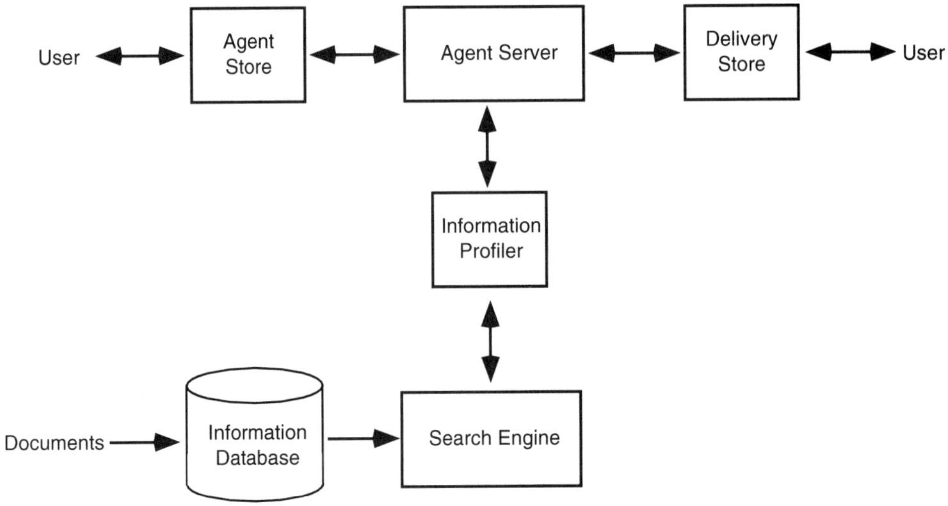

user, interacting with the Agent Store, adds a new agent, or modifies an existing agent, or removes an agent, or temporarily deactivates an agent, or reactivates a suspended agent. Corresponding to each new agent, a profile is added to an internal profile network, sharing any profile substitutes already specified by another agent. New documents from the information database are evaluated against the network of profiles using the prefiltering engine. The engine returns a list of agents and a corresponding relevance score. For each agent with a score higher than a threshold, the information about the document is delivered to the user according to the user-specified delivery format and schedule (e.g., email, Web page, fax, pager format, on-demand; hourly, daily, delayed delivery schedule). The topicAGENT engine has been incorporated into a number of high-volume client applications such as Lotus Notes and Netscape Suite Spot Server.

The shortcomings of the current intranet information filtering agents include the following:

■   These agents promote a separate notification for each user interest, adding to the information clutter in the user's in-box, and increasing the information overload.

■   These agents do not incorporate a user model that can monitor the user's processing of the delivered information in order to learn user's dynamic information preferences, and automatically adapt to them.

The next generation of information filtering agents will incorporate learned user models using components such as the Learn Sesame learning engine (http://www.opensesame.com) for continuous personalization. Such agents monitor user behavior to learn user preferences continuously, and dynamically adapt to changing user interests. In topicAGENT, a learning interface agent would in essence manage the user's relationship with the various topic agents. Figure 4.5 is an example. This type of interface agent can provide the following functionality to the user:

- Recommend an agent for each new learned user interest topic such as books on the programming language Java

- Modify an existing agent based on the learned use of agent recommended information, for instance, learning the specific user interest in books on collectibles in the general category of books on crafts

- Remove an agent when the user repeatedly does not make use of this agent's recommendation, for instance, learning user disinterest in programming books published by a certain publisher

- Temporarily deactivate an agent for time intervals when the user is not interested in that agent's recommendations, for instance, learning user disinterest on entertainment events on Mondays while reactivating this suspended agent when the user interest returns on Fridays

Figure 4.5   Integration of a learning interface agent into TopicAGENT.

Similarly, the next generation of information filtering agents will incorporate collaborative filtering that makes recommendations based on other users' prior experience with an information resource.

Collaboration Agents

Collaboration software is an application that runs over a network and enables a team to work together sharing information. The products Lotus Notes, Microsoft Exchange, Novell GroupWise, and Netscape Collabora Share are examples of commercial software within this category. Other products that focus on specific niches in collaboration software include those for project management, such as GroupWorks from FTP Software, and Workgroup Information Manager from Commence, and those for discussion management such as OpenMind by Attachmate and Team Talk from TraxSoftworks.

Collaboration software is typically built around a messaging system as messaging is a key component of collaboration software. Collaboration software assists the members of a workgroup in:

- Group scheduling
- Discussion groups
- Resource tracking
- Document management
- Collaborative filtering

A collaboration agent is a softvvare component that brings agent functionality into collaboration software. Such functionality allows a user to create task-specific agents to perform a set of actions in response to a trigger-event within the collaboration software environment. Some simple tasks for collaboration software products include the following:

- Save and re-execute sharable queries that search groupware databases.
- Perform a script (e.g., copy to database, send mail message, etc.) whenever a user-specified event (e.g., a document with a matching set of keywords) is added to the database.
- Perform a script according to a time-based schedule.

In the next section, we discuss the agent in the leading groupware software—
Lotus Notes.

Lotus Notes Agents

Release 4 of Lotus Notes introduces agents in the client application. In essence this
is *only* an extension of the LotusScript macros that have been part of Notes since
the beginning. Notes agents are LotusScript programs which a user can attach to
any database or even individual Notes objects within a database with proper authorization access. These agents can then be triggered by one of a number of events
and perform user-defined actions. For example, a user could attach an agent to a
database of enterprise financial data so that he or she would be notified whenever
the database was updated.

Notes agents are easily constructed by selecting the database of interest in the
Notes client and then selecting Create/Agent from the Notes client toolbar. This
presents a visual editor which is not as slick as Visual Basic's but provides similar
capabilities. The agent is defined in four fields:

1. The name of the agent, with an optional comment.

2. A definition of when the agent should run. The options are:

   • Manually from the agent list.

   • If new mail has arrived.

   • If documents (Notes objects) have been created, modified, or pasted.

   • On a schedule of hourly, daily, weekly, monthly (or never). The user can
     specify a starting time.

3. What documents should the agent act on?

   • All documents in the database to which the agent is attached.

   • All new and modified documents since the last time the agent was run.

   • All unread documents in the selected view of the database.

   • Selected documents.

   The agent may also search fields within documents for specific words
   in Boolean combinations.

4. What should the agent do?

   Here the user is able to enter a LotusScript program that can examine
   named fields within documents, apply conditional logic to the contents, and

modify fields. The user also has the option of entering a simple command or a formula, which is a single line statement. The advance that distinguishes Notes agents from their predecessors—macros, which were also written in LotusScript—is the introduction of language support in LotusScript for conditional branching within a macro/agent. LotusScript is a class-oriented language and operates on Notes objects, which are primarily document containers. As a language it is almost, but not quite, identical to Visual Basic, and Visual Basic programmers would have no difficulty in learning the dialect. The advantages that programming in LotusScript has over Visual Basic are:

- *Integration with the Notes framework.* It is trivial to hook the agents to Notes events.

- *Integration with the Notes databases.* Access to database fields is easy.

- *Automatic version distribution.* This is perhaps the best part. Notes has a sophisticated set of mechanisms for replicating databases. Since the agents are part of the database to which they are attached, modifications to the agent are propagated like any other database update. This means that the developer can test the agent locally and have high confidence that it will execute correctly on remote replicas of the database.

For exceptional cases, a programmer can exploit the Notes API to delve deeper inside a Notes object to perform low-level operations programmed in C++.

So how do Notes agents help the enterprise? Although restricted to operations within the Lotus Notes framework, the Notes agent facility provides a powerful and fairly straightforward set of tools for creating helpful agents. Notes provides a highly structured environment for the management and networked distribution of information. The Notes agents can easily exploit both this structure and the support for distribution. So you can attach an agent to the corporate financial database that will notify you, for example, whenever a particular field is updated, and through the replication mechanism you can get this action performed wherever that database is distributed in your network. Furthermore, since the structured documents presumably accurately reflect the logical frameworks of the enterprise's products or services, the agent is provided with a ready-made world view or ontology. So it is very easy to set up watchdog agents. It is also easy to set up information agents, since the agents can perform searches on the fields within documents. So, for example, any time and anywhere a document in a selected database is created which contains the word "encoding," you can arrange to receive a copy of the document attached to your mail. Notes agents benefit also from the very thorough access control system built into the Notes databases; Notes agents can access or act only on databases to which their creator is authorized.

The new Lotus Domino intranet platform extends the capabilities of Notes to a wider range of databases, so that Notes can coexist with, and perhaps eventually take over, an existing enterprise system; at the same time, Domino allows these databases to be accessed as Web servers. The Notes agents remain within the Notes framework, but this framework is now extended to other content sources. In practice, office workers still do not create Notes agents; most of this work is done by the Information Systems groups. So within their own framework—and for the time being, we do not know how to build totally general agents—Notes agents are a very complete and effective tool for automating processes and the management of information.

Process Automation Agents

Process automation agents automate workflow in business applications. Typically, business processes involve the interaction of an employee, customer, vendor with multiple units of an organization. These different units of a business (e.g., shipping, support, sales, etc.) are often geographically dispersed and relatively autonomous, each owning a piece of the task involving a customer's interaction with a single business entity. In a conventional workflow system, automation involves the automatic execution of a sequence of tasks defining a business process. For instance, in a transaction processing system, a workflow engine executes a workflow script. The differences between traditional workflow automation and process agents can be summarized in the following way:

> In a traditional workflow system, the central workflow engine monitors all system events. In contrast, process agents offer a distributed infrastructure where each agent represents a separate business task with local monitoring capabilities, thus offering a more scalable solution.
>
> Conventional workflow automation works in structured environments where the business process is defined for every possible condition. In contrast, process

automation agents typically have the capability of managing resources during task execution, thus offering a more flexible environment.

Traditional workflow solutions support exception handling by defining an alternative path to be followed in case of errors. In contrast, process automation agents have the ability to dynamically negotiate tasks between multiple agents in order to resolve exceptions, thus offering a more robust environment.

Process automation agents employ a language (e.g., KIF (Knowledge Interchange Format) Genesereth, 1995) to describe processes, and enable machine reasoning about the operation on these processes. The language is used to specify tasks formally. Figure 4.6 shows the task model in process automation agents. The task specification specifies the agent assigned to the task, a set of trigger events for interaction of task execution, task description, and a set of stop conditions. The planning stage involves negotiation between agents to agree on scheduling and exception handling specifics for a given task. The execution phase involves monitoring the set of events that initiate a task execution and another set of events to stop task execution. In case of an error, the agent may need to go back to the planning phase to reschedule an aborted task.

Table 4.5 summarizes the attributes of process automation agents in terms of our end-user model. Table 4.6 summarizes the advantages of process automation agents.

Figure 4.6   Task model in process agents.

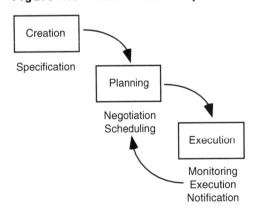

Table 4.5   Attributes of Process Automation Agents

Element	Description
Environment	Intranet
Task skills	Process scheduling, negotiation, execution, and notification
Knowledge	Business processes, resources management
Communication skills	KQML, KIF, CORBA

Edify Workforce—A Process Automation Agent

Electronic Workforce from Edify (http://www.edify.com) is a process agent for automating customer service via Web, telephones, fax, pagers, and interactive kiosks. Edify Workforce software consists of agents, Agent Trainer environment, and Agent Supervisor runtime environment.

> *Task skills:* For a telephone application, Workforce agents can answer, place, and transfer phone calls, assemble and speak prerecorded phrases, and convert text to speech for a Web application. Workforce agents can create and send Web pages and process commands from Web forms. For an electronic mail

Table 4.6   Advantages of Process Agents

Feature	Advantage	Benefit
Task scheduling	Schedule user tasks negotiating with server agents	Alleviate the need for user to be present to execute a task
Resource management	Dynamically allocate resources for task execution	Reduced workload as the user no longer needs to worry about resource availability
Exception handling	Renegotiate to reschedule in response to execution errors	Reduced workload as this is transparent to user
Proactive notifications	Proactively notify user of task completion	Increased productivity by reducing user need to monitor

application, Workforce agents can receive, forward, reply, and send faxes. Similarly, Workforce agents can compose and send messages for pagers.

Agent knowledge: Workforce agents incorporate features that enable interaction with back office systems such as legacy databases and PBX computer telephony integration (CTI).

Task triggers: Workforce agents respond to time-triggered events as part of a workflow process.

The *Agent Trainer* is a misleading term because it does no training but rather provides a visual environment to define and customize interactive service applications that the agents perform. Figure 4.7 shows a telephone service application. In this environment, "action" and "device" icons are paired together on the work-

Figure 4.7   Agent Trainer.

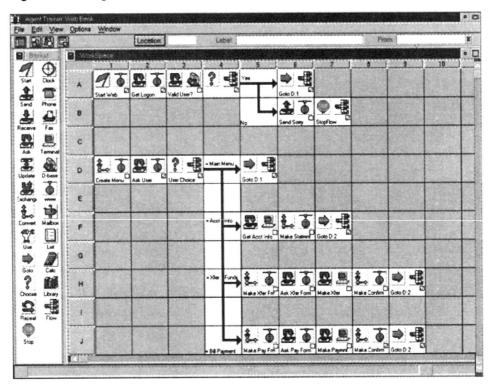

Figure 4.8   Agent Supervisor.

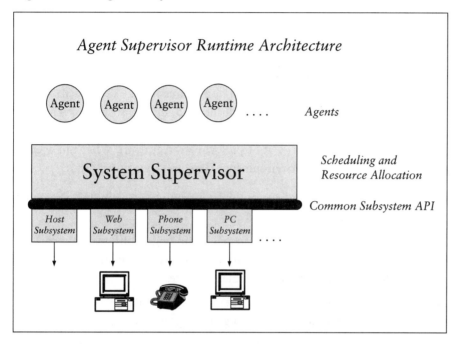

space grid. Each icon pair is an individual task performed by one or more agents at runtime. The left-to-right sequence represents the task flow and branches of the interactive service application.

The Agent Supervisor shown in Figure 4.8 is a depiction of the interactive service application. This runtime architecture schedules resources and activities, manages resource use, tracks application status, and responds to raised exceptions.

Database Agents

Modern enterprise information systems are often client/server solutions where client query tools operate on relational databases on servers. These solutions provide GUI-based data access and report presentation capability to end-users. While these client GUI front ends have improved the legacy-based proprietary database architectures, they still fall short in enabling users to efficiently specify and access desired information.

One of the emerging remedies to the shortcomings of current client/server database systems is to migrate towards a distributed client/server information architecture that supports a multidimensional, conceptual, and hierarchical visualization of information. So can agents be part of a solution addressing the deficiencies of current client GUI/server database solutions? We believe so. In fact, such agent-enabled features are already being incorporated into the next generation of decision support systems (DSS Agent by Microstrategy at http://www.strategy.com). What can agents bring into a client/server database environment? Here are some possibilities:

- Run scheduled database analyses in the background (e.g., running a regional sales-report at the end of each month)

- Exception reporting for operations management (e.g., notifying national sales manager of a monthly sales figure from a specific region that is substantially different from the median sales of all regions)

- Notify a change of information in a user-specified database object (e.g., notify user if the sales data for a given region is changed)

Of course, these kinds of tasks can be programmed for a given database application using the low-level database trigger events such as table inserts, data updates, and so on. What an agent framework brings to this environment are high-level live objects that can be enabled by end-users and that do not depend on a particular database. This functionality allows users to create live objects whose methods are triggered by user-specified events.

Given the amount of investment that corporations have in relational database management systems (RDBMS) it seems logical that commercial database solutions that preserve this investment while enhancing the delivery of information in these relational databases will find a receptive audience. The acceptance of multidimensional database visualization solutions in the market place confirms this view. Just as multidimensional visualization of data can be separated from the storage of data multidimensionality, we believe that the delivery of information to the user can be abstracted out from the underlying database. This is where intelligent agents can fit into existing database applications. In essence, intelligent agents can bring in the indirect manipulation metaphor where agents can monitor, retrieve, and deliver the desired information to users.

Figure 4.9 shows a simplified view of an enterprise data delivery system. Here, the data warehouse is typically a relational database derived from an on-line transaction processing system. The database also contains metadata information to identify the contents and location of data in the warehouse. The engine in the middle dynamically generates SQL queries from the decision support system application outputs. This engine also performs the postprocessing on the RDMBS results in order to provide the requested results format to the decision support system application. Typically, the application allows users a high-level specification of the criteria describing the desired information, and the presentation format of the retrieved information from the data warehouse. Intelligent agents fit into the decision support system applications as data delivery systems. Such agents provide the capability of automating repetitive data analysis tasks and event-based notifications.

Table 4.7 summarizes the attributes of database agents in terms of the end-user model we have been using. The benefits of database agents are summarized in Table 4.8.

Figure 4.9   Enterprise data delivery system.

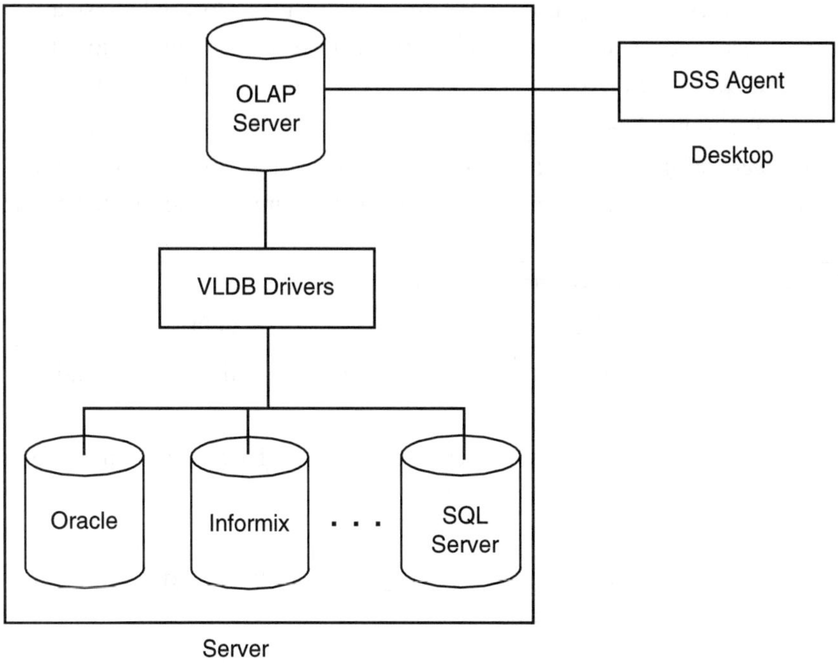

Table 4.7 Database Agent Attributes

Element	Description
Environment	Intranet
Task skills	Data analysis automation, exception reporting, notification of information change
Knowledge	Data warehouse, metadata, RDBMS
Communications skills	SQL, ODBC, OLE

DSS Agent—A Database Agent

DSS Agent from MicroStrategy is a decision support front end designed to bring query reporting and decision support to the desktop.

Figure 4.10 shows how the DSS Agent fits into a decision data warehouse environment. DSS Agent enables users to navigate the data warehouse stored in RDBMSs via an OLAP server. In addition to developing conventional database reports, DSS Agent incorporates the following agent functionality:

- *Exception-reporting alerts* scan the data warehouse in the background, and display messages when exception conditions are met. For example, instead of a user checking the inventory level of an item every day, a buyer could activate an exception alert that warns them when the item falls below a specified minimum level.

- *Time or event triggered report execution* automates data analysis tasks, thus helping the analyst to spend more time applying the information rather than

Table 4.8 Benefits of Database Agents

Feature	Advantage	Benefit
Automatic data analysis	Automates users' repetitive data analysis	Reduced workload
Exception reporting	Reports user-defined exceptions in business operations	Faster decision making
Notifications alerts	Notifies user of changes in information	Increased productivity

Figure 4.10 DSS agent architecture.

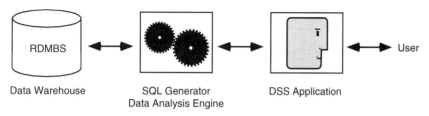

Data Warehouse   SQL Generator   DSS Application
                          Data Analysis Engine

retrieving it. For instance, a sales manager may create an agent that distributes a series of reports to regional sales managers whenever new relevant data arrives at the data warehouse.

■ *Workflow actions triggered by reports* enables an analyst to accomplish a postanalysis task using another desktop application. For instance, a report that retrieves the most recent inventory figures from the data warehouse can then update a forecasting spreadsheet in Microsoft Excel.

DSS Agent represents an innovation in decision support systems with its use of agents. However, DSS Agent does not have any learning agent technology. Learning can be incorporated into a DSS Agent solution in more than one way:

■ *Incorporation of learning into DSS Agent client* would involve the integration of a learning engine that would monitor the user's behavior within the DSS Agent/Client, find the repetitive behavior, and offer to enable agents that would automate the user's repetitive tasks. Figure 4.11 is an example. The incorporation of such a learning feature would increase user productivity as the user no longer needs to keep track of what, when, and how to automate.

■ *Incorporation of learning capability into the OLAP server* would involve the integration of a learning engine that would monitor the behavior of users served by the OLAP server, find repetitive behavior across users, and make a recommendation to create an agent to automate this behavior. Such a learning engine can also find clusters of users with similar behavior, and make agent recommendations based on the group preferences. Such a collaborative filtering would cluster, for instance, buyers into groups where the group members share a common preference for analyzing data. For instance, the system can recommend an inventory agent with a particular

Figure 4.11   Integration of learning into DSS Agent.

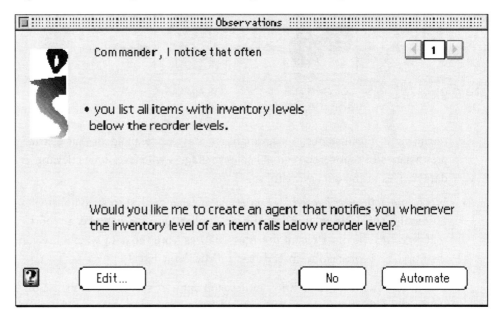

characteristic based on the preferences of a group of buyers whose preferences match that of a particular buyer.

Mobile Agents

Mobile agents are software agents that can transport themselves from a client computer to various servers for remote execution (White, 1996). In contrast to remote procedure calls (RPCs), which are limited to communicating data to a procedure to be executed on a remote server, mobile agents transport both the data and program acting on the data within its specification.

Dispatching a program for execution on a server (e.g., a mainframe or a cluster of minicomputers) as is done in the mobile agent paradigm has been around since the early 1960s. At that time, the motivation was due to the limitations of computing power of desktop CPUs. It is, therefore, not surprising that the most notable application of mobile agents to date has been the AT&T PersonaLink network, providing services to lightweight PDA devices built using the Telescript environment.

Is agent mobility a desired attribute? The answer is not an unequivocal *yes*, given the security issues that mobile agents introduce and the availability of alternative means of accomplishing the same function (Chess, Harrison, and Kershenbaum, 1995). In this section we discuss the pros and cons of using mobile agents after a brief overview of mobile agents.

Figure 4.12 shows a mobile agent environment. Here, an agent encapsulates the procedure that a receiving computer is to execute, the data comprising the procedure's arguments and state. A user's agent on a desktop machine transports itself to a server machine where it performs the user-delegated function (e.g., finding the prices for a number of workstation configurations) by interacting with the server agent. The client agent then transports itself to other servers to complete its user-defined task (e.g., visiting all workstation resellers), and finally, the agent comes back to the client desktop to report its findings to the user.

Figure 4.13 shows the computing model for the client and server machines. Here the agent platform is the agent execution environment in which agents are created, registered, launched, and executed. The security issues involve authenticating the sender of the mobile agent, determining the user's authority to execute agents at the server, and verifying the agent's ability to pay for services rendered at the server.

Figure 4.12   Mobile agent environment.

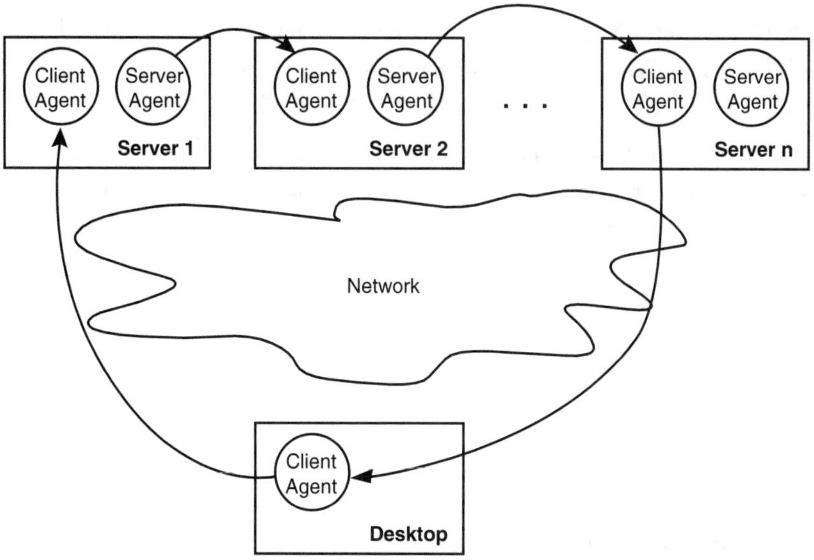

Figure 4.13   Mobile agent computing model.

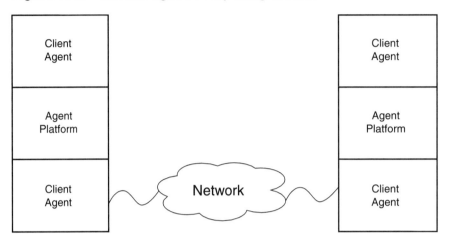

Mobile agents need a programming language that lets agent authors define the behavior of their agents as they travel across a network. There are a number of options in the choice of an agent communication language.

- Tcl and Safe-Tcl is a machine-independent scripting language that uses electronic mail to transport agent procedures as contents of mail messages (Osterhout, 1994).

- Telescript by General Magic is an agent operating environment designed for mobile agents (White, 1995). Telescript is object oriented, where every element of the language is an object, just like Smalltalk.

- KIF (Knowledge Interchange Format) is an extended first-order predicate calculus for agent-server and agent-agent communication. KIF is a product of the ARPA Knowledge Sharing Effort (Genesereth, 1995).

- Java by Sun Microsystems is an object-oriented, platform-independent language suitable for agent applications. Java originated from an effort to develop an operating system for networked devices (Gosling and McGilton, 1995).

Table 4.9 summarizes the mobile agent attributes in terms of the end-user model we have been using.

Table 4.10 summarizes the benefits of mobile agents. The network efficiency of mobile agents provides an advantage for mobile clients of low-band-width net-

Table 4.9   Mobile Agent Attributes

Element	Description
Environment	Intranet, wireless networks
Task skills	Travel, information search, transaction services
Knowledge skills	Agent places, negotiation
Communication skills	Safe-Tc1, Telescript, KIF, Java

works, such as wireless networks. However, this will be less of an issue with the availability of access to packet switching wireless networks. Similarly, the server computing capability of mobile agents provides an advantage for lightweight devices such as PDAs with modest CPU and storage resources. In agent-enabled commerce, agent meeting places can promote open markets where buyer and seller agents can engage in direct commerce on behalf of their users. However, there does not seem to be any compelling reason to adapt network servers to accommodate mobile agents (as discussed in detail in Chess et al., 1995). For each mobile agent solution there are alternative solutions that do not employ mobile agents. On the other hand, a mobile agent framework does offer a generalized framework for the development and personalization of network services.

Table 4.10   Mobile Agent Benefits

Feature	Advantage	Benefit
Remote Programming	Efficient intermittent use of network bandwidth	Reduced network traffic for low bandwidth and wireless networks
Server computing	Uses server CPUs for compute-intensive tasks	Increased functionality for lightweight mobile devices
Server customization	Server agents customize the server for each user	Enhanced user experience
Agent Meeting place	Provides a meeting place where agents meet to conduct transactions	Negotiation-based electronic commerce
Intranet management	System maintenance over an intranet	Server CPUs used for corporate tasks

CyberAgent—A Java-based Mobile Agent System

CyberAgent (Gao, 1996) by FTP Software is an integrated mobile-agent framework based on Java technology. In CyberAgent, the Java language (Gosling and McGilton, 1995) is used both as a programming language and system development language. An agent in CyberAgent system consists of state, code, and auxiliary data, shown in Figure 4.14.

The static state of the CyberAgent represents the agent attributes which remain fixed over the life cycle of an agent:

- Agent name

- Agent identification specifying a specific traveling agent

- A description of the agent

- Agent sender originating the agent

- Date and time of the agent launch

- A list of destinations that the agent may use

- A travel plan specifying the agent's journey

- Security information

The dynamic state of the CyberAgent includes both generic states such as current-stop, failed-stops, unreached-stops, and so on, and agent-specific states representing execution condition.

Figure 4.14 CyberAgent components.

State	Static Atributes Dynamics state
Code	Internal control Agent methods In API Agent task in Java
Auxiliary Data	Machine-dependent executables

Figure 4.15   CyberAgent platform architecture.

Agent code in CyberAgent is a set of Java classes. Each agent includes the Agent class in the Agent API for internal control and public methods in addition to the classes and methods written by the agent author.

Figure 4.15 shows the CyberAgent platform that provides the native environment where agents are launched, received, enabled, executed, packaged, and transported to a platform on another server. The CyberAgent runtime environment consists of Agent Launcher, Agent Listener, and Agent Monitor. Agent Launcher's function is to send an agent to its destination. Agent Listener receives and unpackages incoming agents before passing them onto the Agent Monitor. Agent Monitor is a control facility that monitors agent activities. The Monitor provides agents an execution environment (loads its classes, instantiates its objects, etc.). When the agent accomplishes its task, the Monitor packages what the agent needs and dispatches the Agent Launcher.

CyberAgent provides a number of security features to ensure the following:

- Unauthorized agents cannot he launched. received, and executed.
- Agents retain their integrity while moving from one machine to another.
- Agents are prohibited from performing harmful actions.

CyberAgent provides two authentication (assurance of identity) methods: password-based and encryption-based authentication. Password-based authentication requires that the launching and receiving platforms share a common password. This method verifies the originating platform of the agent but not its integrity. To assure agent integrity CyberAgent uses encryption-based authentication where the agent code and data is encrypted with an encryption key at the launching platform, and decrypted with a decryption key at the receiving platform.

Agent activities at a platform are secured by the security mechanisms in Java. First, the Java compiler provides a first line of defense. Second, Java's bytecode verifier validates code before execution. Third, Java's customizable class header prohibits any authorized classes from loading. Finally, the Java Security Manager class enables an application to check the safety of an operation before execution.

In addition to general security measures inherent in Java, CyberAgent provides additional security features. For instance, only the Monitor starts an agent. An agent has no direct access to other objects in the runtime environment. Also, agents are not allowed to change attribute values such as identity, travel plan, and destinations.

CyberAgent is an example of a mobile agent environment that can be built in Java.

Tabriz AgentWare

Tabriz AgentWare by General Magic is Web software for executing and managing agent-applications built on the Telescript language. The main constructs of the Telescript language are agents, places, and go. Agents are mobile agents that go to Telescript-enabled places to interact with other agents and to perform user-delegated tasks. Tabriz AgentWare includes the Telescript execution environment, and a set of Web class libraries that enable access to Telescript from the Web and HTML support libraries for generating and manipulating HTML pages. Tabriz provides Java support as well. For instance, Telescript agents can set parameters of Java applets, and Java applets can call Telescript procedures. In addition to their mobility attributes, Tabriz agents have persistence and security attributes. Tabriz agents continue a search until specifically instructed by the user to quit. Agent State is preserved across Tabriz servers.

Tabriz offers security at multiple levels. First, Telescript is a safe language that prevents Telescript programs from corrupting system resources. Telescript also provides each agent an authority that uniquely identifies the agent and user permissions. The authority construct uses RSA public key encryption.

In addition, Tabriz agent environment allows servers to provide operations wrappers that, for instance, can verify the identity of an agent and the authority of the agent's user. Using these operations wrappers, a Tabriz agent can be given the following permits for authorized operations:

- Native permits assigned by process creator
- Local permits issued by either the sending or receiving place

- Regional permits covering a particular domain
- Temporary permits good for a limited time

Summary

In this chapter, we presented an overview of intranet agents, and classified intranet agents into collaboration, process automation, database, and mobile agents. We discussed each intranet agent category in terms of the end-user agent model introduced in Chapter 1, and described examples of commercial agents for each category.

We covered the specific agent features that provide increased organizational productivity, reduced operational costs, enhanced corporate communications, reduced workload, increased resource utilization, faster decision making, mobile work capability, and reduced communication costs. In particular, we identified personalization, information sharing, work flow automation, and database notification as applications ready for the introduction of agents into the various functional business units of an organization.

How Intelligent
Agents Work

The Technology of
Intelligent Agents

There's a humorous quiz going around the Internet called "Are you a guy?" Imagine that highly advanced aliens have landed on Earth and you are the lucky person they first encounter. As a gesture of goodwill they present you with an incredibly powerful device from their distant home. This marvel of technology has many wonderful capabilities: it can cure all diseases, produce peace and justice throughout the world, and create economies that generate wealth for all. What would you do with it?

1. Present it to the Secretary-General of the United Nations for the benefit of all mankind?

2. Use it yourself for the benefit of all mankind (and incidentally become rich and famous)?

3. Take it apart and see how it works?

While intelligent agents may not be quite as powerful as this device, we suspect that many readers are in that third category and want to know how they work. But there is another reason for needing a deeper understanding of these technologies.

In the first four chapters we gave many examples of agent products and services that exist today to assist you on the desktop, on the Internet or on your intranet. These are fruitful early application areas for agents, particularly on the Internet where the need to apply intelligence in finding and filtering information is highest. But the greatest value to your enterprise will probably come from applying these techniques to running your business, where agent intelligence can directly affect the efficiency of your business processes. These applications of agents will demand much greater effort on the part of your Information Systems group than simply signing up for Firefly or another Internet-based service, and therefore you will need to understand how agents work and where their limitations and implementation difficulties lie.

So now in this and the next five chapters, we take you under the hood to show you how agents work. While agents may appear to have (or may be claimed to have) wonderful capabilities, Chapters 5 through 9 demonstrate that agents' capabilities are the product of straightforward software technologies. Here are our goals for the coming chapters:

1. To give you a mental framework for assessing which technologies are required for building particular kinds of applications, where some of the challenges with these technologies lie, and how much effort is needed to apply them.

2. To help you distinguish between the reality and the hype of agents. We will try to draw some lines indicating current boundaries between these realms. While you will almost certainly not be starting to build your technology from the ground up—though some large enterprises still do this—you will need to convince your peers that this new approach is realistic and dependable.

3. To prepare you for introducing these technologies in your company. You will need to be able to select among the many different options available to meet both the immediate and long-term needs of your company. As you will see in these chapters, the value of agents increases as they become pervasive, this requires you to be able to develop a plan for initial trials that can also be expanded over time to spread the benefits of agents throughout your company.

In short, the following chapters review the various technologies underlying intelligent agents. This chapter sets the scene by presenting two views of intelligent agent applications. We begin with a historical perspective, which positions the emergence of agent technology in the general development of personal and business computing; and a technology perspective, which provides a framework for the further discussion of existing and emerging technologies for agent applications.

Reality Check: What's an Agent?

People are often confused about "intelligent agents," because the term is applied in so many different ways. This can lead to problems when software developers begin to propose applying agents in their companies, as managers and end-users have widely varying interpretations of the term. Several academic and technical communities have each developed fairly specific definitions. For example, the academic artificial intelligence community has a well-established research field for the study of multiple agent planning[1]; this is particularly relevant to the problem of distributed negotiation and planning, and finds application in information system support for the management of flexible manufacturing systems. Likewise, the network management and systems management communities have for a long time used the term *agent* for the management application which represents a managed system or network element and integrates it with the overall management application. These are very concrete uses of the term *agent.*

At the other extreme we have seen in the last two to three years the widespread abuse of the term by those who primarily wanted to indicate that their application or service was somehow more advanced or "intelligent" or helpful than previously. This use has unfortunately given rise to the mis-impression that there is some "magic" agent technology which can be applied to a given application to turn it into an intelligent agent. The primary message of the following chapters is that there is in fact no such magic technology. All we have to work with are 1s and 0s.

Agents are just programs executing what they were programmed to do—nothing more and nothing less. However, it is possible to start to apply existing technologies in new ways for the realization of end-user applications, and the result of this innovation can be a very compelling new set of capabilities. Compilers, databases, and Java are all examples of innovations that were based on existing technologies, but which created dramatic progress in computing through changing the user's model of how to use the computer. We believe that while there are many ways to define intelligent agents, at their core, agents represent *only* a new application of existing technologies; the new application, however, provides a very compelling set of benefits to the end-user or the enterprise.

---

[1]Stan Franklin's book, *Artificial Minds* is an excellent and readable tour of this field [Franklin (1995)].

The Historical View

The evolution of agents resembles the emergence in the 1970s of the graphical user interface (GUI). During that period the vast majority of applications were written for command line-oriented operating systems and text-based terminals. Some operating systems also offered support for structured programming, which permitted screen-to-screen navigation based on character entry, and much effort was being applied to so-called fourth-generation languages (4GLs), which could automatically generate the successive screens of an application. While the Xerox Star already contained the concept of the "messy desktop," which is still the main visual metaphor for today's GUIs, common operating systems did not provide support for GUIs until the X11 standard became a popular extension on UNIX systems in the early 1980s. Even this was a narrow success at the time.

DOS applications began to explore GUI concepts in the early 1980s as part of the application, but it was really the Apple Macintosh which brought the GUI into the mainstream of PC operating systems. Finally, the rest of the personal computing community caught up in the early 1990s. In 1983, there were essentially no GUI-based applications. By 1985, WYSIWYG text processors and graphical editors began to emerge, extending older, text-only applications to produce higher-quality results, and providing increased user productivity; but many non-GUI applications continued to exist into the early 1990s. Today, there are very few popular applications which do not use the X-Windows, Windows, MacOS, or OS/2 GUI, although text-based applications developed by or for businesses for their own use are still common.

The transition from command line/text-based to GUI applications took several years. In some cases, such as text processing, a large part of the benefit of this transition has been a dramatic improvement in ease of use and in the quality of the results. In other cases, such as presentation tools, hypertext documents, or multimedia applications, the benefit has been the creation of an entire new set of capabilities.

For practical purposes, the GUI component of operating systems emerged as the generalization of specific capabilities that application developers had been putting directly into their programs in the early to mid-1980s. Commercial software developers wanted these capabilities for competitive purposes, and probably did not think of them as a distinct technology at the time. There is in fact a wide range of technologies required to provide a full GUI. These include high resolution, color, all-points addressable displays and corresponding printers; scaleable fonts; pointing devices and direct manipulation; graphical and WYSIWYG editors; the clipboard; and so forth. While these technologies were being developed in the mid-1980s, few people recognized the overall abstraction of this work as "GUI technology."

Today the GUI is recognized as a distinct subsystem within the operating system, which applications can exploit. It provides a set of standards (APIs) for the applications that provide specific functions in the interface, such displaying a bitmap. The GUI ensures that applications have a consistent look-and-feel, which makes it easier for users to learn new applications, and saves the application developers the effort of developing their own standards. The GUI is now such an integral part of personal computing that no commercial developer would think of creating products that did not use it.

The emergence of agent technology is similar in many ways to the GUI story, but also different in at least one important way. First the similarities.

- Agent technology is not a single, new, emerging technology, but rather the integrated application of a number of technologies. Some of these technologies have been around in one form or another for a considerable time. Some are experiencing strong evolution as the richness of the computing infrastructure improves and as users make new demands for usability and functionality. Today the agent developer must still do considerable integration, as did the developers of the early, standalone GUI applications, who could not count on support from the operating system. These technologies will be reviewed in the coming chapters.

- Agents are not necessarily a new, isolated form of application, but will often be new sets of capabilities added to existing applications. The agents enhance the usability and the quality of the applications, but without revolutionizing them, just as the GUI did. This book focuses primarily on this evolutionary approach to agent applications. Agents will also create revolutionary new applications, just as the GUI did. The popular press tends to focus a great deal on this revolutionary approach to applications.

- Agent functions will emerge initially within individual applications, but with experience we will be able to define a set of abstractions that will become part of the operating system or application environment.

- Agent applications inevitably have strong human-computer interaction aspects. Humans delegate authority to agents. Agents proactively communicate with humans. Agents may engage in dialogues with humans.

- In the short term, applications exploiting agent technology will have usability and functional competitive advantages over other applications. In the longer term, agent behaviors will become standard, expected features of all or most applications. Ultimately, applications that do not exploit the agent support in the operating system will be severely disadvantaged. The time frame for this transition is probably shorter than the 20 years required for the emergence of the GUI, but probably still on the order of 5 years.

The key difference between agent and GUI technologies is that various companies and individuals have already been projecting visions of what the endpoint of agent technology will provide. A landmark in this area was John Sculley's 1987 "Knowledge Navigator" video, which portrayed an appealing, anthropomorphic relationship between the end-user and the agent. Unfortunately for Apple, Sculley had no idea about how to turn this vision into a research and development program. Also unfortunately, as a result of Knowledge Navigator and a dozen other visions (for example, HAL in *2001*), a mythical image of a fully realized intelligent agent has entered the consciousness of consumers and software developers. This has led to a fuzzy recognition of "intelligent agent technology," and so, in part, this field has been driven by a series of unsuccessful attempts to do a top-down implementation of this image, instead of the piece-by-piece, bottom-up approach that characterized the emergence of GUI-based operating systems and applications.

Intelligent agents are thus challenged to live up to a level of hype that was not prevalent during the emergence of the GUI. Fortunately, the computer industry has a short memory for visions, and other, newer visions have emerged—browser wars and network computers are the stuff of today's gossip—and we can now get on with the realistic and practical applications of intelligent agents.

Today we may be at roughly the same point that the GUI had reached in 1980:

- It was still an active research area.

- Isolated pioneer products were emerging.

- The full set of required technologies was not available.

- The technologies were not integrated with one another.

- There was no consensus on the required abstractions which could be provided by an operating system.

- Despite the high level of expectation aroused by the hype, the technology was not yet in widespread use, nor had it been widely accepted as an inevitable trend in the evolution of application technologies.

- But there *was* a set of early adopters who were able to demonstrate that there was value in this approach.

Intelligent agents are an emerging technology. We have seen that there are many early examples in use, and their value is well established. But we have not yet mastered the generality of agents in the way that we have for the GUI. This will emerge in the next two to five years, and agent functions will become normal extensions of operating systems and application environments. In five years' time we anticipate that application will include agent functions as normally as today they incorporate GUI functions.

The Technical View

In learning about the commercial agents described in the earlier chapters, you may have hoped for a comprehensive definition of agents with detailed categories. In Chapter 2, we present a good working definition, which we hope is useful in your review of current agents applications. In an emerging field however, definitions evolve rapidly. Is a simple Java applet an intelligent agent? Is a wizard an intelligent agent? Is a helpful user interface such as Microsoft's Bob an intelligent agent?

The working definition given in Chapter 1 will help you decide these questions from an application point of view—which for many purposes is the most important. From a technology point of view, we propose a more open-ended "definition" of an intelligent agent. Agent technology is not generally a structural feature of an application, in the same way that, say, database retrieval or client/server orientation are. Rather it is a pragmatic set of application characteristics, supported by various technologies, which extend the functionality or value of the application. In other words, developers do not set out to create an "agent application"; they set out to add additional value to a new or existing application and find that the agent approach is a unique or at least an advantageous means to this end. So the search for a technical definition of intelligent agents becomes instead a method of describing the "agent" technologies of a wide range of applications.

Intelligence and Agency

As with the GUI, we find that there are several key technologies which combine to produce intelligent agents. Not all intelligent agents employ all these technologies; however, agents or applications which are rich in these technologies will be more readily recognizable as intelligent agents than those that are not. In the following chapters we lay out the landscape of these technologies and describe how they combine to create intelligent agents. The two major dimensions of this landscape are *intelligence* and *agency*.[1]

The dimension of *intelligence* means the degree to which the application employs reasoning, learning, and other techniques to interpret the information or knowledge to which it has access or which is presented to it. This dimension encompasses a number of steps, progressing from marginal intelligence to very advanced intelligence. The most limited forms of Intelligence are modest advances over the customization features of current applications, which allow the user to specify a style or a policy. The first step along this path leads to the expression of *preferences*: relatively formal statements of desired, potentially complex behaviors of a single application or a group of applications. The second step leads to the provision of a *reasoning* capability, in which preferences are expressed in a formalized set of rules and combined with long-term and short-term knowledge in an inferencing or decision-making process, which may lead to some specific action by the application or at least to the creation of a new piece of knowledge. The third and final step along this path is the general ability of the agent application to modify its Reasoning behavior on the basis of new knowledge derived from a wide range of sources; this is generally called *learning*.

The other dimension of the technology landscape is *agency*, which is the degree to which the agent can perceive its environment and act on it. Wooldridge and Jennings' (1995) definition of an agent emphasizes autonomy and perception:

---

[1]We are indebted to Donald Gilbert of IBM for this model.

Perhaps the most general way in which the term agent is used is to denote a hardware or (more usually) software-based computer system that enjoys the following properties:

- *Autonomy:* Agents operate without the direct intervention of humans or others and have some kind of control over their actions and internal state.

- *Social ability:* Agents interact with other agents (and possibly humans) via some kind of *agent-communication language.*

- *Reactivity:* Agents perceive their environment (which may be the physical world, a user via a graphical user interface, a collection of other agents, the INTERNET, or perhaps all of these combined), and respond in a timely fashion to changes that occur in it.

- *Pro-activeness:* Agents do not simply act in response to their environment, they are able to exhibit goal-directed behavior by *taking the initiative.*

This dimension encompasses a number of steps, progressing from standalone agent applications able to accomplish a minimal goal autonomously, up to agent frameworks, which are generally accessible resources for providing intelligence and agency to suites of applications. The dimension of agency begins with the concept of *asynchrony,* which is the degree to which the application can be given a task which it performs asynchronously with respect to the user's requests. Contrast this with the typical behavior of applications as tools, which respond (more or less synchronously) to the user's commands but have no autonomous abilities. The first step along this dimension leads to the application having some *user representation,* that is, a model of the user's goals or agenda.

This model allows the user to describe not just a single task, but a series of related tasks which accomplish a higher-level goal and which can be performed by the agent application. The succeeding steps along this dimension lead to the agent being able to perceive or access data external to itself (*data interactivity*), then to its being able to act upon and respond to other local applications (*application interactivity*) and collections of applications that make up a service (*service interactivity*). The final step along this dimension is *agent interactivity,* in which agent capabilities in independent applications are able to communicate and interoperate with each other. In this form, the agent may be a separate entity from any specific application, existing as a subsystem or resource for agent-enabled applications, and as an asynchronous tool by means of which the user drives other applications.

This capability model is illustrated in Figure 5.1. The model proposes qualitative thresholds for an intelligent agent. This technology-based definition of an agent simply requires that the application exceed minimal capabilities along the dimensions of intelligence and agency. Software whose capabilities position it in the shaded area of Figure 5.1 meets our technology-based definition of an "intelligent agent." Software which lies below the shaded area will resemble an agent in some ways, but will not have the functionality or intelligence to qualify as a real agent. These thresholds are our subjective judgments based on our assessment of which existing applications represent intelligent agency and which do not quite make it; they are debatable and subject to change over time. Agents which are toward the

Figure 5.1   Intelligent agents are software entities whose intelligence and agency exceed certain thresholds.

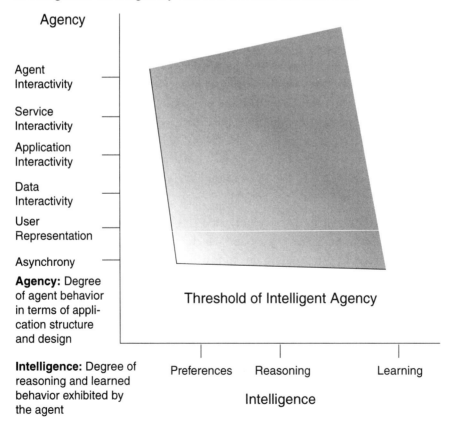

Figure 5.2   Examples of intelligent agent products and their capabilities in intelligence and agency.

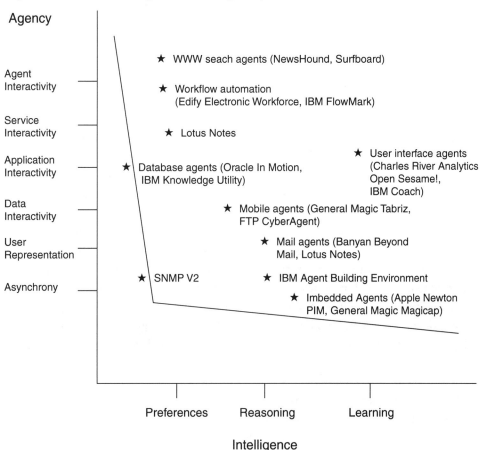

top-right corner of the figure are clearly more powerful than those closer to the thresholds, and few people would dispute their qualifications as intelligent agents. Academic and industrial research will bring us progressively closer to this region. Agents in the regions approaching the thresholds will provoke (heated) debate as to whether they really are intelligent agents.

Figure 5.2 shows a number of the agent applications reviewed earlier mapped onto this model. The Simple Network Management Protocol version 2 employs "agents" to monitor the status of network elements such as routers and switches, filter the information, and pass on to an operator console alarms. While it thus contains elements of intelligence and agency, we feel that these agents are too weak in intelligence to count as true intelligent agents; there are however, more intelligent forms of network management agents, and these will pass our threshold test. Database agents provide valuable functions in making information available to users in the most useful form, and are quite strong in the dimension of agency with their abilities to perform searches across multiple, heterogeneous databases, but they are still relatively weak in applying intelligence.

Web search and filtering agents are our first example of an intelligent agent, with their ability to search widely over the Internet or intranet among millions of Web servers, and to perform very sophisticated searches based on user specifications. This category has much in common with the database agents, and the two categories are converging. Mobile agents permit a user to specify a detailed task to be performed by the agent during its remote execution, giving it significant intelligence, and its ability to visit remote servers provides data interactivity for those servers which are equipped with appropriate execution environments. As such environments become more widespread, the agency factor will become stronger. As more and more reasoning capabilities are provided by either the mobile agent or the execution environment, so the intelligence factor will strengthen. Clearly General Magic wants to strengthen both, but in the short term, FTP's CyberAgent, based on Java, may make faster progress.

Workflow developers, for example, Edify's Electronic Workforce, have created intelligent agents with good access into enterprise data and applications and with a certain amount of intelligence, and these are some of the most valuable early agents for enterprise use. Lotus Notes has added agents in release 4, which can monitor a Notes database or its replicas anywhere in the network and execute LotusScript programs under a limited number of user-specified conditions.

Mail agents are a well-established class of agents, employing rule-based specifications of how to handle various kinds of electronic mail, and they are widely used for simple handling. Moving further along the intelligence dimension, we find fewer examples. The successful application of reasoning and learning in commercial agent products continues to be more challenging than providing widespread access to data and services.

Why is this? One possible answer is that there are far fewer developers skilled in those areas. IBM is trying to remedy this by providing a developer's kit that deals with many of the problems of adding intelligence to an agent. Apple and General Magic (and Microsoft to a limited extent) have tried to incorporate learning in their operating systems for personal digital assistants, so that Newton, for example, comes to recognize what the user means by "Lunch" as a time for an appointment. Likewise, GMI's Magic Cap learns nicknames and other personalizations. User interface agents, which monitor the user's use of a specific operating system or application features and then propose helpful actions of automations score highly in both dimensions; they incorporate quite sophisticated monitoring and learning capabilities and have widespread access into applications and operating system functions. Social agents are brokers of knowledge which they learn from large numbers of interactions with users. Firefly, for example, is knowledgeable about users' taste in music. Social agents are somewhat the mirror image of Web search agents in that the user population is putting knowledge into the network service.

Most of the action in intelligent agents today is in the top-left corner of our diagram (Figure 5.2), possibly since this is where the largest number of interested users are to be found and the value to these users of the intelligent agent functions is quite high. We may therefore expect that investment in this top-left corner will lead to progress to the right, as more reasoning and, eventually, learning capabilities are added to successful searching and filtering products. At the right-hand side, user interface agents may evolve upward to meet the searching and filtering agents by providing hints to the latter on what the user appears to be interested in. Mobile agents are a fascinating technology that has perhaps still not found its true application; mobile agents will probably become stronger as standards emerge in the Web which enable Web servers to directly execute such agents, thus eliminating the difficult problem of propagating separate execution environments.

This is a rich field; there is much to be done in development, but even more to be learned in how to generate real value out of these various classes of intelligent agents.

Machinery, Content, Access, and Security

We have seen how the two dimensions of intelligence and agency are useful in characterizing various kinds of agents. In the following chapters, we will relate these dimensions to several software technologies. For the purposes of these discussions, we will cluster the technologies into four factors (see Figure 5.3):

- *Machinery* and *content*, which are factors of Intelligence
- *Access* and *security*, which are factors of Agency

Machinery refers to engines of various kinds, mainly developed in the field of artificial intelligence, which support varying degrees of intelligence. These engines include:

- Various forms of inferencing
- Various forms of learning
- Tools for the user's creation and modification of rules and other knowledge
- Tools for the validation of rule sets
- Tools for the development of strategies for negotiation and collaboration among agents and among agents and users

Content is the data employed by the machinery in reasoning and learning (not necessarily identical to Knowledge). *Access* (see below) enables the machinery to perceive content (see below) and perform actions as outcomes of reasoning. *Security* is the usual set of concerns related to distributed computing, augmented by a few special concerns related to intelligent agents

Figure 5.3   Agent technology factors.

Intelligence
Machinery:
*inferencing,
learning, validation,
representation*

Agency
Security: *mutual,
public authentication,
privacy, payment*

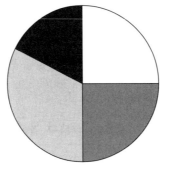

Content:
*rules, context,
application ontologies
& grammars*

Access:
*to applications,
data & services,
networking, mobility*

Table 5.1   The Technology Factors of Intelligent Agents

Factor	Meaning
Machinery	Engines of various kinds, which support the varying degrees of *intelligence*
Content	Data employed by the *machinery* in Reasoning and Learning
Access	Methods to enable the *machinery* to perceive *content* and perform actions as outcomes of Reasoning
Security	Concerns related to distributed computing, augmented by a few special concerns related to intelligent agents

Machinery

Machinery is activated by events. Events are the detection by the agent of some new piece of knowledge or content, signaling a change in the agent's environment. An event may be the time of day, the arrival of a piece of mail, a change of value in some database entry, or a new goal or preference expressed by the user. In other words, whenever the agent's environment changes in a way that the user or developer has defined to be significant by causing it to trigger an event, the machinery is activated. The purpose of this activation is to cause the machinery to determine whether the event requires a corresponding action. Actions are invocations of application functionality; each action requires a binding of some form between a piece of machinery and an application. Thus an agent intended to manage electronic mail must have both an ability to receive events notifying it of the arrival of mail and an ability to manipulate the user's mailbox(es).

Content

Content refers to the knowledge or data which is the agent's perception or awareness of its environment. Content is data for machinery. It includes rules, which are the user's expression of preferences of policies. It is also the interpretable representation of real-world knowledge, so that agents and applications can communicate with one another about goods and services of interest to the user. This kind of knowledge has also been the subject of research by the artificial intelligence community, which has created a valuable set of *knowledge representation tools* and some instances of knowledge bases. Another type of structured knowledge is the grammars required to support dialogues among agents and between agents and users; just as humans have protocols about how one orders pizza or negotiates an appointment, so applications and agent-based applications have expectations of a certain flow of assertion and response.

Next comes nonstructured information. The bulk of the world's knowledge is stored in free text form, with perhaps a few hints provided by formatting, such as HTML. Agents must deal with free text knowledge and must rely in turn on filtering and natural language support tools to extract structured information, which can form the basis for inferencing or learning. Lastly agents must be able to learn from "observation" of user behavior or other heuristics; here the data is structured, but its significance may not be interpretable, and the agent may need guidance from the user or may rely explicitly on interpretation by the user.

Access

Access is the degree to which the agent can interact with its environment. The agent must "perceive" events occurring in its world and must also be able to perform actions upon that world. In most cases, the agent will be developed for an existing environment or for *legacy* applications, which were not created with agents in mind. A major effort is often required to enable the agent to interact with applications which were originally developed for interactions with users, and which do not have convenient APIs to their internal functions and states. These access functions are generally implemented as bindings to the action procedures of the machinery, so that inferencing and learning can lead to actions on the local or external applications.

In the local environment, access may be accomplished by direct binding to APIs, or through shared memory, or through database or file system methods. When the application is remote from the user, the agent may exploit distributed computing techniques such as messaging, remote procedure calls (RPCs), or other standard protocols such as HTTP. A further example of access, however, is mobile agents. These are independent programs, generally written in a script language, which are capable of migrating themselves, including process state and instance data, between the user's computer and one or more remote servers.

Security

Security is a topic whose scope greatly exceeds that of agents. However, the success of agents depends critically on the effectiveness of security services and agents therefore raise new requirements for these services. An agent is in effect acting on behalf of the user. In interactions on public networks—for example, in electronic commerce—the agent may have the legal authority and responsibility of the user. This requires that actions performed by agents carry the same authority as actions performed directly by the user. Agents must carry the certified authority of the user and their rights must be restricted to not more than the rights of the user. In some cases, the agent will be performing electronic commerce on behalf of the user (buying or selling a good or service), and this requires a conventional electronic payment scheme, methods of reconciliation, and auditability.

In many cases, such new security services are being created for user-driven electronic commerce, and agent-based applications will be designed to exploit these, where permitted. Some electronic traders may differentiate nonetheless between direct user commerce and agent-based commerce. One of the potential benefits of the ability of agents to go tirelessly around shopping for prices, for example, is that they can thereby create a more informed market; some businesses have already chosen to resist this by excluding agent price inquiries.

The agent may contain content that is personal information of the user, for example, preferences or a negotiation strategy; these must be subject to privacy and integrity protection. Agents written in Java, for example, benefit from the checking performed by the Java engine on the integrity of the program before it begins execution.

Agents also create new security concerns: like any autonomous system of significant complexity, agent behavior cannot be fully analyzed. Agents may exhibit unanticipated behaviors at times when no human is directly observing them. One set of unexpected behaviors are accidental or intentional viruses; these are benign or malign behaviors which are able to propagate themselves via networks or other means. Another set of unexpected behaviors are collective phenomena that arise from interactions among large populations of autonomous entities such as agents. One question surrounds any form of agent, whether human or computer-based: *Will it do what I want (even if that is not what I said)?* In practice, the risks raised by some of these security issues cannot be reduced by analysis; it may not be possible, for example, to detect a virus without actually executing it. In many cases, the solution may be the human approach of developing trust and providing infrastructures for certifying trustability.

Intelligent agents thus raise a new set of security issues that must be addressed if users and IS managers are to be willing to delegate significant responsibility to them.

Putting the Pieces Together—An Example

Let's illustrate this model with a simple example; consider a news retrieval and filtering agent, as shown in Figure 5.4. The agent uses its access methods to go out into local and remote databases to forage for content. These access methods may include setting up news stream delivery to the agent, or retrieval from bulletin boards, or using a spider to walk the Web. The content that is retrieved in this way is probably already partially filtered—by the selection of the newsfeed or the databases that are searched. The agent next may use its detailed searching or language-processing machinery to extract keywords or signatures from the body of the content that has been received or retrieved. This abstracted content (or event) is then passed to the agent's Reasoning or inferencing machinery in order to decide what to do with the new content. This process combines the event content with the rule-based or knowledge content provided by the user. If this process finds a good hit or match in the new content, the agent may use another piece of its machinery to do

Figure 5.4 A news filtering agent, showing the roles of *machinery, content, access,* and *security.*

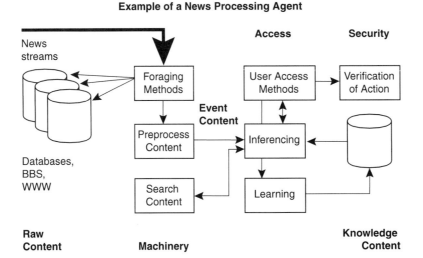

a more detailed search on the content. Finally, the agent may decide to take an action based on the new content; for example, to notify the user that an important event has occurred. This action is verified by a security function and then given the authority of the user. The agent makes use of a user-access method to deliver that message to the user. If the user confirms that the event is important by acting quickly on the notification, the agent may also employ its learning machinery to increase its weighting for this kind of event.

Machinery, content, access, and security are just useful categorizations of the factors involved in developing and running intelligent agents. They do not represent a development methodology, just a helpful way of dividing up a rather complicated topic. You will also find that there is a certain amount of overlap among these factors.

Finally, just to help you see how we view the relationships among these four factors, take a look at the general conceptual model of the functions of an intelligent agent, as shown in Figure 5.5. The basic set of agent functions is to combine

Figure 5.5 Conceptual model of an agent. Knowledge and events are combined by reasoning machinery to decide on the next action. The agent autonomously performs the action through its access methods, subject to constraints and checks imposed by security. Finally, learning machinery is capable of learning from events in the agent's "world" and from actions performed by users. This leads to new knowledge.

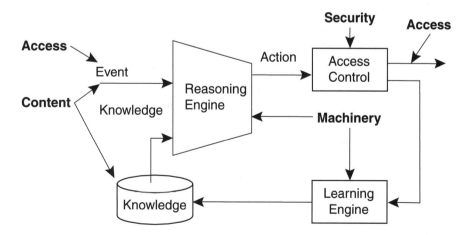

existing knowledge content with new knowledge represented by events and to apply the reasoning or learning machinery to these to determine a desirable action or to extend the knowledge base. Specific agents will exhibit these functions to varying degrees, and some agents may not include the complete set. Generally the agent will not be an entire application; it may be a component of an application or it may be a middleware resource that can be exploited by other applications.

A Development Model

In the preceding sections we saw how the attributes that characterize an agent application can be deconstructed into four technology-based components. For the development of agent-based applications or services for a specific business, in addition to this technology model, we also need a development model. The purpose of this model is to help the developer:

- Identify realistic opportunities for applying agent techniques to business applications.

- Identify the sources of content that are necessary for the desired agent behavior.

- Consider the full set of tools or machinery that are required to operate and manage the agent-based application.

- Ensure that the application will be well-behaved.

- Create a deployment plan for the introduction of the agent-based application.

There are several development models available which could help us think about the application of agent techniques in business. One very early precursor to our work was the effort undertaken in the 1960s to 1970s by the chemical manufacturing industry to automate its processing through the use of computer control. This has led to the development of large-scale process control of all kinds of industries, extending not only to manufacturing but also to service industries. The automation of industrial, particularly chemical, processes is now a highly developed field. A chemical process, say the production of gasoline heating oil, and other products from crude oil, involves the operation of many components, such as pumps, storage containers, pipelines, and heating systems, and these in turn have large numbers of controllable inputs, such as electrical power, pump speeds, and routing. Manufacturing processes are controlled in a *process space;* that is, there are certain combinations of the process parameters, such as temperature, pressure, mixtures, and so forth, which are known to produce high yields of certain outputs, but which are not directly controllable. The first steps in plant automation had been to provide computer control over the basic plant components and the ability to measure the process parameters. This enabled the plant to be centrally controlled, reducing the labor required and enabling the process to be monitored much more precisely. But the plant was still being controlled in terms of basic inputs.

So the second step in automation was to develop functional models of the plant; such a model might describe how the electrical power (input) to a boiler determines the temperature of the water (the outcome). These models are inverted mathematically, so that desired outcomes (water temperature) can drive the required input (electrical power). When these individual plant models are combined, the process engineers have an overall set of tools for controlling the plant in terms of process parameters rather than plant inputs.

The third step in plant automation was to add a process model that represents the relationship between process parameters and different kinds of yields. An additional feature of these control systems is the ability to protect the plant against dangerous combinations of input parameters and also the ability to reconfigure the plant quickly when some component fails. These process control systems are operated via user interfaces which present the information in ways that match the habits and thinking of the process engineers, and run by technicians who may have little knowledge of the chemistry they are controlling. Finally, the process managers had a way to safely control the process outcome itself, and could adjust plant operation to meet customer demand.

Steps Toward Automation

The owner of the chemical plant had some goal in mind for it, perhaps a specific return on investment, and a strategy for attaining that goal: selling a particular product mix. The steps of automation enabled the owner to go from a process control system that was based on basic inputs and required highly skilled chemical engineers to operate it, to one based on outcomes that can be operated by control room technicians. Agent technology is a step forward in enabling us to operate personal and business processes in terms of outcomes rather than inputs. Typical business and productivity applications today enable us to give inputs, such as entering a meeting into a calendar, but do not deal with desired outcomes or goals, such as planning a trip to the customer's office and back. Development of the process model required the chemical engineers to accomplish a number of tasks:

- Provide access to the plant to be controlled (access).

- Develop models (content and machinery) for each plant component to provide control in terms of process parameters.

- Develop an overall model (content and machinery) to allow the plant to be controlled in terms of a desired outcome.

- Develop safety mechanisms to protect the plant against failures of the control system and against failures of parts of the plant itself (security).

Steps Toward Agent-based Applications

Developing agent-based applications will require us to consider a similar set of steps:

- *What are the desired outcomes?* These could range from an absence of spelling mistakes in documents to the ability to set up meetings of a dozen people. It is essential to choose a realistic goal. Automated spelling checking is a feasible goal. Multiparty negotiation may not be.

- *What are the inputs that lead to these outcomes?* These could range from keyboard input to an individual's calendar entries. Are these inputs accessible? Are they sufficiently formalized for an automated process?

- *What are the models that relate inputs to outcomes?* Here we have to consider both content (a dictionary, hierarchical employee/manager relationships) and machinery (string comparison, multiparty negotiation). Do we understand these models adequately to express them and execute them?

- *How can we make sure that we get the* right *outcome?* Does the application do what I want, not what I said? How does it behave under extreme conditions? Most intelligent applications are extremely fragile at the boundaries of their capabilities; we need to provide safety mechanisms that can detect failures of reasoning or negotiation.

Summary

This chapter provides an overview of agents from three perspectives:

- *Where is agent technology in its evolutionary process?* We suggest a similarity to graphical user interfaces in the mid-1980s. Much of the basic technology is available and pioneering applications are in successful use. The software industry is fascinated with the agent concepts, but has not yet worked out how to effectively integrate the various components into operating systems, although that can be expected to occur soon. Agent technology can also be expected to become a pervasive component of all end-user application by the year 2000, and a significant component of specific applications by 1997.

- *There is no "magic" technology for intelligent agents.* Rather, agent-based applications exploit major sets of technologies: one set for intelligence and another for agency. The application's strengths in these two major dimensions will determine whether it is qualified to be labeled an intelligent agent. These two dimensions are further subdivided for convenience of presentation into four technology factors: *machinery, content, access,* and *security.* This technology analysis forms the basis of the next four chapters.

- *How do we plan the development of agents and their introduction into business processes?* Agents are unlike other applications. They have strong impacts on humans, whether employees, customers, or vendors. They span internal computing boundaries within enterprises, creating a level of integration formerly provided only by the management hierarchy.

There is still much to learn about application of agent technology to business processes. This field is still in its infancy and open to innovation. We will try in the coming chapters to ground you in the technologies you will need.

6

Agent Machinery

What puts the intelligence into intelligent agents? In Chapter 5 we associated this with machinery—algorithms and processes—and with content—data processed by the machinery. (We'll discuss content in the next chapter.) The machinery used to make agents is drawn from the research field of artificial intelligence, but it no more represents artificial intelligence than do databases, image processing, and fuzzy logic. From the point of view of managing the business, the machinery of agents is simply that; a collection of practical, down-to-earth techniques for enriching applications and capturing some of the knowledge and experience of your users. (It is not just another attempt to apply "artificial intelligence" to your real-world problems.)

In this chapter you will learn how simple machinery can be applied to the main needs of intelligence in agents, that is, reasoning and learning.

Introducing intelligent agents in your business requires you to think about many aspects of your goals and about how this technology will fit into your operations. Agents are not merely applied technology; they come close to impersonating people. That can be unsettling to employees. Machinery that learns behavior patterns of employees or snoops on service operators brings

Negotiation among Agents

When two or more entities, such as humans or agents, need to work together either to achieve a common goal or to individually achieve their goals, then negotiation must take place. Negotiation is a process that enables each party to try to optimize its approach to its goals by offering or requesting a certain action of the other party or parties. Negotiating techniques have been studied for centuries by diplomats, philosophers, and economists, and they have been joined in this century by researchers in the field of artificial intelligence, who recognized that the societies of agents will need negotiating abilities to resolve conflicting desires.

This is another complex field. In business, negotiation is an important technique in the allocation of scarce resources, for example, time. Negotiating strategies that would allow a society of agents to perform executive calendar management across the entire company would be a major breakthrough. Practical business agents display negotiating skills to only a modest degree, such as in polling a number of electronic commerce sites to find the site with the lowest price. This technique is still primarily in research rather than practical application. This is the front-line of agent machinery.

There are a few kinds of machinery that may be associated with intelligent agents that we will not be discussing. These include: free text searching, speech recognition, text-to-speech, and natural language understanding. While these are all important tools to be exploited by agents, we feel that they lie outside the boundary—which we have to draw, if this book is ever going to be finished—of intelligent agents themselves.

fears of Big Brother. Such machinery is also tricky to get right the first time. Think carefully about how sophisticated your early steps should be.

We will also consider how much machinery you really need for your application. Agent machinery is like any other machinery: it requires maintenance. The more you have, the more maintenance you have to perform. So keep it simple. Now on to reasoning.

Principles of Reasoning

In this section you will learn about the machinery commonly employed to add reasoning powers to agents. Reasoning machinery by itself does not make an agent; a useful agent generally requires all of the four key elements identified in Chapter 5 (i.e., machinery, content, access, and security). Here we are taking a look at the machinery required to make sense of various kinds of content; in the next chapter, we will look at how content provides data that the agent can use for reasoning.

Inferencing Systems

Inferencing systems are software programs that have the interesting property that their logic or behavior is not hard-coded as it is in most applications, but depends on both external event and a set of external data that we will generally call the *rule base*. You could think of them as programs whose logic has been externalized and represented as a set of logical propositions. Many programs, such as interpreters or compilers have very elaborate *case* statements, which provide a range of possible behaviors depending on the values of some (external) data; however the logical flow provided by the case statement is still inside the program and introducing a new case requires editing the program and recompiling it. Inferencing systems, on the other hand, are typically built around the concepts of *production systems* such as the theorems employed by Gödel in his famous proof. These concepts are the foundation of *expert systems*. The goal of an expert system is to capture the logical processes by which a human expert in some field, say, diagnosing a specific illness, arrives at his or her conclusions. These logic processes are represented by the rule base. Large-scale rule bases run to tens of thousands of rules, though many are much smaller, perhaps only on the order of ten. Expert systems have been applied in many domains, from medicine to automobile repair to scheduling cargoes on the NASA space shuttle.

Two of the earliest large-scale expert systems are E-MYCIN, which was developed for the diagnosis of infectious diseases, and RI or XCON (McDermott, 1993), which was developed by the Digital Equipment Corporation to ensure the correctness of the configurations of its minicomputers. However, developing experts systems proved harder than originally expected, in part because of the difficulty of getting experts to reduce their behaviors to sets of rules[1] and in part because it is very difficult to manage large rule bases (or even quite small ones), as you will see. Nonetheless, expert systems are a very valuable technique for creating the small among of intelligence we need for commercially useful agents.

For our purposes, you can think of a reasoning agent as including the following elements.

- *Short-term facts.* This is the state of the program: new facts produced by analysis of events or acquisition of information and derived facts, which are intermediate results of the inferencing process. Short-term facts may be persistent during an execution of the expert system, but may not be preserved if the expert system is restarted. You can think of these short-term facts as the agent's real-time perception of the real-time perception of the world, a set of symbols that represent current facts about significant entities and events in its world. Of course, the agent simply processes them as bits of data (1s and 0s) without any "understanding" of what they mean.

- *Long-term knowledge.* This is generally the working knowledge provided to the agent by its designer or user. Much of this knowledge is encoded in the rule base, but some of it may be in symbolic variables defined to have long-term values. In an adaptive agent, the rule base may be modified either by the agent itself, or by some external process.

- *Control structure.* This is the procedural structure of the reasoning engine, which determines, among other things, when to reevaluate a given rule.

- *Event/action interfaces.* These are the programming interfaces by means of which the agent receives events and performs actions. *Events* are delivered to the agent by other applications or services known as *sensors*. *Actions* decided by the system are performed by *actors*.

Some short-term facts are produced during the evaluation of the rules. Others are created from events presented to the agent. Events usually require preprocessing to extract the new facts; the collection of facts from a single event is called a *fact packet*. For example, a mail handling agent will be notified of the arrival of a new piece of mail and the mail item must be analyzed to extract the significant facts

---

[1]To quote Stan Franklin: "Experts generally do what works, and it generally works." (Franklin, 1995).

(Sender, Addressee, Subject, Priority, Type, etc.). The reasoning system deals with events one at a time and does not generally look for temporal correlations among sequences of events (but see later discussion on Learning for Intelligent Agents).

We add reasoning capability to an agent as follows:

1. The user or developer provides a set of rules that describe a set of desired behaviors: *When X happens, then do Y.* These are composed off-line with a simple text editor, a graphical editor, or other GUI tool. They may be subsequently translated into a different form for processing by the agent.

2. The reasoning system is provided with a set of input events. (This is an aspect of access, which we will cover in Chapter 7.) One or more sources of new information, such as an email post office, such as Lotus cc:Mail or Banyan's BeyondMail or a news service such as NewsHound feedback, is connected to the event interface of the agent.

3. The reasoning system is provided with interfaces to perform or initiate various actions. *Do Y*, for example, may be implemented by sending a message to a system object, or by writing a file or any other typical action that a program may perform. This again is an aspect of access.

4. After the reasoning system is initialized, it will wait until an event arrives. It will extract short-term facts from the event and then evaluate its rules to see if the new facts cause any of them to fire. If one or more rules fire, it may produce additional short-term knowledge or eventually cause an action to be initiated.

Thus the reasoning system provides a means for applying simple, rule-based reasoning to the emergence of new facts in the agent's world and for using this reasoning capability to decide what the agent should do next. You will see below that this is a very mechanistic process; there is no magic involved at all, but some care is required in developing the rules in such a way that the agent does what you want as well as what you said!

Rules for Inferencing

The rules in reasoning systems are often called *production rules*. Each production rule expresses one or more conditions and possibly an action. For example:

```
If Caller_ID_priority is high, then ForwardCall is True
```

Here the condition is whether the value of the short term fact `Caller_ID_`
`priority` is `high`, that is, whether the person receiving the call has defined calls
from this calling party to be of high priority. The action here is simply to set the
short term fact `ForwardCall` to be true; presumably this leads ultimately to the
call being forwarded to the called party. Many languages have been developed
for composing expert system rules. (Note that the "rules" used in this chapter as
illustrations are not expressed in any particular language.) Many of these are ad
hoc languages developed by a programmer for a specific, limited application.
Others are well-specified languages with very rich semantics and vocabularies.

The conditions are symbolic expressions, whose variables are short-term facts.
Here is the typical structure of a rule:

```
IF ((Condition 1) OR (Condition 2)) AND (Condition 3) THEN action
```

The rule consists of a left-hand side (LHS)—the conditions—and a right-hand
side—the action. When the LHS is evaluated, it creates a derived belief, which,
if true, justifies the performance of the RHS. Note that sometimes you will not see
the `'If'` of the LHS, as it is often taken to be implied. Each LHS condition asserts
some relationship (equal to, not equal to, greater than, and so forth) between two
symbols or one symbol and a literal. For example:

```
IF (Subject = 'Bad weather') AND (Current_Time <= Close_of_business)

    THEN (Priority = 'High')
```

These symbols may be assigned values from the long-term knowledge (rules);
thus intermediate inference results can be passed forward in the evaluation of the
rule base. This is called *forward chaining*. In the above example, when the rule
fires—that is, when the LHS is reevaluated and found to be true—the RHS creates
a new short-term fact, which states that this is a high-priority event. This new fact
can now be used in the evaluation of subsequent rules. One of the optimizations
in an expert system is to order the evaluation of the conditions of a given rule so
that the most specific conditions are evaluated first, so that rules which are not
going to fire are discarded quickly.

This ability to create short-term facts for forward chaining is one of the main
advantages of a rule-based system over simple predicate logic. In simple predicate
logic, without forward chaining, each specific combination of possible states

must be represented by a single rule, which leads to very long rules that are hard to manage. Forward chaining allows a complex condition to be expressed over multiple, shorter rules, leading to a higher level of readability and easier manage-ability (see below).

Some conditions may require further processing of short-term knowledge; for example, in a mail handling agent, if the Sender field or fact has certain values, the rules may require a keyword search of the body of the mail item. For example:

```
IF (Subject = 'Bad weather') AND (Body(Keyword = 'snow'))

    THEN Warn_employees
```

This causes the body of a mail message to be searched for a match to the key-word "snow." If the reasoning system supports this kind of syntax, it can enable table-based data to be used instead of explicit rules. For example, instead of having a large number of entries of the form:

```
IF (Event = Mail_Arrival) AND (Sender = 'Robert Smith')

    THEN = (Priority = 'High')

IF (Event = Mail_Arrival) AND (Sender = 'Ann Jones')

    THEN = (Priority = 'High')

IF (Event = Mail_Arrival) AND (Sender = 'George Cohen')

    THEN = (Priority ='High')

IF (Event = Mail_Arrival) AND (Sender = 'Rachel Edwards')

    THEN = (Priority = 'High')

IF (Event = Mail_Arrival) AND (Sender ='Elizabeth Green')

    THEN = (Priority = 'High')
```

the user could maintain a file of very important people (VIP.TXT) and reduce the rule base to:

```
IF (Event = Mail_Arrival) AND (Content(VIP.TXT) = Sender)

    THEN (Priority = 'High')
```

Now instead of adding and/or creating rules as relationships come and go, the application can simply add or delete names from the VIP.TXT file as the user's priorities evolve.

The control structure determines which rule from the rule base will be evaluated next. Rule evaluation consists of determining whether all the conditions of a given rule are true. When all the LHS conditions are satisfied, the rule is said to "fire"; that is, its RHS (action) is asserted. This can be a simple matter of symbol matching or arithmetic evaluation, but it can also be more complex if one of the variables in a condition represents a fact that must be retrieved from a remote application. In large rule bases, the selection of the next rule to be evaluated is a difficult decision, and the control structure becomes quite complex. In the small versions of reasoning systems that are needed for business agents, where the rule base probably consists of less than a hundred rules at most, it is often acceptable to reevaluate all the rules in the set whenever a new event occurs (or periodically, that is, from a Time Event).

If the agent is "shared" among multiple users, the combined rule base may nonetheless be quite large. For example: A mail handling agent may have rules for hundreds or thousands of users. In this case, when a new Mail_Arrival event occurs, the control structure is responsible for selecting the appropriate subset of the rules that apply. It does this by analyzing the fact packet associated with the Mail_Arrival event. In other cases, the rate of arrival of events may be so high that it is not practical to always reevaluate all the rules; here again, the control structure must perform some analysis on the event fact packet to identify the relevant subset to be evaluated.

If the rules in an expert system are modified, for example, through a learning process or by a user, some or all of the rule base must be reloaded into the executing expert system. For high performance, the expert system may preprocess or at least parse the rule base, instead of interpreting it every time. This complicates the process of updating the rule base and creating adaptive behavior, since reinitializing the system may destroy short-term knowledge. Clearly expert systems that can dynamically modify the rule bases are preferable, unless there is a major performance penalty.

Sensors and Actors

Unlike many expert systems, an agent is not merely an observer and commentator on its environment. The agent is embedded in its environment and can perceive much of its environment via sensors and act upon the environment via actors. You could picture the agent as a spider which has built out its web to sense a wide range of events occurring through the (enterprise's) computing system; this is an aspect of *access,* which you will encounter in Chapter 8. The agent may thus be richly provided with facts that can be incorporated in its reasoning and may be able to provide useful control over a rich set of actions.

In the case of RAISE (Grosof, 1995a), described below, the sensor is limited to a single set of events coming from the foraging agents, and RAISE's view of the world is limited to the fact packets extracted from these events. In the case of Doppelgaenger, an agent developed at the Media Lab (Orwant, 1991; 1993), the agent has a much richer view of the world. Doppelgaenger is equipped with a range of sensors that provide many kinds of information about the user population of the Media Lab's computing environment. These sensors can include active badges that provide location information about the user, login daemons that detect the arrival and departure of users on the computing systems, user actions that reflect the frequency and duration of the use of application programs and telephones; in short, any electronically monitorable interaction between a user and the Media Lab can be captured by Doppelgaenger and added to its knowledge base. Doppelgaenger uses this information statistically to construct profiles of user behavior. User behaviors can be analyzed to find clusters of behavior. For example, there might be a cluster of users who frequently read certain Usenet newsgroups between 10 P.M. and 3 A.M.; Doppelgaenger could use this information to ensure that the most recent editions of these newsgroups are available during this time.

Actors are the actions that can be invoked by the agent on its environment. Actors are the machinery that actually pulls levers and turns knobs to assert the agent's actions on the external world. In expert systems, we often think of the output side as being a direct action or at least a recommendation for a direct action: deliver this message, alert this manager, restock this item. In well-connected agents, however, the actors are also often involved in the collection of new information. For example, if you are expecting to leave for the airport to catch a flight, you might have some rules to remind you:

```
IF ((Current_Time + 90 minutes) >= Departure_time(My_flight))

      THEN SendPage ('Time to go!')
```

In this case, `Departure_time(My_flight)` is an invocation of an actor which can query a remote database (the airline's departure schedule) and return a result which is used in the evaluation of the rule. Since it will take some time—at least a couple of seconds—for the actor to perform this operation, this inferencing system must be able to suspend an incomplete evaluation and continue with others until the result is available. If you recall our earlier model of the agent as digital glue, you will see that techniques such as these can greatly increase the richness of information available to the agent. Its ability to use the information, however, depends on the developer's ability to find uses for the information and to express this in the rule base.

RAISE: An Inferencing System for Agents

Production systems are relatively easy to build, at least on a small scale, and many programmers have used this technique for externalizing the setup of an application, for example. The artificial intelligence community has produced hundreds of them for many research purposes and a much smaller number have been developed on a large scale. RAISE (Grosof, 1995a) is an inferencing system developed by IBM Research to provide a reusable class library that can be employed in a wide range of applications and which is now available in the IBM Agent Building Environment. Figure 6.1 shows the major elements of RAISE:

1. The control structure is defined by the *agenda:* which specifies the conditions under which the rules will be reevaluated; essentially this occurs whenever *news* arrives from the *fact packet formation* processor.

2. The *news* interface is the entry point for new fact packets resulting from a new event and also for new facts resulting from additional processing of the event or from the retrieval of additional information.

3. The *Working Knowledge Base* consists of the rule base and long-term and short-term facts.

4. The rules are created and edited by the *Rule Editor,* which also maintains a *Library* of rules for different applications.

5. The *Action Launcher* is a set of access bindings to external functions that are invoked when the RHS of a rule that fires asserts an action verb. In the case of RAISE, there is a final validation of the proposed action before the access binding is actually invoked (see below).

6. The Action Launcher has access bindings to *Other Software Components,* which may be any other applications accessible by the agent (actors). They could include, say, a free-text search tool, forwarding of a mail item to a user,

Figure 6.1   Structure of the RAISE inferencing system.

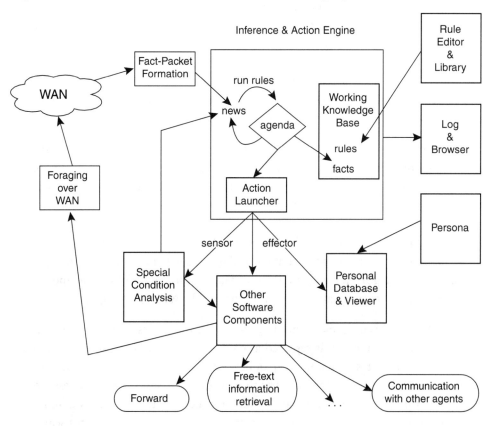

communication with another agent, or remote access to a weather service. One specific database of interest to many agents is the *Persona*[2] of the user.

7. The inferencing system writes a log of all events (fact packets) that it processes and the resulting actions (if any). You will see below that this is a valuable source of content for adaptive agents.

RAISE was developed originally to help to automate an IBM customer support tool called GlobeNet. GlobeNet is an application that searches for appended text

---

[2]See Chapter 7. The Persona is the integrated view across multiple databases of all the information relevant to describing a specific user.

(appends) to public bulletin boards by users or software developers working with certain IBM products. GlobeNet uses *foraging agents,* which periodically dial into bulletin board services (BBSs) or on-line services containing such BBBs and retrieve the most recent appends. These are brought back to the GlobeNet site for screening. The GlobeNet's goal is to find appends from users containing problems or questions, and so it has a good set of tools for searching the appended text for questions. When it finds such an append, it posts it to a database which is periodically reviewed by IBM customer support personnel.

The problem with GlobeNet has been that it performs no classification of the appends—which may cover a very large range of problems—and so each support person must spend a lot of time searching through the appends to find one that he or she can answer. RAISE dramatically improves the productivity of the support personnel by applying a rule base to the classification problem. Each append is processed into fact packets and these are used as short-term input data to the inference system, which uses the content of the various fields to classify the append into a narrow category for which a support team is known to exist. The append is then forwarded to a specific person for study and—we hope—response.

GlobeNet itself is a simple form of agent having the access function and a very limited machinery function. It replaced a manual retrieval scheme, which required on average 30 minutes of support personnel time to identify an append containing a problem (the BBSs contain lots of other threads of discussion). GlobeNet essentially automated that process, eliminating the human time required for retrieval and identification. The support personnel also spent an average of 30 minutes searching through the identified problems to find one that they could solve and then entering the text of the solution. RAISE initially helps GlobeNet only with the classification problem, but removes an additional 10 minutes from the overall process. An ultimate goal for RAISE is to be able to match the user's problem statement to known problems and to automatically retrieve the known solution. GlobeNet and RAISE are early examples of how a relatively simple agent can both reduce operational costs and improve customer service.

The Trouble with Rules

Expert systems would be a lot more useful if human beings actually behaved and thought in logical ways. The whole idea of production systems was to produce virtual machines which could deduce logical consequences when given a set of logically consistent production rules. The problem is that human beings have a really hard time generating logical consistency, even on a relatively small scale. Consider the following trivial example:

1. Suppose you are developing a mail handling agent. You might want to give it a default behavior to store a new mail item at a mailbox. This is to cover cases where no rules fire as a result of a mail arrival event. For example, a user may only have one rule that states that if mail arrives from Robert, then it should be stored in a folder. But if mail arrives from Elizabeth, then no rules fire and no action would be taken on the mail.

2. Now suppose that the user has another rule that fires in some cases that says, delete the mail. This is now in conflict with the default behavior, which is to save the mail. In this case, the delete is explicit (the user specified it), whereas the store is implicit (system default), so the delete should take precedence.

3. It can also arise that two user-specified rules fire, one to store and one to delete mail, through user error. In this case, the store should take precedence as the safe failure default.

In more general cases, it may not be easy to determine which is the "safe" action. Whereas a human being can see a conflict between two proposed actions, to the agent they are just two actions. The agent has no concept of "conflict" nor of "precedence" nor of "safe default." This kind of problem leads to relatively high human involvement in checking the consistency of rule bases. Naturally this problem is a research topic in artificial intelligence, since expert systems would be a lot more valuable if the level of human effort involved in their development could be reduced.

Human beings resolve conflicts by rules of precedence: *When two vehicles arrive more or less simultaneously at a four-way Stop, the vehicle arriving earliest takes precedence.* Research in this area is trying to give expert systems the ability to determine the order of precedence when two or more rules fire simultaneously. Grosof (1995a) proposes the use of trusted advisors or hierarchies of belief as way as of assigning priority to derived beliefs. The basis of the trust or hierarchy can be prior experience (reliability), specificity, "freshness," or authority. Thus if you read a stock recommendation in your local newspaper, you may well give it a lower priority than a recommendation you read in your investor's newsletter.

If the two recommendations are in conflict, you will probably take the more trusted advice.

This is an area that requires some caution. This kind of problem with rule bases tends to quickly exhaust the logical abilities of users, and leaves them frustrated with the rule development process. For this reason, rule-based systems have often failed when the end-users were expected to develop their own rule bases from the ground up. As users—rather than computer scientists—we simply are not used to thinking about our lives in this way. A valuable approach to this problem is to profile the new user and to try to provide him or her with a set of default behaviors which can be tailored. The example given above (VIP.TXT) of further separating the rule content from the behavioral logic can greatly improve the reliability of the rule base and greatly reduce the level of effort required by new users.

The approach taken by GlobeNet/RAISE on this problem is to perform a final screening of each proposed action before it is actually executed. Such an approach can be used to improve the security of agents by applying sanity checks, which may apply statistical or other bounds to reduce the likelihood that the agent does what you said, but not what you meant.

In developing agents for your business applications, you should adopt a methodical approach to generating the rule base and start with a small number of broadly useful rules, rather than trying to go immediately for very detailed cases, as you will almost certainly run into conflicts of this kind. This approach leads to less specific conclusions from inferencing and, therefore, early on in deploying the agent application there will be a significant level of human intervention in narrowing the broad conclusions to specific actions. For example, in our own automated information retrieval profile, which brings a hundred or more potentially interesting news items to our attention every day, we have set a very broad filter that searches for articles containing the keyword "agent." This leads to a wide range of articles on chemical agents, secret agents, travel agents, bonding agents, and so forth, as well as the desired articles on intelligent agents. We could narrow the scope on the filter by extending its specification, but actually eliminating the trash is a very fast and easy task for us and occasionally the trash is interesting in itself.

We believe strongly that this early human monitoring of the agent application is in any case a desirable process for building trust and confidence in the agent's abilities. As users gain more experience by observation of the agent's conclusions, they will learn how to extend the rule base to achieve the needed specificity. That is, the agent teaches the users!

Adaptive Inferencing

Later in this chapter you will be reading about learning in agents. While we are looking at inferencing systems, though, you might be wondering how we can incorporate new knowledge permanently into the agent's behavior. This means in effect modifying the rule base. Users will often want to tune their rule bases as their needs and goals change, but wouldn't it be useful if the agent had a way of modifying its own behavior? As you just saw above, it is all too easy to get into trouble when writing rules, even for relatively simple expert systems, so the idea that you should delegate the writing of new rules to the agent itself may seem ridiculous. However, agents are capable of detecting patterns of user behavior and at least remarking on this to the user. For example, a mail handling agent might notice that the user is beginning to receive a high volume of mail from a sender whose name does not appear in the VIP.TXT file, and it is certainly feasible for the agent to suggest that this sender now deserves special handling (even if it is only to filter out a new source of junk mail).

A valuable extension of the classic expert system which helps with both rule conflicts and adaptation is known as *probabilistic* or *Bayesian reasoning*. Probabilistic reasoning is very helpful in dealing with ambiguity, where the result of reasoning is not a single, clear decision. This approach has been used extensively for many years in developing clinical diagnostic systems, where the outcome of a given diagnostic test (for example, a chest X-ray) can identify the presence or absence of a clinical condition (for example, lung cancer) with a certain confidence level. The outcome of one test may be confirmed by another test in a decision tree structure that ultimately leads to a confidence level approaching 100 percent. In the rule examples given above, the inferencing system uses absolute confidence levels: if a rule fires, then the derived belief is absolutely true and the RHS must be performed. For example:

```
IF (Subject = 'Bad weather') AND (Current_Time <= Close_of_business)

    THEN (Priority = 'High')
```

Here the derived belief is that the weather is bad during working hours, but no confidence level is associated with this belief. Problems arise when the agent finds multiple, conflicting derived beliefs which are all held with the same level of confidence. In a probabilistic inferencing system, the rule might be expressed as:

```
IF (Subject = 'Bad weather') AND (Current_Time <= Close_of_business)

    THEN with probability = 0.8 (Priority = 'High')
```

This leaves open the possibility that some mitigating circumstance, for example, *Today is a holiday,* may make this event of lower significance. You could use systems of this kind to resolve rule conflicts by weighting the proposed actions of each rule and then selecting the action with the highest level of confidence. This still does not guarantee that the correct action will be performed in every instance, but over some sequence of events the selected actions should on average converge to the user's desires. This approach seems to correspond better to the way human beings deal with conflicts and can be used to implement the precedence schemes mentioned above.

Manipulation of the probabilities is also a relatively safe form of adaptation, particularly if the adjustment is performed gradually rather than abruptly. In the following section, you will see how learning techniques can provide feedback to a probabilistic system to improve its behavior.

Learning for Intelligent Agents

Learning is the modification of behavior as a result of experience. You saw above that the rule base and long-term facts are the repository for long-term knowledge in agents with reasoning abilities. That is, the long-term facts define what the agent "knows" in the sense of symbolic artificial intelligence and the rules define the relationships among these facts. Wouldn't it be nice if the agent could develop or at least extend this knowledge by itself, instead of requiring human intervention whenever its world changes? Firefly and Open Sesame! are both examples of agents that learn from their worlds. Firefly uses statistical techniques to identify clusters of musical taste and Open Sesame! uses neural networks to identify patterns of behavior. The search engines of Yahoo! and AltaVista also learn new keywords as they roam the Web and encounter new links; these new keywords are added to their vocabularies and can be searched via the search panel. Such agents would be called *learning agents* or *adaptive agents.* In rule-based agents, learning implies the agent's ability to automatically modify the rule base and the long-term facts in one or more ways:

Adding new rules or modifying old rules. If the agent can recognize a desirable new behavior, it may be able to propose a new rule or at least draw the attention of the user or developer to its belief about the desirable new behavior and invite the creation of a new rule. We pointed out already that this is a difficult task to automate, not because writing rules is difficult, but because maintaining a logically consistent rule is very difficult. Modifying existing rules could involve removing or adding predicates that are invariably satisfied or never satisfied; this is a form of rule optimization. The really interesting problem here, though, is not how to modify the rules, but how to recognize a desirable new behavior.

Adding new facts or modifying old facts. The ability to recognize new long-term facts is even more difficult than creating a new rule, because it implies that the agent can extend its range of concepts. For example, suppose that the agent's user forms a new working relationship as a result of starting a new project. The agent might be able to recognize that there is an important new sender/recipient for email, but has no way to recognize that the person is performing the role of project finance manager (unless it already knows about finance managers and how to identify them). Automatically identifying new concepts is a very advanced problem in artificial intelligence. Modifying existing facts is possible; for example, if the user begins to get a lot of email on financial topics from a new sender, the agent may be able to recognize this new person as the new finance manager—again assuming that it already has the concept of "finance manager." Again the real problem is not how to do the modification, but how to automatically identify the new facts.

Modifying the coefficients of confidence. In a system with probabilistic reasoning, it is very easy for the agent to modify the coefficients specifying the level of confidence in a given belief and this should be safer than introducing new rules. The difficulty here lies in providing the agent with the ability to recognize when the probabilities should change.

Sources of Data for Learning

In our basic model of an agent (Figure 6.2), learning corresponds to the feedback loop that results from the agent's experience leading to modifications of its knowledge. The agent needs access to a stream of data from which it can extract new knowledge. This new knowledge can then be incorporated—automatically or manually—in the agent's long-term knowledge. The agent needs to be able to perceive its world not only for the purpose of reasoning, but also for the purpose of learning, and these two sets of perceptions are not necessarily identical. Reasoning in agents, for example, is about events as specific instances that need to be dealt with individually. Learning, on the other hand, is often about collections of events, so the agent needs access to historical databases or logs of events, which can be analyzed for emerging trends or correlations. If the user wishes to train the agent, this implies that the agent can monitor the user's behavior and learn from this data, which it would otherwise not consider. So the inputs to the learning process could include:

- Events and actions produced by the expert system
- The user's own handling of events known to the expert system
- A range of other events within the scope of the computing system accessible to the agent

Logs of events and actions produced by the expert system can be analyzed for known or likely correlations. For example, it may be that the net result of a complex sequence of rules invariably results in a particular event producing a particular action, even though the rules foresee a much wider range of possible outcomes.

Figure 6.2   Conceptual model of an intelligent agent.

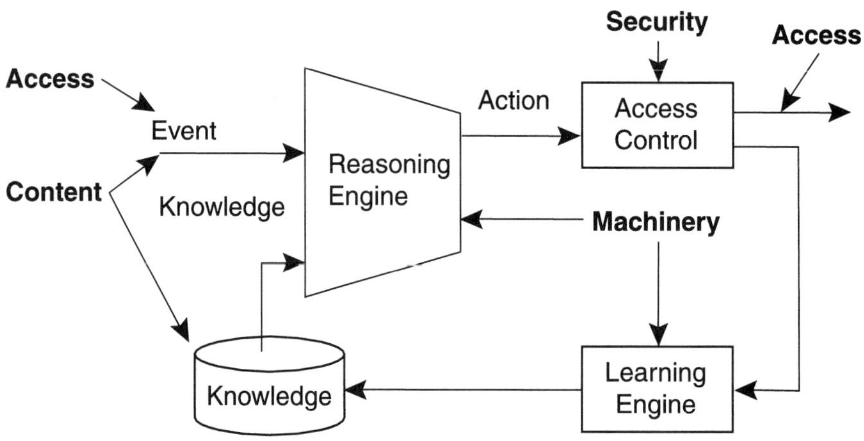

In this case, it may be possible to simplify the rule base, leading to performance improvement and also to a reduction in the difficulty of maintaining the rule base. Alternatively, the log may expose correlations between events that the expert system will miss because it deals with events one at a time. For example, it may be that email from one source is always quickly followed by an identical piece of mail from a reflector. The expert system never looks for event-to-event correlations and so it will never notice this, but a simple analysis of a log of the event processed by the agent and the resulting actions will quickly reveal the duplication. It may be desirable to extend the expert system to maintain a short-term history that it can exploit for these kinds of correlations.

Users of the agent are by far the best source of data for learning, but their actions are also the most difficult to capture and interpret. An agent which can monitor all the user's actions as he or she manually performs the tasks which the user wishes to delegate to the agent has a rich stream of events and actions. However, the agent can only perceive out of the stream of user actions those events and actions which have been identified to it. If the user frequently uses an application which is unknown to the agent, it can form no opinions about it. A difficulty with capturing user actions is that they may be distributed over many systems. For example, you may wish to have an agent perform mail management as an extension of a post office. The problem here is that many of the actions the agent most needs to perceive (delay in reading, duration of reading, frequency of replying, and so forth) are only visible at the mail client. Likewise, a user interface agent needs to have access inside the user's presentation manager in order to be able to capture its most valuable data. These are examples of the problems of access (there are more in Chapter 8).

Finally, the agent could be given access to a much wider range of events within the enterprise's computing systems in order to look for correlations unforeseen or unforeseeable by the developers. This is the realm of data mining, in which the entire data wealth of an enterprise is examined to try to find correlated events.

Basic Statistical Analysis

One of the most valuable adjuncts for a reasoning system is the ability to find correlations among the events that it receives. Inferencing systems generally process events in isolation, not noticing the sequential relationships between events. For highly specific events, for example, mail from Elizabeth, it is straightforward to apply commercial statistical analysis programs to see if the event is highly correlated with time or other events, for example, mail from Robert. It could be, for example, that Elizabeth always forwards to me a copy of any mail she receives from Robert and that Robert always copies Elizabeth on any mail that he sends to me. So when I receive mail from both Robert and Elizabeth within a short time interval, it is quite likely that the events are redundant and I (or the learning agent) should modify the rule base to introduce a probability factor for this case.

Straightforward statistical analysis can also extract simple trends. For example, if the sales of snow shovels suddenly rise dramatically, I may want to check the inventory and possibly have more delivered to a sales floor.

Simple learning of this kind is the basis for several practical agents. The learning functions of Apple's Newton operating system and Charles River Analytics' Open Sesame! (CRA, 1996) achieve useful results from the analysis of relatively simple logs of user actions. Open Sesame! captures a log of user actions on the Macintosh GUI and periodically scans it to find repeated sequences of actions, which presumably represent some habitual task of the user. General Magic's Magic Cap operating system also learns to recognize frequently contacted people by their first names, so that sending mail to "Bob" selects a specific man from the user's address book; similarly, it learns to recognize what time the user means when she says "lunch."

While these are valuable forms of learning, they are limited to a well-known set of possibilities—times of day, the known set of possible user actions, and so forth. To the extent that they extract new knowledge from real-world observations, we are not surprised at the results. These results are knowledge that we could have given the agent ourselves—had we had the time or inclination. The great value of this kind of learning is that it is automating the transfer of knowledge from the user to the agent. This is a significant achievement already, as users are notoriously unwilling to devote time to this activity. An agent which starts a user off with a useful default set of behaviors, based on an analysis of the "typical" behaviors of a user class to which the specific user is believed to belong, and which then applies simple techniques such as these to capture the specific behaviors of this particular user is one of the best approaches to introducing agents to a new user community. However, to get beyond this level, to results that are genuinely novel—and perhaps surprising—we need more powerful tools.

Discriminant Analysis

Another area in which users are unwilling or unable to provide complete knowledge to an agent is in searching and filtering. We mentioned above our own approach to this problem, which is to specify a very loose filter and then perform rapid manual filtering of news articles. However, others will want a much more automated searching or filtering capability from their agents. Ted Selker (1994b) has demonstrated an example of improving the user's filter specification by automating the determination of the user's real discriminants. This demonstration was known internally as Relevance And Trash (RAT). In RAT, the user provides an initial search specification which is applied to a database and yields a certain number of hits or matches. The user is then invited to review a subset of these matches and to rate each one for its relevance or level of interest. RAT can then apply rankings to the keywords of each article and determine combinations that have very high relevance and others that have very low relevance. These discriminants can then be applied to the rest of the search results to yield a much improved selection of articles.

As in the cases of General Magic's Magic Cap and Charles River Analytics' Open Sesame!, these techniques are capturing knowledge that in principle could have been provided by the user, though in this case the user may be even less inclined to try to specify the knowledge explicitly. By iteration, the learning process is able to develop much more complex specifications of the user's interests than he or she may be able or willing to enter. Here again, though, there is no magic. The user still needs to get the agent "into the ballpark" of his or her interests and while the techniques will reduce the level of "trash," it is unlikely to be eliminated completely. For example, Web surfers following the 1996 U.S. Presidential campaigns found that an interest in Senator Robert Dole led them also to the Dole canning company's Web site.

Data Mining

Data mining is a powerful new set of tools for distilling learning out of observations of real-world behavior. It has primarily been applied to very large corporate databases, for example, for detecting potentially fraudulent credit card transactions. But these techniques are just what is required to help an agent extract new knowledge from the streams of events and actions that it processes. Like reasoning, however, data mining is not magic. Human judgment is still required to validate its discoveries. For example, a negative correlation between utility bills and order processing delays could occur as a result of a failure of the electrical supply to a warehouse.

While it was originally conceived as a way of extracting unforeseen information from massive corporate databases, data mining will provide a growing set of tools for the agent developer to perform temporal correlation over event logs, to look for hidden relationships between different events and their associated actions. Algorithms developed in this area of research can automatically discover all associations and patterns within a collection of data, for example, an event/action Log. These associations are extracted by applying statistical correlation techniques along all dimensions of the database. For example, events which frequently occur together can be automatically identified even though a user or administrator would have never thought to program a statistical search for such a correlation. Or an interface agent could use such patterns to prompt a user who begins a known, but rarely used sequence of actions and then becomes lost and starts searching for the next step. Trends could be identified, in which the strength of a given belief, for example, that mail from a previously unknown sender is important, may increase over a period of days.

While the core statistical techniques employed in data mining may not be new, the value in these tools lies in their ability to out-perform blind searching in the discovery of unforeseen relationships. For small agent systems this may be unimportant, but its importance rises dramatically as the scale of the database to be studied grows. Data mining is finding important applications on large-scale commercial databases (for example, in identifying fraud or people with poor credit histories), but has not been closely associated yet with popular intelligent agent applications. It can be expected to play a significant role in extracting knowledge from the vast amount of data available on the Internet (see Chapter 3). For example, IBM recently announced a pilot service (ICE) (http://www.nhl.com) with the National Hockey League to perform on-demand mining for particular combinations of events during NHL games.

Nonsymbolic Learning

So far in this chapter we have been concerned with elaboration and refinement of knowledge represented as a rule base for reasoning or, similarly, a filter specification for searching. Rule bases evolved from the application of formal logic techniques to symbolic reasoning, and this has been one of the mainstreams of artificial intelligence research. Symbolic knowledge representation has the advantage that it can be directly interpreted and manipulated by humans. But knowledge can also be represented by purely statistical results. The most elaborate form of this approach lies in neural networks.

Firefly (1996) is a commercial Internet agent, which was derived from an earlier project on social agents originally known as Dylan (Maes, 1994). The core technique in Firefly, is the ability to recognize population clusters in a multi-dimensional space. Firefly acts as an advisor on musical taste (mostly rock music). New users are invited to submit a list of their favorite CDs to Firefly, which then responds with suggestions of other CDs that the user will probably also like. How does Firefly know this? It does not have a complex rule base of factors in musical appreciation, still less an ability to extract from the user's submission what the user's taste may be. Firefly's knowledge is based on the identification of clusters of people who have similar taste or at least similar lists of favorite CDs. That is, empirically one can find groups of people who have the same or similar combinations of CDs; in some cases, such as fans of the Grateful Dead or the Rolling Stones, there may be a very strong disciminator. In other cases, there may be a more diffuse cluster over a number of performers with similar styles or content. This leads to a finite number of clusters, which represent statistically the musical tastes of a large user population. We could call this an "aesthetic taste hashing function." When the new user submits his or her favorites, Firefly determines which cluster or clusters are closest (in statistical space) to these favorites and it then returns other CDs which are popular in this cluster or clusters and which were not mentioned by the new user.

Thus, while Firefly contains no conceptual knowledge about music or performers, it is nonetheless a repository of statistical knowledge about the musical tastes of a large population. We could say that Firefly has automatically identified patterns in musical taste from the large set of input data presented to it. So although Dylan does not use an inferencing system, it is nonetheless an intelligent agent in a specific domain and one can foresee other applications of this approach to providing guidance to individual users from a large population with clustered interests or behaviors. There are no examples of the combination of the statistical approach with the rule-based approach. However, we have already suggested that there is likely to be great value in identifying the group to which a new user belongs and using this to provide a default rule base derived (manually) from the personal rule bases of the members of the group as a way to provide initial value to the new user.

Neural Networks

Neural networks were developed as analogs of biological brains. It has been demonstrated that learning in humans and higher animals results from the formation of complex "wiring" among the brain's cells, so that the excitation of a given cell depends on weighted functions of the inputs from many other cells to which it is "wired." The knowledge is encoded in the wiring and weighting factors of the various neurons. In a neural network, a set of external inputs is presented to an initial layer of summation units, which also receive inputs from their outputs and from the outputs of eventual other layers. The outputs from the final layer of summation units can be observed. The neural network is trained by presenting it with sets of known input vectors and a corresponding set of desired output vectors. By repeatedly applying these vectors, the weight factors for the connections among the various layers can be made to converge, so that whenever a member of the set of input vectors is presented, the correct output vector will be produced. The neural network is then said to have learned to recognize the set of input vectors. Moreover, the trained network is able to recognize input vectors that are similar but not identical to the training set.

Neural networks have been shown to be very effective at dealing with unstructured data or with noisy input data (events), such as handwriting and speech recognition and various forms of image processing, which are very difficult to process with the (rigid) reasoning techniques of inferencing systems. In agent systems, they could find application in identifying approximate sequences of events or user actions which are approximate matches to known behaviors, and their output could then become input to inferencing systems to determine a required action. A disadvantage of neural networks is the relatively long training period—large numbers of stimuli must be applied and the desired outcome asserted in order to perform the learning. In many cases, this training can be performed as a background task, working on data collected over a period of execution. A further disadvantage is that the learned knowledge cannot be systematically modified or transferred to another network. While this is a very powerful technique, it seems unlikely to make a big impact on intelligent agents in business applications in the near future.

Principles of Negotiation

Neural networks bring us to one of the research frontiers in intelligent agents, one that is concerned with various kinds of societies of agents. One very powerful model of intelligence, for example, considers hierarchies of agents with various kinds of capabilities. The highest-level agents are given goals, which they deconstruct into subgoals recursively until the subgoals are sufficiently primitive that they can be executed by one of the lower-level agents. Achieving a goal may have a cost associated with it; for example, in order to get an appointment on the calendar of a co-worker, an agent may have to agree to move another meeting. In order to decide whether to agree to this cost, the agent must have some idea of the importance or value of achieving its current goal. Will it exceed the imposed cost? Thus there is some metric for the achievement of a goal and for the associated cost. The agents' user probably has many high-level goals, and an optimization strategy for the agents would be, in economic terms, to maximize utility—the difference between the value of the achieved goals and the cost of achieving them.

For example an agent managing the flow of traffic across an intersection in the middle of the desert can develop a strategy to maximize the overall throughput of cars across the intersection (value) and to minimize the waiting time for individual cars (cost). However, if we now put two such intersections one block apart, each having its own agent, then (above a certain volume of traffic) the two agents will have to collaborate to achieve their goals. This interaction becomes a negotiation, in which each agent tries to maximize its own utility by adapting its strategy to its observations of the other agent's strategy. Here we are at the intersection of AI and economics, a fascinating research area, and in the long term very relevant to agent activities such as purchasing, auctions, or meeting-scheduling, indeed any form of decision involving more than a single party. But these are not immediately relevant to today's practical, business applications; there is still much to learn about how to apply even simpler agents in the real world. The book *Rules of Encounter* by Rosenschein and Zlotkin (1994) is a fascinating study of this area.

Machinery for Your Business

We led off this discussion of how agents work with this chapter on Machinery, because it can be for some readers the most worrying. We have tried to portray these mechanisms for adding intelligence to agents as very practical, concrete technologies, and not distant theories of AI. The subsequent chapters on content, access, and security will seem much more like familiar territory to application developers than these concepts of reasoning, learning, and negotiation. So our first recommendation is to think about how complex you need your machinery to be. Remember that you are already running a business today—your organization is already applying reasoning, learning, and negotiation, but these processes are being accomplished by people. How much machinery you want to invest in depends on how much of your organization's mental processes you want to bite off.

If your main goal is to improve employee productivity or the quality of certain work functions, you could start with reasoning. Reasoning allows you to capture in machinery the expertise of some classes of employees and either to improve their productivity or to displace—or *disintermediate*—them altogether. This was, after all, the original goal of expert systems. It has proven difficult to achieve the hoped-for staff reduction by this means, because while reasoning agents can be very effective in their defined domains, human employees often add tremendous value by being able to work—to some degree—outside the narrow domain represented by the rule base. In other words, while it may appear that the bulk of a given task can be represented by some finite number of rules, human beings are able to deal with a very large number of exceptions to those rules. These exceptions often have to do with the application of the very large body of nondomain-specific knowledge to the task. Thus the agent may in many cases be best viewed as an adjunct to the human rather than a replacement.

In this light the agent can add value in various ways:

- *By automating or verifying the hard factual, domain-specific knowledge required for the task.* Here the archetypal example is probably still Digital Equipment Corporation's R1 (McDermott, 1982) or XCON (Barker, 1989), which can validate the complex configurations of minicomputer systems for a sales representative, who adds value through his or her knowledge of customer preferences and equipment availability.

- *By reducing the level of skill required in the employee.* This was the goal, at least, of the extensive work performed to develop medical diagnostic tools such as E-MYCIN. The hope was to enable medical personnel, trained to below the physician level, to perform primary screening tests in underdeveloped countries. Similar tools have been successfully developed to raise the accuracy of specialist, but nonexpert, physicians in diagnosing, for example, breast cancer from mammograms. Such tools are particularly useful in less specialized professions where there is a high turnover in staff and long training cycles cannot be justified. Thus sales agents for goods less complex than minicomputers can also benefit from agents to automate and verify their transactions.

■ *By enabling management to impose a defined business process as an alternative to formally training employees.* The agent's reasoning capabilities can be applied to guiding and requiring employees to perform a task in a specific manner or sequence as part of a quality control process. Here intelligent agents overlap with workflow, which has similar goals, and may also use rule-based systems to define business processes.

Your ability to introduce reasoning agents in your business will depend primarily on your ability to define useful initial rule bases. We suggested earlier that it is important to begin by introducing rule bases whose behavior is sufficiently simple to be readily understandable by the user and yet which begin to provide some useful function. Clearly this entry point will depend on the skill level of your users. If you begin in this way and add function and complexity at a rate that most of your users can absorb, experience in other fields suggests that even nontechnical users can eventually deal with very complex systems. Of course, you will need to deal with new employees and you may need to be able to back out of an unsuccessful new version.

For many tasks you will also need to provide users with the ability to customize their agent's behavior; it is very important that the user be able to explore nondestructively the effects of introducing new behaviors and also be able to revert to an earlier version if the modification is unsatisfactory. A key tool here is the application used to modify the behavior (more on this in Chapter 7).

Alternatively, you could start with learning. Every business relies on watchers who are uniquely skilled at discovering trends or noticing relationships. As the pace and scope of businesses expand, these tasks become harder to accomplish in useful times, although agents will probably never compete with talented people at these tasks. Learning agents, and their relatives searching and filtering agents, can powerfully complement these people by keeping silent watch on a multitude of databases around the world and providing filtered and informed summaries of their observations to the human agents. Learning agent are less well developed than reasoning agents, but are expected to become valuable tools in recognizing automatable processes within an enterprise.

You will need to think carefully about the complexity of the task to which you would like to apply an agent. As humans, we tend to overlook our amazing abilities to process, say, visual information, and assume that some task, say, managing the distribution of incoming fax mail, can be easily turned over to an agent. In fact, the "simple" task of reading the "From" and "To" fields reliably may be well beyond current sensor technology. Can the rules that define the agent behavior be completely defined *a priori* with no need for automated extension? Such tasks, if you can find them, are excellent starting points. Is there a single set of rules or do large numbers of employees have individual, personalized sets of rules? Nobody likes to be told that "one size fits all." While Henry Ford was able to impose that uniformity on the production line, information workers believe that they bring individual skills to their work, and consequently any agent assistance will need to be tailored to their styles; but are there users willing to do this work? The Doppelgaenger approach of performing user modeling from large-scale observations is a valuable but potentially expensive way to generate these models. From these, generic rule bases can be abstracted by the application developers, and these rules can then be customized to fit specific users.

If the users truly do have highly developed individual skills, it may be worthwhile to experiment subsequently with learning techniques that can capture these nuances and evolve as the user himself or herself evolves in response to his or her own learning and to the evolution of the user's world. The more highly skilled the user, the more valuable (generally speaking) it will be to apply agent machinery to assist him or her. But equally, it will be more and more challenging to provide a useful tool.

Starting by attempting to apply agents as assistants to radiologists is probably not a good idea, although expert developers have achieved valuable results even in this profession. Better starting points may be found among lower-skilled employees in jobs with a high turnover rate. Here there is probably already a well-developed knowledge base for performing the job. The degree of individuality is probably low, so a generic agent knowledge base will apply, and the complexity of the knowledge will be manageable. Use a number of simple applications to develop your team's skills with these new tools and with capturing and maintaining business knowledge. At the same time, define a measurement system so that the value of the agent application can be assessed. This can be in terms of employee productivity, or accuracy, or reductions in turnover, or reductions in training costs. Productivity gains from agents are real, as we have shown in earlier chapters, and you will be encouraged to try harder cases.

Summary

In this chapter we have looked at the techniques employed to bring intelligence to agents. The two main features of intelligence for business agents are Reasoning and Learning and we have shown that there are very pragmatic mechanisms for producing these; intelligent agents do not depend on magic. Good, commercial examples for these exist and are cited in Table 6.1. The usefulness of intelligence depends on capturing accurate and consistent sets of knowledge about how the agent is supposed to behave. The production and maintenance of this knowledge is one of the chief problems to be solved in developing a practical business application, and developing an agent application will entail a significant effort to capture and validate this knowledge of how some part of your business operates. Once the skills exist to create and maintain these knowledge-based applications, you will be ready to investigate the application of learning to the automated maintenance and fine tuning of these knowledge bases; here again, there is no magic, just the careful application of statistical analysis or data mining techniques. At heart, intelligent agents still depend on 1s and 0s, like any other software.

Table 6.1 Intelligent Agent Products

Intelligent Agent Product	Source
AgentBuilding Environment	http://www.raleigh.ibm.com/iag/iagsoft.html
Magic Cap	http://www.genmagic.com/MCW
Open Sesame!	http://www.opensesame.com/

Agent
Content

How do you talk about your car? When the conversation turns to cars, do you say it's a Chrysler four-door sedan with a V6 and everything automatic? Or do you start by explaining that its most interesting feature is the variable timing for the cam shaft which enables the valve opening to be optimized for the engine speed? Or perhaps you start by listing the 16 visits it has had back to the repair shop since you ran into a deer and bent the chassis. A conversation about cars brings with it a large set of assumptions that we make about each other's knowledge of cars. Do you remember when you were ignorant of cars, and someone asked if you could help jump start her car? Were you in doubt about who was supposed to do the jumping? Do you remember when you first joined a conversation about cars, and you realized that beyond counting the wheels you were pretty lost? And if you feel on pretty firm ground with cars, let's try you on music, and see how quickly we can get you out of your depth.

We have divided up our social world into thousands of domains, such as cars or music or gardening, and further specialized these into detailed topics, whether it be about how to play marbles in Italy, as opposed to the Netherlands, or how to play arbitrage games on Wall Street. These *domains* each have their own vocabularies, which label the various topics within them which can be very esoteric, as in medicine or wine tasting, or can be fairly evident. Vocabularies are the lists of names of the elements that make up a topic. But domains also have implicit structures, which define relationships among the various elements within them, and which are often hard for an outsider to discover. For example, the car's transmission has close relationships to the engine and to the drive wheels, but it does not have a relationship to the passenger seat. We could call this structuring the "world-view" of the domain. Taken with the vocabulary, this world-view is a definition of how we think about and talk about that area of life. In the world-view of a car, transmissions and engines are fairly close—not as close as, say, cooling systems and engines, but much closer than transmissions and passenger seats. Elements that have close relationships can often be associated by verbs; we say that the cooling system *cools* the engine, or that the engine *drives* the transmission. But the transmission does nothing to the passenger seats.

How do we develop agents able to interact with servers or other agents on the topic of cars? or shirts? or futures positions? How should they know to ask about the paint scheme when the bodywork is being discussed, rather than the electrical system? How should they know that there was an error when the color scheme was described as "radial"?

Welcome to Content

Simply put, content is the stuff that machinery operates on. It is both the means by which the agents interact with one another and with other entities and the means for the expression of the information that the agents process for decision making, information filtering, and searching. When agents interact, they need to know what they are talking about. If you were able to send BargainFinder (see Chapter 3) out to search for car prices, you would like it to be able to express complicated requirements such as your desire for "engine front and drive rear." Content is the means by which an agent develops competency in a domain.

One immediate example of content is the directions that we want to give to a personal agent via the user interface. It would be very convenient to be able to give orders such as: "Set up a meeting with Bob on the performance problem." Leaving aside the speech recognition problem—you did want a speech-based user interface, didn't you?—this form of content input raises some very difficult problems:

- *Parsing.* Despite decades of research, there is no machine that can reliably parse unrestricted free speech, that is, analyze a sentence into its grammatical elements: subject phrase, verb phrase, object phrase, and so forth. Whatever language we use for expressing content among agents is going to have to be a lot more explicit about such things.

- *Context.* It is not that human languages are ambiguous—a well-trained assistant would know immediately what to do with this request (including possibly ignoring it). The problem is the massive amount of contextual knowledge—or awareness—required to classify the sentence. Who is *"Bob"*? What *performance problem* is in question here (Bob's? the company's? the product's?)? How urgent is this meeting? How much time should be allocated to it? Then there is the general knowledge required to fully express the sentence's implications. For example, the world-view of *meeting* implies time, location, people, facilities, and possible preparation. But how much of such general knowledge do we expect an agent to understand? Should it be evident that all the participants in a meeting need to be physically present at a single location and that the room should be large enough to hold all of them?

- *Dialogue.* If we limit the agent's awareness to a small number of human concepts, for example, let it deal only with setting up meetings, then it would still need to prompt the user for the missing information. In the case of meetings, we could think of it filling out a form or template which describes the meeting: starting time, duration, participants, location, audio-visual facilities, and so forth. In order for the agent to solicit this information, it needs to know the order in which details are defined—for example, we generally choose a day before choosing a time (but not always). So the world-view has to lead to a logical sequence of questions and answers; we call this an *application grammar* for defining a meeting. Since the agent is dealing with a human, it will also have to be able to deal with our difficult habits of presenting information out of order. ("oh, we need this meeting before the board meeting") and of changing our minds ("no, let's have Bob lead the other meeting").

It is when we ask agents to step up from dealing with the administrivia of operating systems, and to help us in the real world, that we have to realize the tremendous amount of content that we routinely handle in order to accomplish what we think of as mundane tasks. We can see from this example that there are three major communication patterns that agents will have to deal with if they are to be integrated effectively into real-world environments:

1. *Human-agent dialogues:* setting goals, giving feedback, giving priorities and preferences

2. *Agent-human dialogues:* reporting on goals, soliciting information, reporting on information discovered

3. *Agent-server and agent-agent dialogues:* negotiating a common language, verifying identities, soliciting capabilities, agreeing on the topic and the world-view, expressing desires, expressing responses, proposing compromises, commanding an action

For each of these situations, we need a world-view for which all the parties have a common definition. Interactions among agents and between agents and humans and agents and server consist of sending messages—by one means or another—using vocabulary drawn from this world-view and conforming to its structure. It is through these dialogues that the loosely coupled, flexible "glue" of intelligent agents is implemented.

Let's contrast here the way that clients and servers interact and the way that we would like agents to be able to interact with servers and with one another. First, we could say that client-server applications have a "world-view" which is defined by the application interface. The two parties each have detailed knowledge of this interface, because they were compiled with a common, fixed definition. Certainly the interface has a vocabulary, for example, methods to which messages can be sent, and a very well-defined structure. But it would be an exceptional interface that was capable of expressing all the facts about a car, except perhaps at the level of a small ad. Second, the client/server API is passive; the server will wait a long time, perhaps forever, for the client to provide a query specification. It would never occur to the server to prompt for additional information. Neither could the server deal with ambiguity in the specification.

Compare this with the idea of an agent contacting a server and beginning a dialogue by asking if the server knows how to talk about passenger cars. The agent and the server have never previously talked to one another, and have no prior knowledge of each other's capabilities, but can negotiate whether to talk about cars from the point of view of a consumer, a repair mechanic, or an insurance company, all of which have their own perspectives on the world-view. In an agent-based approach, an agent "client" should be able to open a dialogue with any server. That is, "clients" are not hard coded to communicate only in the parameters of a medical application, and "servers," while they may contain highly specialized data or services, are able to engage in an openly expressed dialogue. Thus an agent will be able to open a dialogue with a server, and may quickly discover that a given server has nothing of interest to it; but with luck, it will find a server that can recognize the topic of interest to the agent and is able to perform the agent's request—even though the two had never encountered one another previously. This is what we mean by "openness" and "flexibility" in agent systems.

Note that the expression of information used among the agents may or may not be the form in which the information is stored. Human languages are not the means by which information is stored in our heads, even at the conceptual level. We have both an abstract form of representation used in our brains, as well as the thousands of human languages that we can employ to transmit that information from person to person. It would be much simpler if we could just mandate the use of a single language for agents. But there is already a world full of content out there, so we shall have to accept the existence of multiple languages. Therefore, there is a need for one or more *metalanguages* in which to negotiate or express the content language (restaurant waiters in Europe are superbly skilled at discerning the appropriate language from styles of dress and body language).

So what is the nature of the content that businesses need to deal in? We have presented agents as being "aware" of their world and able to "act" upon it, so basically we need a language that can describe the world that we want the agent to deal with and provide the agent with an appropriate set of actions. An agent system for managing a company might need to be aware of the organization and hierarchy of the company, the employees and/or their functional positions, the policies established by the company for various activities, the goals that the agent is supposed to accomplish and the processes that it can invoke to accomplish these goals, and where it can go to gather information and perform actions. As human office workers, we bring to this situation the accumulation of many years of general knowledge, professional training, and organizational experience, plus wonderful abilities to observe and learn. To express this we will employ two types of languages: *knowledge representation* and *agent communication* languages.

Knowledge Representation

A knowledge representation language provides us with tools for representing information in one or more specific domains. For example, suppose we needed our agent to be able to deal with the world of shirts. Such an agent system would need to have a content structure which reflects the world-view of shirts. That is a vocabulary for describing shirts: long sleeve, short sleeve, button-down collar, turtleneck collar, cotton, denim, striped, tie-dyed, and so forth. It would also cover the structure of shirts: sleeves, types of collars, types of cuffs, button left or button right, types of fabric. The world-view is the framework that differentiates a shirt from, say, a skirt, and the vocabularies enable us to describe specific instances within these domains. Of course, we can use inheritance to describe shirts and skirts as subclasses of the class of clothing, and in this way we can build up knowledge representation schemes that cover large and useful domains.

So if we want to construct agents that know how to be aware of how our businesses are run, we will need knowledge representation languages that represent the types of objects and types of processes that are employed in those businesses. For example, in medicine there is an elaborate terminology for describing a patient's condition and the doctor's orders for treatment. This terminology exists in various forms—there is a learned language employed by the practitioners as a professional extension of the vernacular, and there is also an homologous codification of this learned language developed by insurance companies for their own data processing needs. While these languages were not designed with intelligent agents in mind, they are an established content base for this profession and any agent system working in this domain will have to be able to deal with them. Similar specialized languages or jargons can be found in all trades and professions, and codifications of them exist typically in professions that already exploit information systems extensively.

Agent Communication

An agent communication language, on the other hand, is the vehicle for moving information among agents. A message expressed in the agent communication language allows an agent to instruct another agent to perform a certain action. It may also transport information encoded in a knowledge representation language. We could think of these as routing slips in a process line, where a batch of production is handed off from station to station, each station being able to perform one or more processes that are specified on the slip. Each agent (processing station) has a certain repertoire of actions that it can perform; for example, an agent may be able to return the current weather forecast or it may be able to extract potentially interesting correlations. So we need a language that can express these requests and the resulting responses and that is recognized by all the agents. The agent communication language must also express the type of knowledge representation employed for the information which is being passed around; that is, the agent communication language is a metalanguage for the knowledge representation languages.

While there are many instances of knowledge representation languages in commercial use already (although not for agent purposes), agent communication languages are only now beginning to emerge from research and development laboratories. Consequently, there are no widely established bases to which an agent system must conform. As a corollary, this has led to the widespread invention of ad hoc agent communication languages by researchers and developers. In most agent systems, the agent communication language and the knowledge representation language are completely separate languages. An exception to this is General Magic's Telescript, which combines the roles of a programming language, an agent communication language, and a knowledge representation language.

An Agent Content Example

Consider a system of agents that produces various representations of digital video. The video itself is represented in a defined format, and there is associated metadata which describes the video frame structures, the sequences of types of frames, the peak and average bit rates for transmission, and so forth. There is probably also information describing the subject of the film, the scenes, the actors, the types of people, the location, and so forth. The agent system is responsible for producing three versions of the original video:

1. The keyframe storyboard (the static images of each scene)

2. A low-resolution version of the video suitable for free distribution on the Internet

3. Several high-resolution versions with different edit sequences

This is a simple kind of production line for manufacturing various digital products from an original content base. The system might consist of a manager agent that receives each production request and prepares one or more routing slips which it dispatches to production agents that can interpret the production requests and perform the appropriate processing. So here we have the two types of agent content plus the actual image content:

1. The metadata expressed in a knowledge representation language that describes the video at two or more levels (frame and visual/audio content)

2. The processing instructions expressed in an agent communication language that describes the agent's goals

Some of the metadata can be expressed in terms of professional languages—in this case, standards defined by the Society of Motion Picture and Television Engineers—and some of it will require either an ad hoc language or one of the many knowledge representation languages. Likewise for the processing language— some of it can be fulfilled using industry standards, but more than likely the developer will have to create a language that describes the industry-specific world-view for postproduction processing of video.

So in this chapter we consider how content is represented. This turns out to be mostly a discussion about employing languages for the benefit of intelligent agents, rather than about the content itself. We presume that you, as an IS practitioner in your industry, are aware of the specific world-view of your industry. As we saw in the chapter on Machinery, the field of artificial intelligence (AI) has produced an extensive body of research and practical results in the area of both these kinds of content representation, but there are also a number of ad hoc languages that different industries and professions have developed. Since this field forms the context for much of the work on agents, we'll give you a little tour of some of these.

Our goal here is not to make you an expert on AI languages, but to help you apply agents in your own business by enabling them to access your company's content and to express and execute goals that serve your company's needs. The vast majority of the content you will need for your agents already exists in your information systems. Your challenge will be to understand how to enable your agents to talk about what your business already knows.

World-Views

Every business relies on some conceptualization of the world to meet its specific needs and to exclude irrelevant factors, thus simplifying the world that it has to deal with. For example, the business of shipping household goods around the world deals in terms of households, crates, local agents, forwarding agents, customs agents, road transport, sea transport, and air transport, among other things. This conceptualization contains timetables for the departure and arrival of boats and airplanes and their carrying capacities. It knows about customs regulations that may forbid the shipment of certain kinds of goods.

On the other hand, it has no view about the color of clothing that is shipped, nor about the metagoal of why the owners want to move their homes around the world. It is a submodel of the world—necessary and sufficient to the business of shipping household goods. Indeed, a successful enterprise of any kind must have such a submodel, since it would be impossible to run a business that tried to deal with every aspect of the world. We call this the world-view of the domain.[1] It provides a concept of some specific aspect of the world, and deals in objects, actions, distinctions, and relationships that matter in that particular domain.

Normally when we write application programs, even client/server programs, this world-view remains outside the software in the heads of the people who defined the application. The application writers create machinery that operates within the context of this system but is unaware of it. For example, one could write a program to monitor historical trends in checking account minimum balances. The people defining the application know how to access the account databases and extract the daily balances and it is then a simple matter of programming to keep track of the monthly and yearly minimum balance. The program is merely a specialized calculator; it knows nothing of accounts, or minimum balance requirements, or associated accounts that need to be included—it just does arithmetic. All of these objects, actions, distinctions, and relationships are external to the software in the heads of the application designers.

---

[1]Such a model or view in philosophy is called an *ontological system*.

World-Views for Agents

In developing agent-based systems, however, a key feature of the approach is that (some of) that world-view has to be expressed in the software, since much of the flexibility of agent interactions stems from their ability to form loose-bindings with servers or other agents, through exchanging descriptive messages, rather than by using rigid, coded client/server messages. A collection of knowledge-based programs that work together must have a common commitment to a world-view which represents the domain in which they are going to collaborate. We saw above in the clothing example that a world-view defines a set of classes (objects, relationships, and distinctions) and functions (actions) for a certain domain.

A group of agents that manage the production of customized jeans must have such a common view of what constitutes a pair of jeans—for example, what dimensions are required to define specific instances, where the denim can be ordered into the production line, and what sequence of processes it must pass in order to create a garment. One of the key decisions that you have to reach in designing an agent-based system is related to the context problem—how much of the world-view on which Levi-Strauss bases its business should be captured and expressed in this agent software? You might choose to make the goal of the agent application development narrowly defined—a single style, a single fabric, a single gender—because you were basically interested in testing the end-to-end process rather than being able to produce a wide range of garments. In that case, you could employ a very narrow world-view model—not much different from the checking account minimum balance case. But when the agents need greater flexibility in expressing among themselves the tasks they ask of one another, then more and more of the Levi-Strauss world-view will have to be captured. If the agent-based application is limited to the garment production process, that defines the bounds on its model. If, on the other hand, Levi-Strauss wanted to apply agent-based techniques all the way from the retail store back to the fabric manufacturers, the agent system will need to capture more and more of the world-view.

A Geographic Example

This problem of defining world-view models is central to creating distributed agent-based systems that can span large real-world domains. It is similar to the design problem in object-oriented programming in that it requires careful thinking about the objects and relationships within the model. Even relatively simple domains can yield complex models, as is shown in Figure 7.1, which illustrates a world-view for travel planning within a small geographic region of Japan (Takeda, 1995). Here the model is based on three primary concepts: Places, Location Points, and Boundary Lines. What is the distinction here between Places and Location Points? A Place appears to be an area or district, while a Location Point is a narrower place, a single building or alternatively a route. Another ambiguity is that lakes show up as Places, whereas rivers—which would seem to be closely related to lakes in some ways—show up as routes. There seems to be some conceptual overlap here, but as a scheme it probably works in the specific application. The developers could get into trouble with this, however, if they try to extend this model by including it in a larger scheme. Just as in object-oriented design, as world-view models get larger

Figure 7.1   Example of a world-view model for Travel Planning (from Takeda, 1995 simplified).

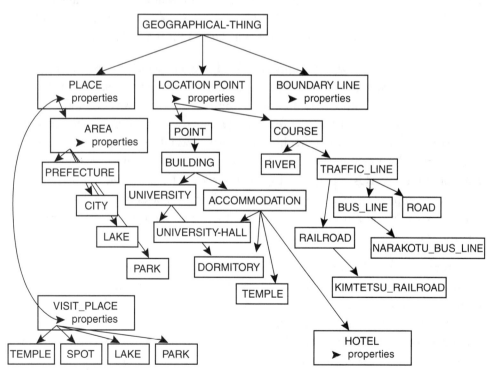

they become progressively more difficult to get right, as concepts from different regions of the model become confused. Design approaches are emerging—as in object-oriented design—to facilitate the clean separation of concepts, and ultimately these should be developed as design tools.

Topics: Classes of World-Views

A similar difficulty exists when applying agents to the problem of information retrieval from unstructured databases. Many corporations have vast archives of documents which represent the company's knowledge base in its field of business. Examples are technical reports, financial reports, bids, and requests for proposals. A prospective customer comes and asks: "What can you tell me about the digital library solutions you have delivered over the last two years?" Can you search through the archive to extract and format all that information? Generally you can't and you rely on what remains in the minds of the engineering and marketing teams. But assuming that you have a world-view model for digital libraries, tools exist which can do an effective job of finding such structured information in unstructured databases by applying the world-view to define a set of empty classes and then searching the databases for the instance data to fill those classes.

Verity (Mountain View, CA) supports a kind of agent which is a permanent query against a database. Whenever the database is modified, the agent scans the change to see if it should report the change to the user. Verity was originally in the business of developing customized retrieval systems for customers, and found after some years of working with individuals who were specialized in various fields that it had acquired very specialized knowledge about how these industries think and talk about their worlds. Verity encapsulated this knowledge in libraries of Topics, which were applied to searching private and public databases not just by trying to match keywords and returning free text, but by extracting industry-specific representations of, say, digital libraries.

A Topic is a multilayered tree whose branches represent a view of the structure of an industry, together with weights for each branch that represent the user's level of interest, and operators that define the way retrieved data is combined to identify a meaningful passage in a document. The structure, the weights, and the relationship operators in the Topic Tree effectively define a concept—for example, descriptions of digital libraries that were sold in the last two years to the major networks

Figure 7.2   Example of a Verity Topic Tree for airline 100 concepts.

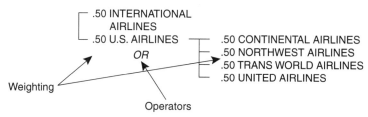

and which provided an interactive browsing capability or which were sold to radio stations and had a query facility for artists, composers, titles, and recording date. This Topic Tree can now be applied to a nonstructured database, such as a collection of reports and proposals. During the search, Topic treats specific words and phrases in a document—weighted and combined as specified in the Topic Tree—as evidence that the document is dealing with the required concept. It also recognizes that one concept may imply other concepts. If the evidence exceeds a threshold, the document is retrieved and presented with a relevance ranking.

Topic Trees can be combined to extend the coverage of the industry. For example, Figure 7.2 shows a simple Topic Tree for the airline industry, which views that industry as consisting of International Airlines (not defined) and U.S. Airlines, where only four of these are of interest. There could be subtrees below each airline reflecting different services, such as frequent flyer programs, vacation deals, and rules on transporting pets. The person requesting the search assigns weights to each of these factors, and these are used to determine how important each branch of the tree is to that person. Figure 7.3 shows the combination of the Airline Topic Tree into a larger Transportation Topic.

World-View Models for Your Business

So a key step in introducing agents into your enterprise is to think about the conceptual model for your agent application. Few examples of these models for specific enterprises exist in commercial tools. Those that do tend to be biased toward information retrieval (such as the Verity case given above), rather than process-oriented tools. Some support for this exists in workflow tools, but these tools, like many others, rely on extensive customization rather than providing deep libraries of models. This is an opportunity area for agent-based application developers.

Figure 7.3   Topic Tree of Figure 7.2 incorporated into larger transportation tree.

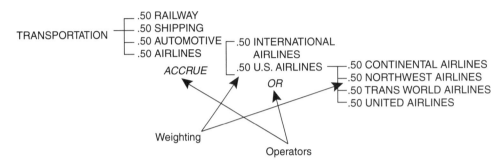

However, it is not an isolated exercise. These models would emerge, for example, from a study to build an overall functional model of the business, which is an aspect of contemporary management science. Extracting this model and making it explicit is an excellent discipline for analyzing what your business does, and this forms a precursor to various forms of reengineering. What is unique about applying it to agents is the need to express this model in machine-readable form and that is the reason for employing knowledge representation language.

Knowledge Representation and Agent Access

So what is so magical about this knowledge representation stuff anyway? How is knowledge different from, say, a database? Content comes in many forms: free text, unstructured documents; highly structured, indexed databases; rulebases; and binary content such as video. Any or all of these may be relevant when defining the world viewed by our agents. For content to be a part of our agents' worlds, it must be logically accessible (see Chapter 8 on Agent Access), but also semantically accessible. How do we accomplish this?

First we should recognize that databases—indexed collections of data, which can be viewed in different ways according to the criteria used in retrieval—were originally invented by the artificial intelligence community as a more flexible method of storing and retrieving data than the record-oriented systems that were in use at the time, so we should not be surprised if "plain old databases" prove to be quite useful for agent applications. Databases manage the collection of values (e.g., checking account balances by day of the month) through a table or set of tables that define a schema. Once you know the schema, you can add data to the database or perform queries against it. Here we come back to the question of how much of the conceptualization of the data is made implicit in the application by the developers.

Information represented in a database requires the application program to have implicit knowledge of the structure of the database; this implies a relatively tight conceptual binding between the application and the database. But information represented through a knowledge representation scheme provides the application with not only a description of how the data is organized and what the fields are called, but also a world-view model that allows the agent application to determine what kind of a database this is—whether it deals with weather or video clips or clothing—and hence, what kind of model will be applicable.

A Meteorological Example

Consider a database that stores the weather each day for a number of cities. The data consists of temperature, precipitation, cloud cover, hours of sunshine, and so forth, and for each of these there will be a numeric value for each day and each city. So we can imagine a two-dimensional table (days, cities) each of whose entries stores a tuple of weather data. Now (depending on the sophistication of the query system) we can ask questions such as "What was the highest temperature in each city during July 1995?" or "Which cities had no sunny days during March 1996?" and the database management system will return a vector of results.

When this application was written, it would have been implicitly a program about processing weather statistics (or whatever), and it would have been given a direct method for acquiring the schema of the database. Just as in the check balance application, the program would be manipulating "temperatures," "rainfall," and so forth, but purely as numbers; if you wanted the program to also deal with, say, per capita income in each city, this concept would have to be coded into the database or the program explicitly. Most likely, weather information and income information are kept in different databases, so the application would now have to deal with two databases.

In a knowledge-based version of this problem, the agent application and the information server will have an explicit world-view that represents information about cities. Part of it might look like the travel planning world-view of Figure 7.1, but it would also now include concepts for weather and days. An update application could send the information server a message that says "I am information about a Place (Tokyo), a Day (July 4, 1995), Weather (Precipitation, 0.0), and Monthly Income (Y2,000,000)." The structure of the message is flexible, because it describes itself in terms of the shared world-view, and the agent application is unconcerned about where and how the information is stored in one or more databases. The agent server can parse the message—having been told the language in which it is represented—and store the data in one or more databases using whatever format is required. (We assume that ultimately the data is captured in a conventional database as the persistent storage mechanism.)

Intelligent Databases

In recent years, database products have advanced in this direction themselves, and some have been referred to as "agents." Products such as IBM's Knowledge Utility allow the user to create *virtual databases* which span multiple real databases and can provide views—for example peak temperature versus per capita income—which do not exist in an single database. Figure 7.4 shows IBM's Knowledge Utility, part of the Information Explorer product. The key components are the "grinders" and the "Persona." The grinders retrieve information specified by the user, either from structured databases or by filtering it from unstructured sources, and compose it into a Persona database specified by the user. The user can request the "database agent" to maintain such a database as a shadow of the real databases by acquiring or pumping the required information either periodically or whenever the database is updated. While these abilities to perform joining across multiple databases and to create virtual databases to meet the needs of an individual user greatly enhance the flexibility of the system, this flexibility is still essentially static, whereas one might argue that part of the essence of agents would be to be both flexible and dynamic in their access to content.

The distinction between one of these advanced database systems and an agent server is subtle and perhaps ultimately not very relevant. This is why in Figure 5.2 (Chapter 5) you will find IBM's Knowledge Utility *just* outside the intelligent agent threshold.

Figure 7.4   The IBM Knowledge Utility is an intelligent data retrieval system that has agent qualities. The user can specify a desired database, and a set of sources to be searched; this information is stored in the connection server. The grinders are the retrieval and search engines which contact the specified sources and search for information relevant to the user's specified interests, and then format it into the Persona database.

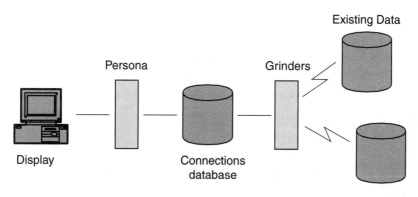

Structured databases differ from most other sources of information in that there is a well-defined front-end retrieval mechanism (see McKay, 1990). Unstructured databases, file systems, and so forth generally provide no front-end; so to make these useful to an agent, the agent developer will have to create such a front-end. A typical approach to such a front-end is a free-text search engine which can access a structured request from the agent, using the agreed world-view, and which can then open the files and perform searching. This is essentially what the Verity product does. Likewise, an expert system could be provided with a front-end that can accept the agent's requests—say for the consistency of a product configuration—and return an answer.

An Agent Content Framework

These approaches to generalizing agent access to content lead to the view shown in Figure 7.5. Each source of content has an appropriate front-end, which can process messages from the agent expressed in the agent communication language, translate

Figure 7.5   An agent framework. Agent applications can communicate with agent servers by sending messages expressing their desires in the agent communication language and using an agreed world-view.

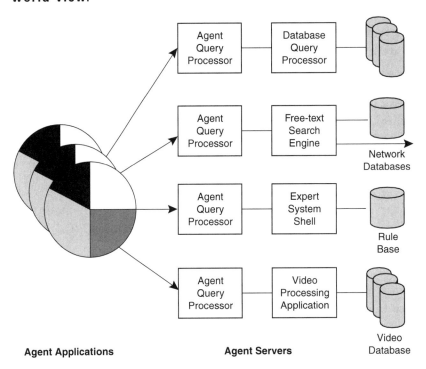

| Agent Applications | | Agent Servers | | Video Database |

them into a form appropriate for the source of the content, and perform the requested action. The agent application is thus independent of the nature of the content storage mechanisms and can use a consistent communication protocol with any content server which understands the agent's world-view. The servers in turn can advertise their expertise in the domain of the world-view to any agent that wishes to use their services.

Such an environment is another form of agent framework. It is an environment in which all relevant resources are accessible through a common interface that has the following characteristics:

■ *Platform independent.* That is, independent of processor, operating system, and application languages.

- *Loose binding.* Interaction among the agent applications and agent servers is purely a runtime activity; there is no a priori requirement for the members of the framework to be aware of one another at compilation time or load time.

- *Common communication protocol.* There are many protocols to choose among for these interactions. Email protocols such as MIME have been used, for example, for communication among Tcl front-ends. This function can also be served by HTTP. General Magic's Telescript provides its own proprietary messaging system. KQML (Knowledge Query and Manipulation Language) also provides its own nonproprietary messaging protocol.

- *Common agent language.* The agent must employ one of a set of agreed languages that the front-end can process. This may be a programming language such as Tcl, or Telescript (see Chapter 8), or a language expressly designed for agent communication, such as KQML.

- *Common world-view.* As we discussed above, the world-view defines what it is meaningful to communicate about in a given system. Asking a video processing server about shirts will not produce a meaningful response. So the servers need also to be able to express what ontologies they can deal with when they advertise their capabilities.

The final element which is missing from Figure 7.5 is a brokerage service, which enables the agent application to ask where it can find services that it needs. You can think of this as simply another agent server, but one which needs a "meta-world-view." That is, the agent application needs to be able to ask the broker "Who can I talk to about processing video content, using the following world-view?" The server maintains a registry of servers that have advertised. The servers are configured to contact one or more such brokerage servers when they become operational and to inform them of their services and commitments to various ontologies, and the agent applications are configured to contact one or more brokers when they need help. Brokers can also advertise other brokers.

Agent Communication Languages

Now we have seen why we need to define concepts that describe the agent "world," and that we can thereby create an agent framework that allows easy access for the agents into its content. So finally, what is an agent communication language?

Burkhard (1994) gives a good overview of aspects of such languages from the point of view of their suitability for creating "open systems" such as the agent framework discussed above. Wooldridge (1995) also surveys several of these languages, in particular noting that concurrent object programming languages "are in many respects the ancestors of agent languages. The notion of a self-contained, concurrently executing object, with some internal state that is not directly accessible to the outside world, and responding to messages from other such objects is very close to the concept of an agent as we have defined it." We have already noted this similarity between object-oriented programming and agent language in our discussion of world-view above. A review of this area is given by Gasser (1992).

One example of such object-oriented programming languages for agents is DAISY (Poggi, 1995). Here's quite a sophisticated example drawn from this work that illustrates a dialogue between a customer (agent) and an airline reservation (agent):

> *There is a customer that must book a seat on a flight from Milan to Amsterdam on August 7, 1994. Therefore, he goes to the airline office and negotiates the booking with an airline clerk. Initially, the customer asks the clerk the flights from Milan to Amsterdam on August 7, 1994. The clerk informs him that there are three flights: the first at 7.05, the second at 10.30, and the third at 16.40. The customer asks if it is possible to book a seat on the flight at 10.30. The clerk answers that it is not possible, because the flight is full. The customer asks if it is possible to book a seat on the flight at 7.05. The clerk answers that it is possible. The customer asks the clerk to book the seat on that flight. The clerk does it and confirms it with the customer.*

Poggi (1995) then goes on to show how this scenario is modeled in the DAISY language:

```
(defclass airline_clerk (agent)
  symbol behavior := 'clerk.engine;
  bool clerk.engine(msg inmsg);
    (seq (symbol customer, label; list flinfo;)
      (if (received inmsg
```

```
              '(?.customer ask ? (flight +.flinfo) :reply with ?.label))

            (inform customer (query (cons 'flight flinfo)) :in_reply_to

            label)

        (if (received inmsg

            '(?.customer request ? (book flight +.flinfo)) :reply_with

            ?.label}}

          (if (is_seat_free (cons 'flight flinfo))

          (accept customer :in_reply_to_label)

          (reject customer :in_reply_to_label)))

        (if (received inmsg

            '(?.customer commit ? (book (flight +.flinfo)) :reply_with

            ?.label))

          (if (assign_seat (cons 'flight flinfo))

          (accept customer :in_reply_to_label)

          (reject customer :in_reply_to_label)))))


(defclass airline_customer (agent)
 symbol behavior := 'cust.engine;
 bool cust_engine(msg, inmsg)
   (seq ()
     ... some code ...
     (:= flights (ask airline_clerk flight_desc
         :reply_with 'flights :comm 'blocking))
       (if flights
         (seq (bool asserted := FALSE; list bestflight;)
```

```
(while (and flights (not asserted))
  (:= bestflight (best_flight flights))
  (remove bestflight flights)
  (if (received (request clerk (cons 'book bestflight)
       :reply_with 'reqbooking :comm 'blocking) 'accept+))
    (if (received (commit clerk (cons 'book bestflight)
         :reply_with 'combooking :comm 'blocking) '(accept
         +))
      (:= assert (assert (cons 'booked bestflight))))))))
... some code ...
)
```

The reservation negotiation scenario is then executed as a dialogue between the two agents. For example:

```
customer:         (request airline_clerk
                   '(book
                       (flight 345 KLM Milan  Amsterdam
                         10.30 "7 August 1994"))
                       :reply_with 'reqbooking
                       :comm 'blocking)
airline_clerk:    (reject customer
                       :in_reply_to 'reqbooking
                       :reason 'no_seats)
```

What we see here is that the language contains a world-view for making airline reservations: verbs asserted by the customer agent (*reqbooking, ask, combooking*) and by the reservation agent (*accept, reject*) and nouns relevant to reserving an airline seat (*flight, customer, airline_clerk*). The language also contains semantics that permit each party to unambiguously communicate with and understand the other; thus *msg* is defined to be a list containing the name of the sender, the verb asserted by the sender, and the operands for the verb. See Poggi (1995) for a complete explanation of the example.

The Knowledge Sharing Effort

The multiplicity of these languages is itself an inhibitor to their use. Why would anyone make a major effort to create content in a given language if the language itself is likely to become obsolete? Recognizing this some years ago, ARPA sponsored a research program known as the Knowledge Sharing Effort (KSE). KSE generally deals with the development of conventions which will facilitate the sharing of knowledge bases and knowledge systems. Its goal is "to define, develop and test infrastructure and supporting technology to enable participants to build much larger and more broadly functional systems than could be achieved by working alone" (Patil, 1992). Not surprisingly perhaps, KSE has itself focused on developing two related languages: Knowledge Interchange Format (KIF) (Genesereth, 1992) and Knowledge Query and Manipulation Language (KQML).

The goal of KIF is to create a *lingua franca* for the development of intelligent applications with an emphasis on interoperation and a common interchange format among knowledge representation languages. In essence it provides a syntax for the content of the messages exchanged among agents, which is based on a version of First Order Predicate Calculus (if/then/exists . . .) with extensions, declarative semantics, and the ability to express metaknowledge. It looks like LISP. KIF is expected to be standardized by ANSI. The point of this is not to create yet another language, but to provide a common interchange format among multiple agent languages, thus facilitating the reuse of content by agents employing different languages. Translating among languages is possible given that they have certain grammatical and semantic similarities, and KIF provides constraints on these to facilitate the design of translatable languages. It also reduces the number of translators required for N languages from $N \times N$ to $2N$.

Within the KSE, the Shared Re-usable Knowledge Base group has worked on the construction of world-view models. The models are written in KIF using the definitional vocabulary of Ontolingua (Gruber, 1992) and have been constructed for various domains.

Knowledge Query and Manipulation Language

KQML (Finin, 1994) defines a syntax to be used in messages among agents—as opposed to the syntax of content, which is covered by KIF. In particular it includes a set of *performatives,* which are verbs, derived from speech acts, that are useful in dialogues among agents. Examples of performatives are: achieve, ask, deny, evaluate, forward, monitor, reply, subscribe, tell, and so forth. KQML messages are exchanged among facilitators, which are similar to the brokerage agents discussed above. Facilitators are able to send and receive messages and to execute a dialogue to complete the definition or accomplishment of a goal. The communication is asynchronous and can be transported over a variety of protocols, such as email or HTTP. Here's an example of a KQML message:

```
(tell   :sender       Colin

        :receiver     Colin_Persona

        :in-reply-to  msg498

        :ontology     Genealogy

        :language     Prolog

        :content      "father(John, Eve)")
```

Each message has one performative, in this case *tell,* that is, assert one or more facts contained in the body of the message. In this case, the sender is *Colin* and the receiver is an agent server called *Colin_Persona,* which is an interface to Colin's database of personal information. The message declares its world-view model to be *Genealogy,* that is, the contents of this message should be interpreted in the domain of genealogy. The language of the content is declared to be *Prolog,* and finally the content asserts that *John is the father of Eve.* Each performative has a defined list of attribute pairs, such as those shown here, which must be part of a message using that performative.

KQML permits the construction of agent frameworks. In the context of Figure 7.5, each agent application or server is equipped with a KQML processor which can communicate over a computer network using, for example, an email protocol. A KQML processor receiving a message parses it and verifies that it is syntactically correct and then passes a tokenized version of it to the backend application, for example, a database query application. The backend application is bound to the KQML front end by functions provided in a Knowledge Representation Interface Library (KRIL), and this enables tokenized query messages and retrieval responses to be exchanged.

Commercial implementations of KQML processors are available (Virdhagriswaran, 1995), and it is being proposed to the Object Management Group (1995) for the implementation of the Agent Facility of the OMG's Common Facilities Architecture.

Agent Content Creation

So you're thinking: Do we all have to learn these weird languages now in order to use agent applications? Probably not, although some of your programmers will. Most of your content already exists (see the next section) in the databases you already use. What has to be done is to expose this to the agent applications using the techniques described above and in Chapter 8 (Agent Access). Where new content is needed, your users will probably be able to make use of a graphical editor. Figure 7.6 shows a graphical editor used in BanyanMail to create the rule base that is used for managing the user's mail. The user "composes" a rule by selecting one of a number of options from three fields:

- *When.* In this case, when a New Memo arrives in the mailbox.
- *If.* If there is a match to the various header fields such as From:, cc:, Subject:, and so forth and the priority expressed by the sender.
- *Then.* Perform an Action, such as sending a reply message and moving the memo to the Urgent folder.

The user deals only in real-world concepts and the editor is responsible for producing content in the defined language. Many such editors exist, for example, the Agent editor in Lotus Notes (Chapter 4), or can be created relatively easily for your own needs using a high-level programming language such as Microsoft's Visual Basic.

Figure 7.6   Banyan BeyondMail rule editor.

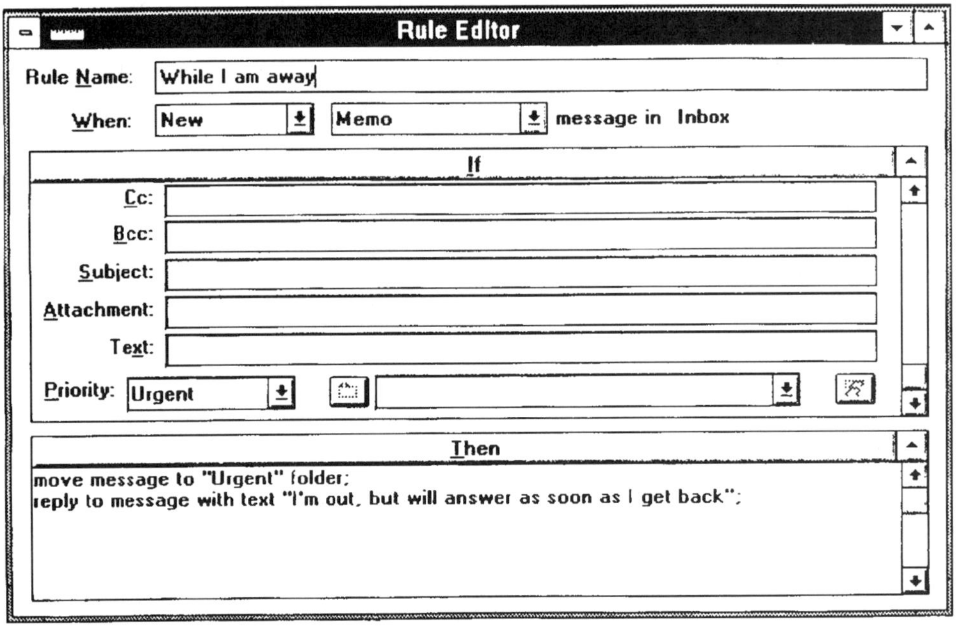

Sources of Content in Your Business

We have shown in this chapter several examples of where businesses already have what is in effect content for agent applications. We have discussed the need for a world-view model—a formalized vocabulary and language that the agent applications and servers can agree on so as to obtain the flexibility of interaction that is a characteristic of agent-based applications. We have shown how to adapt the existing databases into an agent framework within which agents can interact using messaging protocols to exchange requests and information. So now you need to consider what content you have that would be valuable to an agent application. Here are a few examples:

- *The business hierarchy:* Its organization into functional departments, the responsibilities of those departments, the reporting relationships, the managers and employees within those departments. You may object that it is impossible to keep that information up-to-date—but perhaps therein lies an opportunity for an agent-based application!

- *Trading relationships:* How do goods and services flow into and within your company? How do you interact with your trading partners? How do you create and maintain bills-of-materials for each product you produce? How do you specify to them what you want to buy, and how is this material integrated into your operational planning?

- *How do you maintain profiles of your employees?* Can the employees securely update their own profiles? How do you perform annual certifications and elections of health plans and so forth?

- *How do you collect and maintain information about your customers?* Do you have a mechanism for capturing their detailed preferences and the record of their interactions with the company?

There are many opportunities to apply agent-based techniques to creating, managing, and using content databases such as these. Here's an example of one such database that you might want to set up as an exercise: the Persona. Figure 7.7 shows the collection of information associated with a single employee in your company. Some of this information is produced by the company.

- A rule base that defines our company's procedures for certain processes, or policies for travel or purchasing.

- A database of relevant business data—budgets, project timetables, design or performance data—that is needed or created by this employee.

- The business hierarchy that defines the reporting and working relationships for this employee, and which can be used for routing information or requesting authorization for actions or decisions.

Some of the information is the personal preferences of the employee:

- *Travel:* Airline seats, types of rental car, types of hotel room, restaurants, and so forth. These can be used, in conjunction with the business policies, for guiding a travel reservation agent.

Figure 7.7   Persona—a database of personal information for use by agent-based applications.

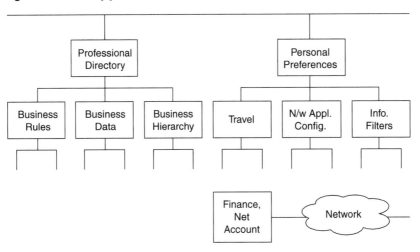

- *Network application configuration:* If your company encourages sharing of computers, this defines how this employee wants his or her computer configured. This may also soon be useful with network computers that gain all of their application software configuration as Java applets. This can also hold the rules that express how the employee wants telephone calls and electronic mail to be managed.

- *Information filters:* The searching and filtering profiles that the user has defined for managing the flow of information.

- *Personal finance:* Network connections to the employee's bank and other institutions allow him or her to include bank accounts, credit card accounts, and electronic cash accounts into the Persona.

Each of these different types of content is adapted into the agent framework by, for example, KRIL interfaces and KQML processors associated (logically if not geographically) with each database. The result is a set of databases that are uniformly accessible to any authorized agent application. Such agent applications could thus have an integrated view of the employee's work life or personal life, and are thus enabled to act upon his or her behalf over a wide range of services.

Summary

Content is what defines the agent's knowledge about its world. The agent's machinery can only process what it can see and understand. Understanding requires having a model into which specific instances can be fitted; we define this via the worldview model. Understanding requires having a common language for expressing requests and responses; we define the syntax and semantics of this via an agent communication language. Access to existing databases—whether structured or unstructured—may require their adaptation into the agent framework via translation of content from the original representation into the representation of the agent languages. Integration of multiple sources of content enables many new applications. Some will produce improved efficiency by replacing clerical staff with agent applications. Some will permit new applications that perform "mass personalization" of our company's products and services. Some will enable your customers to interact directly with your business, improving their perception of your responsiveness and reducing your investment in customer support agents.

Note that formal world views exist already in many fields, such as medicine, and understand the importance of these as bases for emerging business-oriented agents, where the flexibility of the agent in providing integration among many different business processes will bring big rewards. Relatively few structured knowledge bases exist today to which these techniques can be applied (medicine and bio-chemical databases being major exceptions), and hence they have seen little application in Internet agents. The world views that will prevail in the Internet are being developed heuristically today by the great search engines at Yahoo!, AltaVista and the news filtering services such as NewsHound, AdHound, and Silk. The vocabularies and structures extracted statistically from searching millions of Web pages will provide the world-view for most public information. An initiative in this direction is the IDML language (see Chapter 2), which provides a keyword self-description of a Web page. This approach meets the basic needs of searching or filtering information, but will need extensions when the need arises for more complex transactions between a client and an arbitrary Web site.

Chapter

8

Agent Access

In Chapter 6 we looked at the specialized types of processing employed by agents: inferencing, learning, and negotiation. In Chapter 7 we reviewed how agents can express themselves to one another in a flexible but formal way. In this chapter, we look at how the agents interact with the world they occupy, how they learn about events in that world, and how they act upon that world. We call this topic "access."

Access refers to the ability of the agent to observe and control its environment. Without ascribing artificial intelligence to the agent, we could say that the agent needs to be "aware" of its world and to "participate" in it. But what should be its world? And how should the agent become aware of it? How should the agent exercise control over the world or manage the applications to which it has access? (And how can you trust it to do so safely? But that's a question for the next chapter.) So this chapter deals with the integration of the agent into the business environment. You could say it's a chapter about "plumbing," the interconnections between the agent and the programs and services that make up its environment.

There are many other reasons for needing to develop access among groups of (legacy) applications, and so, fortunately, most enterprise Information

Service organizations are well versed in these (often ad hoc) techniques. The combination of agent requirements for access and these other motivations may lead over time to generalized frameworks for interapplication communication. The idea of interapplication communication is of course well-established; what we are thinking of here could be called "late binding" or "loose binding" of applications, particularly for preexisting applications. In applying agents to your business, what we want to do is to develop links among programs that were never originally designed to work together.

One way to think about the agent's role in assisting the user is the "glue" model, illustrated in Figure 8.1. The idea is that the machinery of the agent processes events from various sources, including the user, and this leads to various actions, including possibly some learning (see Figure 5.4). The glue represents the integration by the agent of various software tools which are normally integrated by the intelligence of the user. Access is about this glue, the integration of applications and services and their operation by the agent, instead of an end-user. Today, a user works with one application, sees something in that application's user interface that makes her think of a related item, and switches to working with a different applica-

Figure 8.1 The "glue" model of an intelligent agent. The agent provides the glue that joins many diverse applications together.

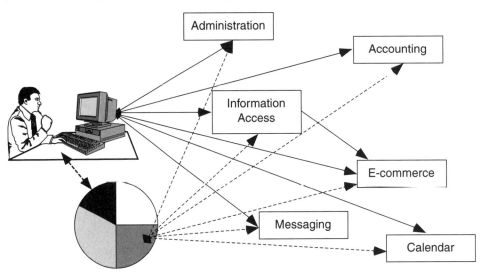

tion, carrying in her head the details that were spotted in the prior application. We might call this "human glue"; what we need in order to provide an intelligent assistant to the user is the equivalent of "software glue." The glue is the binding between the event/actions/content/security interfaces of the agent and the corresponding interfaces of the managed applications and content databases.

So how do we create this glue? The answer to that question will vary widely depending on the nature of the applications to be glued together and the goals of the integration. In this chapter, you'll read about the concept of an access framework, which is a general and powerful solution to this problem, and which is an excellent application of emerging software technologies. There are various encapsulation techniques that can be applied that will enable applications of all vintages to be incorporated in that framework. However, in many cases simpler methods may suffice. An important and difficult access is that of the user. How should users, particularly unsophisticated ones, interact with the agent and vice versa? Later on you'll look at the novel approach of *mobile agents,* which move among the applications and services that they wish to integrate. The Internet and Web protocols also offer important opportunities for agent access and get a brief mention here, but for a more detailed discussion see Chapter 3 (Internet Agents). Finally, you'll get some thoughts on applying access technologies to your business needs.

A Framework for Intelligent Agent Access

There are two sides to access: awareness of the environment and the ability to participate in it. Without access, the agent by itself would be only aware of its internal state and have no direct ability to act upon its world; it would be a eunuch. To be aware, it needs to be told about what is going on or to be able to go and find out what is going on. To act it needs to have access to software machinery that knows how to produce the required actions. Ideally, we need a general framework which provides the agent with access to a wide range of applications and data; we call this the *access framework.*

An older approach to such frameworks, derived from work in AI, is the "blackboard" model. A group of applications interact by writing significant information to a common blackboard. A server application will examine each piece of information posted to the blackboard, and forward it to applications (agents) that have registered interest in that type of information. Blackboard systems are falling out of popularity, in part because they have scaling problems, but also because this functionality is beginning to be provided by operating system function or middleware.

A more recent approach to the agent access framework could be called a "software bus." We can think of this is as a piece of middleware which provides a communication infrastructure among a number of unrelated applications. This is not the same as client server computing, where very specific point-to-point connections among applications are created to accomplish a specific task. The software bus is a structure for passing information, typically in the form of messages, *among unrelated applications*. This approach requires that each application is written with some specific features for this software bus:

- When the application is initialized, it must be registered with the bus. This may occur as part of the application's own initialization, or the framework may detect the presence of a new application and request it to register. In this registration it declares its identity, the kinds of events that it can produce, and the kinds of events it can process to accomplish certain tasks. Events are structured messages conforming to some ontology, so that they can be interpreted by appropriate applications. An application can request to be notified of specific kinds of events.

- The application can also discover from the registry how to communicate with other applications that can perform specific kinds of actions. This may be implemented by a brokerage function, which can match a request for a service to an application which has advertised the ability to provide such a service.

- When the application executes certain functions, it sends events (messages) to the bus—not to any specific application—which are notifications of significant changes of internal state or of significant external information received by the application. These messages are distributed by the bus to applications which requested them when they were initialized.

- When an application receives a requested event, it must handle it in a well-behaved fashion. Each event must be examined for relevance, and, if the application can make use of it, the event will cause the application to perform an action.

Figure 8.2   An access framework for agent-based applications.

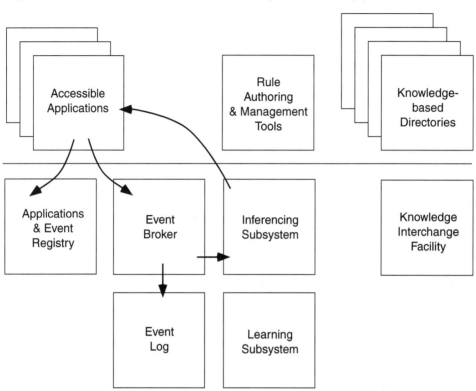

You could use this software bus to create an access framework as shown in Figure 8.2. In this framework you find the Application and Event Registry and the Event Broker, which combine to create the software bus. In addition to simply transmitting events as they occur to applications which have requested them, the Event Broker may also provide certain kinds of filtering. Thus an application may register an interest in events containing, for example, financial transactions; and the application may specify that it is only interested in events where the monetary amount exceeds some threshold, say $100 or 2,000 pounds. The framework also contains an Event Log, which records all events, and which may be read by interested applications. Attached to the access framework, there may be various pieces of agent machinery, such as an inferencing component or a learning component and gateways to various content databases, which may include knowledge-based directories. This framework is now capable of supporting our agent glue.

Let's look at an example of how you might exploit such a framework. Suppose you wish to create a Financial Monitor agent, whose purpose is to keep an eye out for large transactions and to try to determine if they represent unusual, perhaps fraudulent behavior. The enterprise integrates its financial trading applications with the framework so that the applications produce events corresponding to every buy or sell action. The Financial Monitor agent registers its interest in transactions that exceed, say, $100,000, and is given a set of rules that define "normal" and "abnormal" trading behaviors, including correlations between trades over a period of a day or several days. In operation, the Financial Monitor agent is notified only of large transactions and uses its rule base to try to identify abnormal trades.

The Event Log provides content for the learning component. The Financial Monitor agent might periodically scan the log looking at the trading positions of the enterprises' traders, looking for trends that may cause concern or for trading positions with high levels of risk. It may also look for correlations among the many events, trying to identify patterns using data mining techniques to spot hidden relationships among the complete range of events. If significant trends or relationships are found, the Financial Monitor agent may decide to take an action, perhaps to notify a supervisor or to alert the trader of an exposed position. The agent may be required to act directly upon one of the integrated applications, perhaps performing an automated trade by sending a message directly to a trading application.

So the software bus helps us create an access framework that enables one or many agents to provide integration across a wide range of applications (Bacon, 1995). The software bus is one approach to developing an access framework, and you will read about others (Shoham, 1993). The hidden problem in these approaches is: *the enterprise integrates its financial trading applications with the framework*. This is often easier said than done. Few enterprises have the luxury of rebuilding all their existing applications to add these kinds of features. We will discuss below some of the approaches to this legacy application problem. However for the future, consider a couple of approaches that may enable new applications to easily incorporate this kind of facility.

Among operating systems, the Apple Macintosh[1] operating system (MacOS) has been a pioneer in supporting this approach. MacOS provides the Apple Open

---

[1]Apple Macintosh and Apple Events are trademarks of Apple Computers, Inc.

Scripting Architecture (OSA) (OSA, 1995), which is based on the Apple MacOS Inter-application Communication facility. MacOS applications can produce "Apple Events," which are high-level events that comply with a protocol known as the Apple Event Inter-process Messaging Protocol. This provides real-time messages among all installed applications. MacOS applications are all constructed around a main loop and the event messages are made available directly to this loop. The application's main loop provides handlers for one or more suites of events and many such suites have now been defined. For example, all applications must support the Required Suite: *Open Application, Open Documents, Print Documents, Quit Application.* Other defined events that can be sent to an application are: *Cut, Copy, Paste, Get Data, Set Data, Move, Delete.*

This is the basic behavior that enabled the Macintosh to create the early drag-and-drop user interface. An application developer wishing to create, say a telephony application, can refer to a suite of Apple Events defined for telephony applications, to learn what events the new application will need to support. The Apple Open Scripting Architecture enables compound operations to be performed by executing scripts of Apple Events against the applications, in effect driving the applications "externally" and thus emulating the actions of a user, exactly the capability we want for agent access. One product which has exploited the Apple MacOS to create an intelligent agent is Charles River Analytics' Open Sesame! (CRA, 1996), which has been described in detail in Chapter 2.

A second such framework is the Object Management Framework (OMF) (OMG, 1993), which is a specification developed by the Object Management Group (OMG) and implemented by various companies. The OMF is built upon the Common Object Request Broker Architecture (CORBA) (OMG, 1992). CORBA defines among other things, a standard for interface definitions for software objects, using the Interface Definition Language (IDL), and a CORBA Event Channel, which enables typed events to be passed among CORBA objects. The OMF extends this model by introducing a Notification object, which receives notification from all objects registered with the broker whenever their interfaces change and which can redistribute these notification events to other objects. Just as in the Apple OSA framework, this model can be employed to develop an agent framework in which an agent can arrange to be notified of events of interest and to then perform actions upon objects controlling specific resources. Unlike OSA, the OMF is a completely distributed framework, possibly spanning many heterogeneous systems joined by networks, and so may one day provide object frameworks that cover an entire enterprise computing infrastructure, although this is some way off in the future. A current lack is a Trader object, which can serve requests from an application for access to an object with some specific attribute, although such an object is being discussed for a future OMG specification. Also lacking are a scripting language and the ability to define filters in the Event Channel, though again discussions are beginning in this area.

Similar services are appearing in the Microsoft world. For example, NeXT Software's D'OLE provides a set of remote access services for distributed object frameworks by adding function to Microsoft's OLE and Microsoft has now introduced a much-enhanced set of capabilities in Active/X.

These frameworks were not designed with agents in mind. But it turns out that they provide some of the advanced software technology required to implement agents efficiently.

Agent Access for Existing Applications

While the technologies described above suggest a promising future for agent frameworks, don't hold your breath. Remember the GUI story (Chapter 5). In luring you into thinking about elegant agent access frameworks, we are looking forward to their emergence over several more years. For today, you will need more pragmatic approaches for the present reality of existing applications. In some cases, where a framework such as OMF is being introduced for other purposes, the agent development may be able to arrange for wrappering (see following section) of the existing applications to attach them to the framework. But in many cases, the agent developer must arrange access for his or her agents without a formal framework separate from the agent application itself. The agent must establish direct linkages with the applications that it manages. In this section you'll see some of the options for establishing this kind of access. The exact circumstances confronting the agent application developer may cover an enormous range of possibilities, so here we do no more than provide broad suggestions. Fortunately, these techniques are already in widespread use for other purposes and so most enterprises will have already some experience with this process.

Figure 8.3   Approaches to application access for intelligent agents.

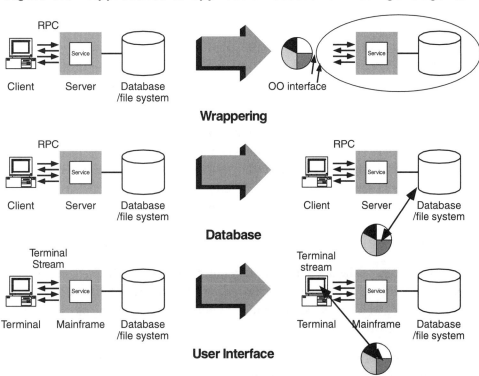

Figure 8.3 shows a range of approaches to the introduction of agent access into existing applications. The first approach binds the backend of an application into an agent's object framework by putting an object-oriented (OO) wrapper around the backend server (and an eventual database), exploiting a defined remote access API. The application is now represented within the agent's object framework by a proxy object, which incorporates the client-side of the remote API and possibly some application logic. Lotus Notes is an example of an object framework in which databases are wrappered into the framework (although most Notes databases are created directly within the framework), and in which agents can be directly attached to the databases themselves. In the second approach, there is no defined remote access API, and the agent's access is at the level of the database or file system where the application stores its data. The agent can employ the standard methods for

reading and writing the file system or performing database transactions, but needs to supplement this with an understanding of how the application uses the database or file system and how to parse the stored data. In the third approach, there is no software interface available at all, and the agent couples to the legacy application by emulating a terminal operator. While the last two methods are more primitive than the first, they can all be employed to create a proxy object for the application and bind it into the agent or into an access framework.

Be aware, though, that human users add a lot of value to the operation of computer applications. They learn to accommodate illogical navigation sequences and misbehavior of the application and to recognize input errors that are not correctly trapped by the application itself. Trying to reproduce this human intelligence in the agent access software is frequently a difficult and frustrating task.

Wrappering

Wrappering refers to the development of an object-oriented (OO) interface for an application, where the application itself does not offer an OO interface or has an OO interface which is based on a different object model than the developer is using. There are two steps:

1. Define the required OO interface in the current IDL, creating stubs for the methods to be provided by the application.

2. Link the stubs to the application using one or more of the techniques described below (client/server access, database/file access, or terminal emulation access).

Step 2 is the difficult part, and the success of this technique, as with all the legacy access methods, depends on how effective this linkage is. While wrappering may seem a heresy to OO purists, it is a practical necessity in a world where not all software can be rewritten to the OO programming model.

Client/Server Applications

The movement toward client/server applications began in the late 1980s and so in many organizations there are already many server applications with well-structured APIs for RPC or IPC access by a client. In these cases, the agent can readily be made a new "client" of the server application and exploit the existing API. The agent application emulates a normal client being operated by a human user. However, there is quite a range in the division of application logic between the client and the server. In many cases the backend server is a relatively standard database or transaction monitor, which provides no logic or protocol specific to the business application. That is, the database knows nothing of, say, the valid configurations for a complex product, but simply accepts inventory and order requests. In these cases, the application logic resides in the client and must be replicated by the agent application. In other cases, the front-end client may do little more than collect individual data fields from the user interface and perform individual checking on this data before passing a request to the backend server to complete the transaction. In this case, the agent application's job is simpler, but it still needs to know how to generate the input requests and parse the responses. If the application logic is known, it is desirable to reuse it in the agent event/action interfaces, so that the agent deals with high-level content, rather than having to interpret database record fields in order to extract the real content. The emergence of network computing, where the client side of the application logic is provided by Java applets that are downloaded at runtime to a Web browser, offers a new opportunity for constructing the agent-equivalent of a Web browser: an application able to interpret HTML and execute the applets to emulate a human user.

Database and File System Interfaces

If the agent developer does not have access to the application logic, there may be no better alternative than to work at the level of the database or even the file system behind the application. While this is feasible and can be made to work, it is undesirable for two reasons.

First, the agent must now deal with content at the record level or byte level, rather than with structured content messages. This may require considerable work to provide the required interpretation and to track the application's use of the file system. The agent is now rather indirectly coupled to the application data formats; that is, there is no direct method to keep the agent's perception of the data in sync with the evolution of the application itself. If a new record structure is introduced, this new structure must be manually transferred into the agent's access methods.

Second, the agent is now rather weakly coupled to the application semantics; that is, the agent may have no way to tell if the record it is currently reading is about to be updated by another application. This method is thus exposed to potential race conditions, in which actions performed by the agent conflict with operations produced by a human operator. This can be avoided if the intent is to completely replace human operators, but the agent interface must still provide the application logic for transaction semantics if multiple agents are permitted to drive the application.

User Interface

The last resort for obtaining access to a legacy application, where no other possibilities exist, is to emulate the user interface. This has become a time-honored technique for legacy mainframe applications, where the only available application interface is the terminal stream. The application incorporates an emulator for the system's terminals and engages in terminal sessions with the legacy application, accepting and generating terminal character streams in such a way that the application believes it is interacting with a real terminal driven by a human operator. However, instead of displaying the terminal stream data on a display, the agent application extracts the key fields and passes their values to other parts of the application for processing. Similarly, the agent can output terminal field data and send it to the legacy application. While it may seem like a perversion of software technology, in practice it can be quite workable, especially since there is no further development of these legacy applications and the user interface is thus stable. The tricks in this approach lie in being able to correctly parse the terminal field data and in generating the correct input sequences to navigate through the legacy application protocol. The agent access interface must be able to follow the screen sequences of each application and to extract and modify the screen fields. Here again the agent is only weakly coupled to the application and is thus very susceptible to uncoordinated changes in screen sequences. Later versions of the popular terminal protocols (IBM 3270 and Digital Equipment Corporation VT200) do permit tagging of the screen fields, so that the agent interface is at least protected against rearrangements of the fields on the screen, but if the screen-to-screen navigation changes, the agent application could become completely desynchronized from the legacy application.

One could imagine a similar approach with the GUIs of PC applications, in which the agent application captured the graphic interface output and extracted the fields. In practice it is only marginally feasible, because in addition to the problems of terminal emulation, the agent application must in effect perform character recog-

Table 8.1   Types of Access for Intelligent Agents

Access Method	Approach	Application
Access Framework	Exploit interapplication notification mechanisms in the operating system or middleware.	Very general, but only useful by itself in completely modern systems.
Wrappering	Create an object interface definition for a non-OO application.	Integration of older (legacy) applications into OO framework.
Client/Server	Agent emulates the client.	Integration of c/s applications, especially if most of the application logic is in the server.
Database and File System	Agent monitors and updates a database or file system directly.	Integration of c/s or other applications where there is no convenient API.
User Interface	Agent emulates a terminal, incorporating the application logic needed to navigate the screens.	Last resort for older, legacy applications, but quite effective in practice.

nition. It has been developed for remote access to PC (for example, PC Anywhere), starting with bitmap copying and evolving to do some character recognition.

User Access

While agents can serve many different kinds of masters, most often we are thinking of agents as assistants to individual users, or possibly groups of users. In these cases, the most important form of access is to the end user and the agent needs to be able to interact with the user in several ways.

The agent needs to be able to engage in dialogues with the user to capture new goals and rules and to report on events and actions. For many people, this in itself is the most important aspect of agents, although we clearly do not share that view. Large efforts have been mounted to create animated avatars, which attempt to emulate human expressiveness in communicating with the user (Halfhill, 1996). While we accept the view that the interaction between users and computers has a similarity to human interpersonal relations (Reeves and Nass, 1995), we see little value in "talking heads." Schneidermann, at the University of Maryland, a key figure in the development of the graphical user interface, also inveighs heavily against the notion that the application should permit the user to believe or pretend that there is a quasi-human intelligence inside the computer (Schneidermann, 1993). He has several arguments against this anthropomorphism, for example, that this leads to unjustifiable levels of trust in the computer or agent on the part of the user.

Conversational User Interfaces

Agent technology permits a different style of user interaction, in which the user and the interface converse by means of dialogues. We have been accustomed for several decades now to interacting with computers by filling in the fields of electronic forms. The application generates a form on the screen, we fill in all the information requested, and finally it will go off and perform the task for us. In a conversational interface, the user can engage in a free-form exchange, which incrementally captures input related to one or possibly several tasks that the user is concerned with. The user interface agent is responsible for maintaining a number of conversational contexts and assigning each piece of user input to the appropriate context. The agent will also know of task-specific grammars; so that when the user opens a dialogue about arranging a meeting, for example, the agent knows that the ontology of meetings includes two or more people, a place, a start time, an ending time, and so forth. The agent uses this knowledge both to solicit complete input from the user, and also to clarify the free-form dialogue. When this form of user interface is done well, it is almost impossible to avoid falling into an anthropomorphic relationship. One of the best commercial examples of this is the Wildfire telephone management agent, which uses several forms of speech recognition, speech output, and task-specific grammars to emulate a human secretary managing an executive's telephone calls and meetings (Wildfire, 1995).

User Events and Actions

In addition to the dialogue aspects of the agent-user interface, the user is a rich source of input for the agent:

1. *Events and Knowledge.* Some of these will be entered explicitly by the user as he or she gives instructions to the agent.

2. *Actions.* Two of the most important verbs for the agent are *Ask* and *Tell*. The agent needs to be able to get the user's attention, sometimes synchronously, sometimes asynchronously, to solicit content needed for a decision, to request approval for a proposed action, or to notify the user of some interesting combination of events and content.

3. *Implicit knowledge.* You saw in Chapter 7 that the end-user is a major source of content, that is, the means by which the user exports his or her goals, intentions, desires, preferences, aversions, and so forth into the agent. A major difficulty with users is that they do not want to spend a lot of time giving this information to the agent. This obstacle has been the downfall of many agent applications: the agent was never able to do anything useful for the user, because the user would not or could not enter (provide access to) the necessary content. You saw in Chapter 6 that there are methods for inferring some of this content, but this inferencing or learning again requires access to the end user. So in developing agent applications, it is often valuable to look for opportunities that enable the agent to get a look at what user is doing.

So what are some good vantage points for getting access to the user?

- *Redirecting the user interface.* The agent interposes a filter between the user input devices (keyboard, speech engine, and handwriting engine) and searches this input stream for relevant Events. Ted Selker has exploited this in his COACH interface agent, which provided intelligent assistance to users learning LISP programming (Selker, 1994a), and this concept has since been extended to providing intelligent help for the IBM OS/2 desktop user interface. This can also lead to the kinds of task automation exemplified by Open Sesame! (see the section on A Framework for Intelligent Agent Access, earlier in this chapter).

- *Redirecting client server messages* (client-end and server-end). Similarly the agent may be able to intercept the dialogues between a user client application and backend server, for example, by monitoring the content of search messages to Web sites such as Lycos or Altavista. This enables the monitoring of user activities with more context than is possible at the user interface level. If the agent is actually a filter in the transmission of client/server messages, the agent could eventually provide the same kind of automation at the task level that Open Sesame! provides at the user interface level.

■ *Monitoring email* and the user's handling of email with different subjects (Lashkari et al., 1994). Email is certainly a rich medium for observing the user's current interests, but extracting good data from it is very hard. Many users have a large number of current interests, and identifying the categories and then using them accurately is a complex problem.

■ *User–operating system interactions* (logon, logoff, level of activity/page demand rate). With appropriate access rights, it is possible to obtain a lot of information from the operating system about user behavior. What applications are frequently used and how intensively? When is the user present or absent? When is the user present and busy or present and idly working? These are all clues to current user interests. A wise interface agent would always try to determine if its user were busy before intruding with a question or a report. This approach has been exploited at the Media Lab in the Doppelgaenger project (Orwant, 1991; 1993).

■ *External sensors,* such as identity badges, telephone call logs, credit card records, automated toll booth systems (such as New York's EZPass). With more effort the agent can extend its monitoring of the user outside the computing environment and into other electronically integrated-sensors. In the early 1990s, Xerox PARC's experiments with mobile computing led them to give radio-frequency badges to the employees, which enabled the security system to determine what room an employee was in and what telephone was nearest. (Employees were not forced to wear the badges and were free to remove them, if they wanted privacy, but many found that being able to be found for unexpected telephone calls was quite an advantage and usage was high.)

These and other accessible streams of user interaction are extremely valuable sources for intelligent agent applications (Rich, 1996). Network services, such as email or telephony, are especially able to capture this kind of information and exploit it to optimize the behavior of the service for the user. In addition to the individual behaviors which can be inferred out of these streams, group behaviors can also be identified and exploited. For example, the Doppelgaenger project found that it could identify significant differences in behavior among faculty, students, staff, and visitors at the Media Lab: they employed different applications, they were interested in different newsgroups, they worked at different times of the day. It may be possible to define default behaviors for a group which are more specific and consequently more helpful than a single set of defaults for an entire population. Thus a new secretary could be assisted meaningfully by an agent using initially the default behaviors for the secretarial group. He or she could then do a smaller amount of data input to personalize the agent behavior than if he or she had had to start from a generic set.

While this is an important area for intelligent agents, it is also one that is relatively unexplored by commercial agent software, perhaps because it is so demanding of specialized access methods. It is an area which also requires a great deal of human factor experimentation. In the short term you may not be able to exploit the agent-user interface; but keep an eye on it—great things will happen here as research turns into products.

Mobile Agents

You saw briefly in Chapter 7 some of the concepts of mobile agents in the discussion about agent communication language. In this section you will learn about mobile agents from the viewpoint of access. Mobile agents are programs, typically written in a script language, which may be dispatched from a client computer and transported to a remote server computer for execution (Chess et al., 1995). The idea of performing client/server computing by the transmission of executable programs between clients and servers goes back a long way in the history of computing, but has been popularized in recent years by researchers and developers interested in intelligent network services, most notably by White and Miller at General Magic, Inc. (White, 1995), but also by the developers of Tcl and Sun's Java[2]. The most significant of the extensions lie in the area of security, since an important goal of this work is to enable spontaneous electronic commerce— that is, commerce which does not require the prior conclusion of a trading contract between the two parties. Security is a significant concern with mobile agent-based computing, as a server receiving a mobile agent for execution may require strong assurances about the agent's intentions. Chapter 9 examines this in detail.

---

[2]Java and Hot Java are trademarks of Sun Microsystems, Inc.

Mobile Agent Languages

The mobile agent program may be written in a compiled language or an interpreted (virtual machine) language. In order to support heterogeneity, it is often preferable to write mobile agents in either an interpreted language or a language which is compiled to a virtual machine instruction set, for example, Java. The agent applications are highly portable, because it is sufficient to port the language interpreter or the virtual machine onto each required platform in order to enable their execution. There is a performance penalty for this, but since most of the agent processing is done not in the agent itself, but rather in the functions to which it binds, this may be acceptable. Performance improvements in Java execution, for example, are now achieved by "just-in-time compilation." Interpreted languages also have the advantage of late binding; this enables the agent to contain references to functions or classes not present on the system at which it is launched, but which are available at its destination. Interpreted and virtual machine languages are also easier to render safe than real machine language, since the language interpreter or processor at the point of execution explicitly controls what system resources are accessible.

It's useful to draw some distinctions between the species of remote execution:

- A program which is sent without execution state to a remote CPU executes there, possible communicating by RPC or other means with other CPUs (including its origin), and then terminates. Java programs would fall in this category. We consider this *remote execution.*

- A program which carries execution state with it and is sent to a remote CPU executes there, possibly communicating by RPC or other means with other CPUs (including its origin), and then moves again to a third CPU or returns to its origin. We call this a *mobile agent.*

These are not dogmatic distinctions, but merely useful classifications.

Mobile Agent Principles

The mobile agent concept is illustrated in Figure 8.4. A client system consists of an application environment, for example, Apple MacOS, IBM OS/2, or Microsoft Windows, which contains one or more applications for interaction with a remote server. These applications may include information searching and retrieval, transaction front-ends, or mail clients. These applications are bound to an execution environment for mobile agents. Via the interfaces between the client applications and the mobile agent execution environment—the Agent Meeting Place—the application can pass parameters to various classes (not necessarily object-oriented classes) of agent programs, and likewise the agent programs can return parameters to the application programs. These classes may be part of the basic agent execution environment, agents distributed with the applications or agents received by the client from a server or other peer on the network. In principle there may be no application program; the agent programs can themselves perform presentation on the client device's user interface and collect information directly from a keyboard or other input device. In this case, the agent programs—or the Agent Meeting Place—must bind to the user interface libraries of the client's operating system. The Agent Meeting Place will also need to bind to other operating system functions, such as the memory manager, the timer, the file system, and so forth. In particular, the Agent Meeting Place needs to bind to the message transport service in order to send and receive mobile agents via the communication infrastructure. The Agent Meeting Place concept is embodied today in products such as Sun's Hot Java Web browser, General Magic's Telescript Engine, Sun's work on Secure-Tcl, and a large number of research or prototyping efforts.

When an application needs to send mail or perform a transaction, it will assemble the required information and then pass this via the API into the Agent Meeting Place. This will initiate the execution of an instance of a particular class of agent as

Figure 8.4   Basic model for mobile agents.

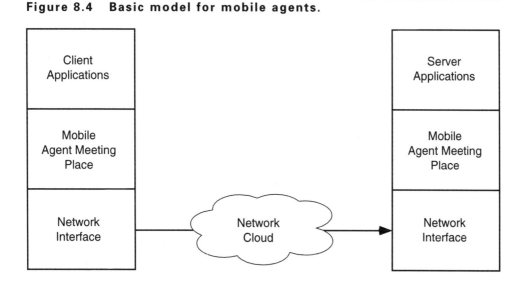

a process within the Agent Meeting Place. This may correspond to an operating system process or an operating system thread or it may be managed by a threads package within the agent execution environment. The Agent Meeting Place will have access to many different agent programs, which provide different services to the client applications. For example, one may act as a delivery agent for electronic mail; another may deliver a database retrieval request to a server, submit the request, and return the result to the client application; yet another may navigate its way among multiple servers, asking each in turn for updates on a particular topic.

The agent program may be built from procedural components or from classes of objects. In either case, the agent has bindings to functions within the Agent Meeting Place, including functions imported from the operating system, the application or other subsystems, as well as other agent programs.

The information assembled by the application is accepted by the agent as part of its initialization. At a certain point in its execution, the agent will execute an instruction which has the following effects:

1. Either the current agent process is suspended in the agent execution environment, or a new agent daughter process is created.

2. The suspended process or the new process, including its process state, stack, heap, and all external references, is collected and processed into a message expressed in a machine-independent form. This step is facilitated if the agent is built from object classes and in an interpreted language. In particular, if it is known that the identical classes are resident at the destination, the agent may be reduced to object references, instance data, and process state data. If the agent is expressed in an interpreted language, the state data is captured on the stack and there is no need to save registers.

3. The message may be addressed explicitly to a final destination, or it may be directed initially to a post office function which can perform address resolution, or to intermediate designations, which route the agent on the basis of its content (semantic routing).

4. The message is handed to the message subsystem and routed directly or indirectly to the destination server, where it is delivered by the server's message subsystem to the server's agent execution environment.

5. In the agent execution environment the received message is reconstituted into the executable and the process or thread is dispatched. If the sending (client)

agent environment had accurate knowledge of the classes available at the server, an agent which had been reduced to object references and instance data can be reconstituted; if there are missing classes, this step may fail, unless the server and client have a means of propagating the missing classes.

6. Execution continues at the next instruction in the agent program following the instruction that initiated step 1 of this sequence.

This is effectively a process migration, one that is performed for the purpose of moving the agent from a client which has an access need—for information, for a transaction, for mail delivery, for a specialized resource—to a server which is capable of satisfying the need. During execution at the server, the agent passes the information it received from the client application to server application functions and perhaps receives other information in return. Alternatively, it may engage in a dialogue with other agents which have been sent to this server. At the completion of this stage, it might perform one or more of several functions:

- It might terminate its execution.

- It might simply suspend its execution at the server, waiting for some event to be delivered from a server application or from another agent. In this latter case, we would say that it has become a "resident" agent at the server. A resident agent may become permanently resident if there is some repeated service desired by the user.

- It might repeat the migration progress, either by forking a new daughter process or by suspending and migrating itself. This second migration might return the agent to its originating client or it might continue to another server or another client. In particular, the agent may be able to perform a recovery action and visit another server if the required service is not available or is otherwise unsatisfactory, or (equivalently) the agent may be able to determine that it should also visit another server based on data it has received from the current server.

Motivations for Using Mobile Agents

Why is this extended form of client/server computing desirable or valuable? There are many motivations for using mobile agents (Chess et al., 1994). They fall broadly into two categories: (1) support for mobile computers or lightweight devices and (2) the emerging need in rapidly evolving networks for an asynchronous method of searching for information or transaction services. For example:

- The reduction of overall communication traffic over the low-bandwidth, high-latency, high-cost access networks typically employed by mobile computers

- The ability of the agent to engage in high-bandwidth communication (with server, for example) to search through large, free text databases

- The ability of lightweight mobile computers to interact with heavyweight applications without prior detailed knowledge of the remote server's capabilities

- The ability of the agent to integrate knowledge from the client and server and perform interfacing at the server

- The ability of the user to create "personalized services" by customizing agents that take up residence at a server

Mobile Agent Scenario

Figure 8.5 shows a travel reservation scenario[3] that illustrates many of the features of an agent framework based on mobile agents. A mobile employee needs to fly from New York City to Austin, Texas on a Thursday evening. His business will be completed by Friday evening, but if there is a significant fare saving, he is willing to stay in Austin until Sunday. He has a portable computer, which is able to access his company's LAN via a public network and a secure gateway. He uses a local Java applet to generate a Web browser form and states his need by filling in the form. The applet translates this need into a task expressed in agent communication language, using a vocabulary standardized for travel reservations.

This task specification is used to create an instance of a Transaction Agent in the portable computer. The Transaction Agent is a program, expressed in a script language, that is able to interact via an Agent Meeting Place with a transaction server, assess the results of the transaction, make a decision, and commit a purchase. The Transaction Agent is also given the user's preferences for travel reservations (expressed as rules), and the agent is digitally signed with the user's authority.

---

[3]We do not claim that this is an accurate method for purchasing airline tickets, but it serves to illustrate many of the features and operations of a mobile agent framework.

The user's employer has a travel policy and a number of preferred providers of travel services, so the agent is sent initially from the laptop to the employer's Business Policy Server. To achieve this, the agent is partially encrypted with the Business Policy Server's public key, and then passed to a messaging system for transport via the LAN gateway to the server (step 1 in Figure 8.5). The mobile user then disconnects his computer from the network. At the Business Policy Server's Agent Meeting Place, the incoming agent is decrypted and authenticated using the Agent Meeting Place's private key. The agent and the Agent Meeting Place engage in a dialogue in which the agent communicates its task, which is to perform a transaction to obtain airline seats. The Business Policy Server's Agent Meeting Place verifies that the task does not violate current policy by employing an inferencing system to see whether the expressed facts conflict with the company's policy.

Figure 8.5   Travel reservation scenario using mobile agents.

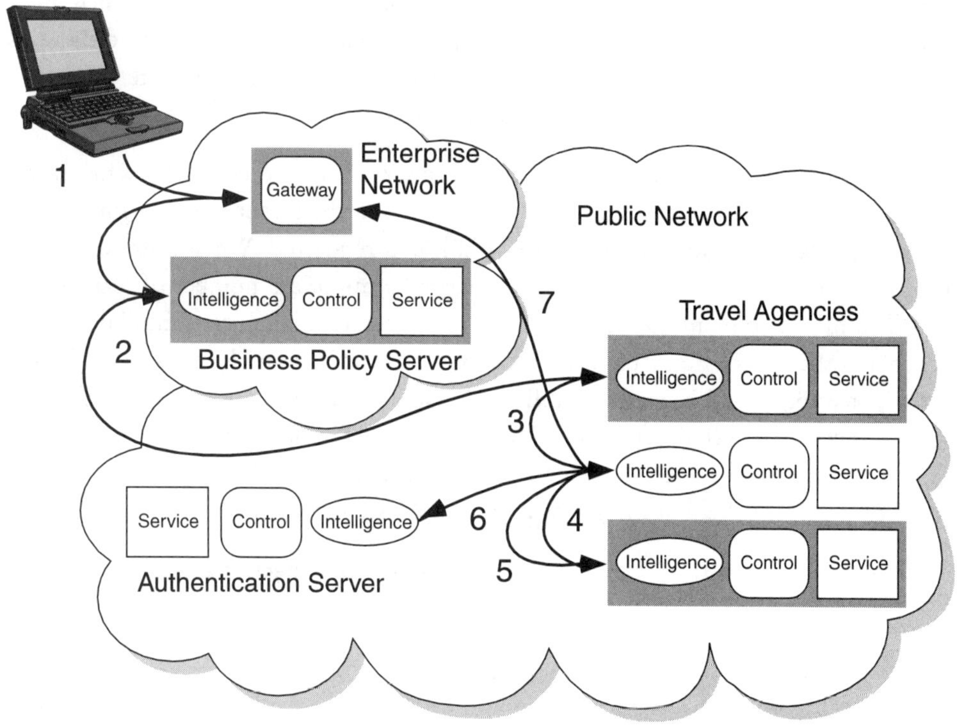

If all is well, a subset of the policy rules is attached to the agent, it is given a list of approved travel agencies and their public keys, and the agent is encrypted with the key of the first agency's Agent Meeting Place. The agent is now passed to a messaging system for transport to the first server to be visited (step 2). At the first server, the Agent Meeting Place uses its private key to decrypt the agent, ensuring that the agent can be executed only on the intended servers. The Agent Meeting Place then verifies the authority of the agent by examining the credentials it carries from one of the public security services to which the travel agency subscribes. The agent and the Agent Meeting Place engage in a dialogue in which the agent communicates its assignment, to obtain airline seats. The travel agency Agent Meeting Place accepts the specification of the transaction and passes it to the on-line reservation system, parsing the agent communication language expression of the task into the semantics of the reservation system, and performing the transaction dialogue. The reservation system returns (we hope) a number of candidate seats and prices for return flights on Friday and Sunday. The agent employs a local inference engine to process each of these candidates against the user's travel preferences and the company's travel policy. After ordering the candidates according to preference, the agent selects the best candidate and requests the Agent Meeting Place to hold the seat for a certain time, say 10 minutes. The agent is then reencrypted and transferred to the next server on the approved list (step 3).

The agent repeats this process at each of the servers visited (step 4).[4] Whenever it finds a better candidate, it sends a message back to the server where it found the previous "best" selection, releasing the hold it had requested. When it has examined a minimum number of candidates or visited a minimum number of servers, as specified by the company policy, it returns to the server of the best candidate and completes the transaction (step 5). This server's Agent Meeting Place issues a Ticket Agent, encrypted with the user's public key, obtained from the public security service, and sends it to the user (step 6). It then sends a Billing Agent (also encrypted), to the security service (step 7). Since the user has disconnected from the network, the Ticket Agent is held at the gateway until the user reconnects.

This scenario illustrates the major features of a mobile agent framework:

---

[4]The methods by which an agent can be authenticated at these servers are discussed in Chapter 9.

- The ability of the mobile user to dispatch an asynchronous task and receive a response at a later time

- The ability of the mobile agent to collect various kinds of knowledge to be applied to the execution of the task at the Agent Meeting Places

- The ability of the agent to migrate from place to place, accumulating information until it is able to complete its task

- The ability of the agent framework to employ various public security services for its own protection, the protection of the servers, and the completion of a payment method

- The ability of the agent to employ the visited Agent Meeting Places for its own execution purposes (selecting the best seat) in addition to simply interacting with the server's resources or static agents

Languages for Mobile Agents

Several script languages have been developed which can be employed for mobile agents.

- Java (FTP Software, Inc., 1996)

- Telescript, from General Magic, Inc. (White, 1995)[5]

- Tcl (Ousterhout, 1994; 1995), especially Safe-Tcl (Borenstein, 1995) (version 7.5 or later) Agent-Tcl (Gray, 1995)

A Telescript Example

Telescript has seen the greatest application as a mobile agent language in the Personalink[6] service from AT&T. This service was not commercially successful—not necessarily for reasons connected to Telescript—and GMI has now reoriented Telescript toward use in the Internet, specifically in conjunction with the Web and Java. This new approach goes under the name Tabriz Agentware and its aim is to make the high function classes of Telescript—for email, for transactions, and so

---

[5]Telescript, Teleaddress, Telename, and Teleclicks are all trademarks of General Magic, Inc.

[6]Personalink is a trademark of AT&T.

forth—accessible to Java applets. Telescript is a strongly object-oriented language, in which a process thread is a base class and all agents are processes. Programs are written in "high Telescript" and compiled into "low Telescript," which can be executed by the Telescript Engine. Agents are executed in Telescript Engines and can meet there with resident agents called Places. Places are stationary (nonmobile) agents that can interact with mobile agents, when they enter the Telescript Engine, meet with the Place and finally exit the Telescript Engine. There are several predefined classes of mobile agents, such as Courier agents, which are able to deliver electronic messages, and corresponding classes of Places, such as Mailboxes. Mobile Telescript agents are launched from a Telescript Engine on a user's client device and are named with the Authority of the originating device's (user's) Region and Telename (identifier). A Region is a collection of Telescript Engines owned by an Authority. A Telescript Domain is a Region and its Outposts. An Outpost is a Telescript Engine owned by an Authority on a server operated by another Authority; for example, a Mailbox Outpost is owned by the user, but executes on a server owned by the service operator (AT&T).

When an agent is dispatched by the user, it is given a Ticket, which enables it to move from one Region to another. The Ticket contains a Permit, the Telename or Teleaddress of its destination, a Way (the immediate destination Region), a Means (access network), and a Class of Service. The Permit (GMITS, 1995) is an object held by an agent or a place that helps to define the agent's or place's capabilities and to control its consumption of resources. The agent's ability to consume or buy resources is measured in a kind of currency called a Teleclick. When an agent meets a Place, the Place checks the number of Teleclicks in the agent's Permit and may reject the agent if the number is too low (not sufficient to pay for the Place's services) or too high (likely to consume too many of the Place's resources). If the agent is admitted by the Place, its Teleclicks are consumed by (and transferred to) the Place during its execution. If the agent runs out of Teleclicks at the Place, it dies; the agent can, however, hold some Teleclicks in reserve to be used for this emergency.

Figure 8.6 illustrates a Telescript environment consisting of three Regions. We may think of Regions 1 and 2 as the client PCs of two users and Region 2 as the servers and networks of a service operator. Region 1's user runs a Courier agent which executes the (pseudocode) "go to A3." This causes the Courier agent to be suspended, encoded, and transferred via the Access/Egress link to the Communi-

Figure 8.6   Telescript mobile agent framework consisting of three regions.

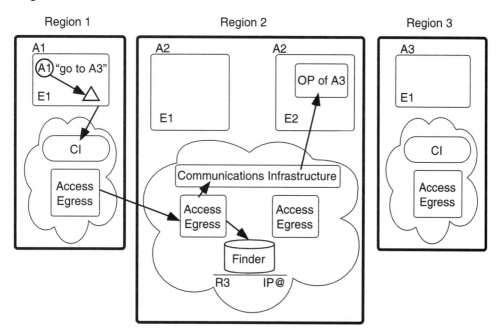

cation Infrastructure of Region 2. Here the destination "A3" is resolved to an Outpost of Region 3 in Region 1 (that is, a Mailbox), and the agent is delivered to the Mailbox place, which is in Telescript Engine E2 of domain A2. If Region 3 were collected, the agent would be forwarded by the Mailbox to Region 3. Since Region 3 is not connected, the Mailbox may have been given rules that cause it to notify Region 3 by means of a pager portal, for example.

Here is a Telescript code fragment for a shopping agent:

```
goShopping:   op (warehouse: ClassName)

throws ProductFailure =

{

        //go to the warehouse

        *.go(Ticket(nil, nil, warehouse));
```

```
//show an interest in prices

*.enableEvents(PriceReduction(*.name));

*.signalEvent(PriceReduction(), 'responder');

*.enableEvents(PriceReduction(here.name));


//wait for the desired price

actualPrice = desiredPrice+1;

while actualPrice > desiredPrice

{

        *.getEvent(nil, PriceReduction());

        try

        {

          actualPrice =

                here@Warehouse.getCatalog()[desiredProduct].price

        }

        catch KeyInvalid (throw ProductFailure())

    }

};
```

The shopping agent is sent by the user to a class of Places called `warehouse`:
`(*.go(Ticket(nil, nil warehouse)))`; in this example, there is assumed to
be only one instance of the class `warehouse`. The agent's next instruction
`(*.enableEvents(PriceReduction(*.name))` is executed at the warehouse
Place. The agent declares its interest in price reductions on a product class
`(*.name)` (not defined in this example) and registers a desire to be notified by
receiving signals of price reduction events. It primes itself by capturing the current
price (`actualPrice`) and then enters a loop in which it waits for price reduction
events and tests for a reduction in the price of the desired product. If the price is
still too high, it continues waiting. The agent also hints at an error procedure: if the

desired product does not exist at this warehouse (`KeyInvalid`), the agent throws an exception method (undefined in this example). This example does not show what happens when the required price reduction actually occurs, but the agent can arrange to be sent home and to report to its originator.

A Tcl Example

Tcl is a procedural language originally written for scripting the execution of multiple tasks on a single CPU. It has become very popular in academic environments, since it has been freely available and is simple to learn. It has been widely modified and extended; in Chapter 9, we will look at how the Tcl group at Sun Microsystems has extended it to provide secure execution of (foreign) scripts. For comparison with Telescript, here is an example of a similar electronic commerce application written in Tcl-DP, a distributed processing extension of the original Tcl:

```
#Create price list

set price_list {50 62 75 18 12}


#Define GetPrice procedure for extracting item price from list

proc GetPrice {stock_number} {

    global price_list;

    set item_price [lindex $price_list $stock_number];

    return $item_price;

}

#Open listening on TCP socket #4251

dp_MakeRPCServer 4251


#Establish RPC connection with remote server on socket &

#save identifier in variable 'server'

set server [dp_MakeRPCClient colin.watson.ibm.com 4251]
```

```
#Remote invocation (after transport) of defined procedure

set price [dp_RPC $server {GetPrice 3}]
```

This code fragment mixes client and server operations. It starts by creating a price list for four items at a "warehouse" server. Then it defines at the client a procedure (GetPrice) which can return a price from a price list given an item number. The client then opens an RPC connection to the server, captures the server identifier (server), and makes itself a client of this server. Finally it uses the dp_RPC function to remotely execute the GetPrice function at the server and return a price. In a strict sense, we would not classify this as a mobile agent, since the mobile program (GetPrice) does not itself return to the client, nor does it have a means to accumulate and transport state. Nonetheless, it provides a very simple and effective means of providing remote access.

Mobile Agent Issues

The goal of the various efforts to develop itinerant or mobile agent frameworks is closely aligned with the topic of this chapter: How do you enable the agent to be aware of its environment—possibly including the entire Web—and how do you allow it—safely—to participate in that environment? The mobile agent approach scores highly against the goals for agent access by proposing frameworks based on Agent Meeting Points, which—if deployed pervasively at Web sites—would produce a global agent access framework. This is General Magic's current hope. We can confidently expect that a dominant, portable programming language will emerge to support the access needs of many Internet applications. Today, Java is the leading contender for that role, but Tcl and Perl are also widely used in research applications.

While much discussion of mobile agents centers on the particular programming language employed, we believe that this is not the essential point. There are many portable languages;[7] in addition to the three cited here we could also mention IBM REXX, Logicware, Microsoft Active/X, Obliq, Perl, SafePython, and, of course, C itself. They all have merits and drawbacks as programming languages. Some of them, as we have seen, are capable of implementing mobile agents. We believe that beyond basic expressiveness as programming languages and the ability to execute

---

[7]Dan Connolly at the World Wide Web Consortium maintains a Web page on mobile code systems [http://www.w3.org/pub/WWW/MobileCode/].

remotely or to transport state, a mobile agent framework needs also to include the following:

> *Agent communication language support.* In a closed system, which may be the case for many enterprises, this may not be necessary, because the enterprise may be able to enforce uniform standards for a script language. In a public network this is probably not possible, and hence the Agent Meeting Places need to be able to handle agents which employ various script languages to express their execution intent, but which employ a common language for the interaction with the server. This is an aspect of content and was discussed in Chapter 7.

> *Security support.* The whole idea of admitting foreign applications to a server—let alone one's own workstation—makes a lot of people nervous. How do I know what a new mobile agent is really going to do? How do I know that it is

Table 8.2   Comparison of Java, Telescript, and Tcl

Java	Telescript	Tcl
A complete "safe," interpreted, language.	A "safe," interpreted, scripting language.	A "safe," interpreted, scripting language.
Widely supported for downloading Web browser applets; not originally designed for mobile agents.	Designed for mobile agents, with many specific features, recently adapted by GMI to interwork with Java.	Adapted for building mobile agents from the earlier scripting language.
Applets can be signed to establish trust and access to system resources.	Telescript Engines provide isolation from underlying systems, strong security walls between agents. Strong security mechanisms for authentication and payment.	Safe-Tcl isolates untrusted programs in "Padded cell" for safe execution.
Widely available from many vendors with many development tools.	Only available from General Magic; development environment only on Sun workstations.	Freely available for many platforms, but not commercially supported.

not a malign virus? How do I know who sent it? How does the sender of the agent know that the server will actually honor the agent's requests for service? If the agent carries state around with it, how does it know that the server will not spy on that state or modify it? These are some of the security issues of mobile agents and are discussed in Chapter 9.

Management support. After I launch a mobile agent off into the network, how will I know what happened to it? Suppose it dies before it returns home or returns a result?

Given these concerns, is this really a useful model for remote access (Chess et al., 1994)? While the idea of agent programs literally running around networks and interacting with servers is intellectually fascinating, it does raise a lot of problems. However, there are applications where the ability to execute an application remotely on a server is a significant advantage:

- *Support for mobile computing.* The absence of a session relationship between the originator and the server is an advantage for mobile users, who are often only intermittently connected to a network. This was an early goal for GMI.

- *Support for browsing large, unstructured, or noncoded databases, such as digital libraries.* If the user wishes to search a very large corpus of noncoded or unstructured data, it may be more efficient to send a searching agent to the server where the content is stored and do the filtering there, than to bring the content back over the network and do the searching locally.

- *Real-time interaction.* If the server application requires very low-latency decision and control, for example, running a robot, the latency of remote control via a packet network may be unacceptably high. Sending the control program to execute locally at the server can eliminate this latency.

Internet Access

One of the richest access hunting grounds for agents is of course the Internet, with its tens of thousands of FTP sites and Web sites. These and other protocols were specifically designed to encourage remote access to information throughout the world and the community of agent developers has been quick to exploit them. The Web browser itself is also an excellent point at which to capture input from the user for learning purposes. Chapter 3 provides many examples of such Internet agents.

Access in Your Business

What kinds of access are important for the introduction of agents in your company? You may be already considering this question for other purposes—for distributed object frameworks to form the basis of new applications, or for workflow-based applications. This goal of integrating applications that were never originally created to work directly with one another is increasingly important for many reasons other than agents. So in many cases, agents will be just another motivation for enterprise integration efforts already under way. Alternatively, you may be launching some completely new application, say a collaboration tool. In this case you may have a unique opportunity to design a set of access points for agents.

Access is the most ad hoc of the four key technology factors. How you do it will depend largely on the circumstances of your company's application base. In a way it is also a necessary evil, ultimately requiring a large investment to get at all the data and controls. Here's a number of issues to look out for:

Level of Access. Does your agent goal require detailed knowledge of the internal state of an application or is it sufficient to see the outputs of the application as expressed by a database or file? The KISS (Keep It Simple, Stupid) principle suggests that you would be better off trying to keep the agent and the applications as decoupled as possible. Do not assume that you need client/server APIs in order to have effective access. Try first to see what you can accomplish by giving the agent the simplest possible access. Much of the learning that you need in getting started with agents comes not from the details of how to develop tight coupling between the agent and the application, but from gaining insight into how to best use the information and the controls that are readily available. In the long term you are likely to make a large investment in access methods, but unless you are already developing such methods for other purposes, you should not make a big investment here at the beginning. Start ad hoc and aim to develop corporate standards after you have experience with the benefits of agents. If you find that the agent application you have chosen is leading you to a disproportionately large effort in developing access methods, you might want to reconsider the application.

Performance Requirements. As in any kind of service, your agent will have a certain latency between the time its world changes (events) and the time the agent decides on a new action. It will also have a certain throughput—the number of events it can process in unit time. If low latency is important in the agent application you have in mind, then having access to files and logs may cause too much delay, and you will have to find how to get access to the data and controls inside the applications you are integrating with the agent. Remote access may itself introduce too much delay, and you may find that this is an opportunity to use the remote execution techniques offered by itinerant or mobile agents. On the other hand, if you want the agent to do significant processing (machinery) on each event, then you may need to apply discriminating filters between the application and the agent to reduce the number of events presented. You also have the option of dividing the agent application between two or more agents. You could build one that can provide high throughput or low latency to deal with real-time constraints produced by high event rates but that can perform only minimal processing of each event, and another that can perform, say, detailed data mining on an event log to extract new long-term knowledge. The two agents then need common access methods to exchange knowledge and actions between themselves.

User Interaction. How are you going to present the agent to your end-users? Will it use only nonintrusive access methods, monitoring the user's actions via the GUI and never explicitly communicating with the user? This can cause the agent to seem like a management snoop introduced purely to monitor the user's productivity in, say, a Call Center. On the other hand, an intrusive agent can become a nuisance if it continually interrupts the user to ask questions or provide suggestions. Remember that you have lots of choices for how the agent interacts with the user. Monitoring is often possible at several points (GUI, transaction log, billing records, HTTP requests). Communication with the user can be by a pop-up window, but asynchronous communication via email or telephone can be much less intrusive. This aspect of access deserves a lot of thought. If done badly, it can doom efforts to introduce agents by antagonizing or threatening the users. If done well, the users can strongly appreciate the value that the agent is adding to their work. Remember above all that, just as GUI-based applications are by no means intuitive for unskilled users, so agent-based applications can be hard for them to comprehend. Unskilled users are already likely to attribute anthropomorphic properties—both positive and negative—to the computing system; agents can make the systems seem even more confusing by reducing the repeatability of the system behavior.

Standards for Access. You have noted already that the value of agents increases as they become more pervasive within an enterprise; that is, as their scope of access increases. If you are successful with your first agent-based applications, you will want to quickly bring the benefits of agents to as many applications as possible. You will soon need to create a set of access standards for your company. You should take advantage of this effort to capture as much as possible of your developers' knowledge about the nonstandard interfaces in your enterprise applications and to drive toward a set of enterprise standards for application integration; this can include any of the access methods described above as needed. These standards will describe the access methods you are providing for various existing applications and also how you want new applications to be written to enable access. In essence you will be creating an agent framework for your company. The benefits of this framework can extend well beyond support for agents and should be incorporated in your overall strategy for maintaining and developing enterprise applications. As agents become more widely used within enterprises, industry standards for these frameworks can be expected to emerge, such the KQML proposal to the Object Management Group (see Chapter 7). These are currently being debated in the software technology community, and are probably two to three years from widespread introduction.

Summary

A key role for intelligent agents is to provide integration across many existing or new applications within your company or among your company, your customers, and third parties. This leads to a need for a wide range of methods of providing access between the agent and data and applications. For existing applications, these methods are essentially ad hoc, exploiting whatever interfaces happen to be available. For new applications, access methods can be integrated into the design. The ultimate goal of the development of these methods is to construct a uniform enterprisewide framework which provides the access needed by a large number of agents. The essence of these methods is flexibility, not elegance. The agent should be able to plug into new sources of events or knowledge or new controls with a minimum of modification. Frameworks of this kind are emerging based on event channels in operating systems (Apple Open Scripting Architecture), languages (Java, Tcl), middleware (Active/X, OMG CORBA Event Channels), and on process migration (Telescript mobile agents). Mobile agents provide especially powerful access methods for large-scale networks, notably the Internet. As with the other agent technologies, access is an area where standards will emerge in the next few years, driven in part by the needs of agents, but also by the use of distributed frameworks as part of a new paradigm for enterprise applications.

Table 8.3 Intelligent Agent Product

Intelligent Agent Product	Source
Agent-Tcl	ftp://bald.cs.dartmouth.edu/pub/agents/agent.1.1.tar.gz
Apple Open Scripting Architecture	http://www.apple.com/
CORBA	Implementations available from HP, IBM, Orbix, and others.
CyberAgent	FTP Software, Inc., 100 Brickstone Square, Andover, MA 01810 http:/www.ftp.com/cyberagent
D'OLE	http://www.next com/
Java	http://www.javasoft.com and dozens of other software houses
OLE	http://www.microsoft.com/
Safe-Tcl	ftp://ftp.smli.com/pub/tcl/stc10.2.tar.gz
Telescript	General Magic, Inc., 420 North Mary Avenue, Sunnyvale, CA 94086. http://www.genmagic.com

Agent Security

I t's ten P.M. Do you know where your agents are, what they are doing, and who they are talking to? Maybe you'd like to read about security?

In this chapter we will make you aware of the additional security problems posed by intelligent agents, and go on to suggest that these are not major threats (compared to conventional security problems), and that reasonable methods exist to deal with them. Security is central to all forms of enterprise computing, whether distributed or purely desktop. Business information systems are under threat from viruses, hackers, fraudulent customers and suppliers, and employees who may be curious, mischievous, criminal, or even well-intentioned, but incompetent. It really makes you want to go back to decks of punched cards; at least you could *see* your programs and data then!

If the operation of your business depends in any way on the use of computers, you should already be thinking about security. Intelligent agents, therefore, do not introduce security as a new topic for your concern, and many of the security needs of agent-based applications should already be addressed in your information system for other purposes. But the use of agents does require you to think again about this complicated topic. You may need to modernize your overall security systems to prepare for electronic commerce. In this chapter we will consider what security measures are needed in agent-based systems in order for you to sleep well at night—the idea of using agents was to reduce the burden on human beings, remember?

But first a disclaimer: Technology by itself cannot solve security problems. Technology for security must be complemented by an awareness of security issues and disciplined application of the techniques. No matter how many bolts, locks, and chains your company may introduce, if you have employees who are ignorant about security or who are sloppy about security measures, or who are disgruntled, then sooner or later you will have problems. Security is tricky stuff. Even the best programmers can accidentally create security loopholes through ignoring the possibilities created by great new features in the software. Even software designed by experts to be secure, when poked at by determined hackers, will often prove to have loopholes. If you have any doubts about the security of your information systems, and especially if they are connected to external networks, we strongly recommend regular audits by security consultants.

What Does Security Do?

Security systems attempt to get you reliable answers to the following kinds of questions:

- Who is accessing our information systems (*identification*)?
- Can I be sure who made this request (*verification*)?
- Can I be sure that this message has not been modified since it was sent (*integrity*)?
- Is this user entitled to make use of this resource (*access control*)?
- Will this program cause damage or disruption (*viruses*)?
- Can I safely send this message on a public network (*privacy*)?
- Can I be sure that this user will actually pay for the service he or she is requesting (*nonrepudiation*)?
- Can I be sure that this server will do what I want (*reputation*)?

Table 9.1   Leading Causes of General Security Failures and Their Preventative Measures

Security Failure	Consequence	Security Measures
Unencrypted information transmitted on public networks (PSTN, Internet, X.25 . . .).	Unauthorized access to private information; other security measures compromised.	Enforce encryption policy. Use secure transmission methods (Secure Sockets). Use physically controlled networks. Do not transmit sensitive information.
Lack of a disaster recovery plan.	Going out of business while trying to recover from an "accident."	Identify mission-critical resources. Develop and test a plan for recovery from loss of resources. Backup!

This chapter will not attempt to be a general textbook on all these topics, but will limit itself to how they relate to agent-based systems. For general texts on computer security we recommend Rivest et al. (1978); Kaufman et al. (1995); and Schneier (1996). Table 9.1 lists some of the most common security failures, their consequences, and what to do about them. As an IS manager, if you are not totally sure that you have already taken care of all of these problems, stop reading this book right now, and go and read one of these books on general security and put your shop to rights! Then come back and think about the challenges of introducing intelligent agents, whether for use within your company or as a way of doing business with the public over the Internet or other public network.

Security for Agents

The topic of security for agents is relatively new, with little literature, but there are a few products that promise hope (Chess, 1996; Ordille, 1996). The agent group at the University of Maryland has a subpage on agent security (UMBCSEC, 1996), the OSF has some thoughts in this area, and for those of you who can read German, Fritz Hohl's (1995) thesis has a section on agent security. What is different about security in agent-based systems? Here's a short list:

- *Delegation*: You are delegating to the agents some of your authority. Think of them as subordinate employees, but without the attitudes. Among other problems, this means that agents are doing things you cannot always see (just like employees).

- *Mobility*: Not only can you not see what the agents are doing, they may be off doing it on the other side of the planet. Still worse, agents from the other side of the planet may be doing it on your servers.

- *Viruses*: Agents share many characteristics with viruses. We might call viruses "agents with attitude." Exposure to viruses is not unique to agent-based systems, but in creating an environment for agents there is additional risk that we expose weaknesses or loopholes that may enable viruses to breed.

- *Trust*: One of the main motivations for using agents is to get human beings out of some of the mundane tasks involved in running a business. However, human beings not only perform tasks, they are also exquisitely sensitive to the results and side effects of processes. They have precise expectations about outcomes. They have particular ways of verifying the correctness of their work. They have classified their co-workers into those who are reliable and those who are not (and no amount of management investigation will discover these webs of trust). How is trust developed in an agent-based system?

This chapter looks primarily at those additional security issues raised by the use of agent-based systems, exploring the risks and proposing security technologies and methodologies. It is difficult to exaggerate the value and importance of security in enterprise information systems. It is, without a doubt, one of the cornerstone issues. While the availability of strong security features does not necessarily make agents immediately appealing, the absence of security would certainly make them very unattractive. Machinery, content, and access all present technical challenges, but nothing is more certain to sink your agent plans than having the agent applications be the source of security problems.

Some Security Basics

We have tried to emphasize above that a good knowledge of security is a foundation of IS management, and therefore we might reasonably expect you to know the basics. However, for those of you who haven't quite managed this, here's a short primer.

Security shows up in many areas of computing systems, from memory management to electronic commerce. The core principle is to isolate sensitive resources, such as the operating system kernel or the personnel records, by means of hardware and software barriers and then to employ hierarchies of privilege to determine who can cross those barriers via controlled gateways. These barriers may be created by the core architecture of the host processor, by the file system, by a firewall in a network interface, or by a resource broker in a distributed object framework. The highest levels of security require specialized hardware architectures and dedicated processors (Palmer, 1994). The barriers are constructed by isolating the protected resource using a hardware or operating system function and then providing a carefully designed access method as the only means for users or applications to gain access to it. The access method will allow only specific forms of interaction with the resource, for example, UNIX file system semantics, and will only permit this interaction if the user or application requesting the interaction is privileged to that resource and that form of interaction. The goal of unethical hackers is either to find an alternate path to the protected resource, or to dupe the verification or authentication methods (usually the latter).

The simplest identification is based on a unique token associated with each user, the *userid,* which is passed on to processes started by that user. The operating system can always authenticate who is requesting access to a resource by consulting the process control table, and the application can also provide (assert) that information to other applications with which it interacts. The user asserts his or her identity when he or she logs in to the system, and proves it (weakly) by entering the password. Basic operating system security generally stops at that point. It is moderately difficult—but not impossible, depending on the operating system and how well its security mechanisms are maintained on a given computer—to spoof a userid. The most common violations at this level come from usurping a legitimate user's userid by acquiring the password, often by "social engineering."

A higher level of security is achieved by having the user's identity verified by a certification authority. Certification is typically associated with public key cryptography (Kallski, 1993); that is, it relies on encryption algorithms to conceal information during its transmission between the parties. The encryption keys are managed by a key management service (Molva et al., 1992) so that any party can locate a second party's public key and encrypt a message for the second party, but only that party can decrypt the message using its private key. The certified is an application—

typically on a remote server which is physically secure, that is, in a locked room—which can engage in a dialogue with a client application employed by the user. In practical systems, the certifier and the user have a piece of shared, secret knowledge and via encrypted messages they prove to one another that they each possess this knowledge. The familiar login protocol is a very degenerate form of this. If this authentication process is successful, the server will issue to the user a certificate, which is an encrypted message stating that the server certifies the user's identity. The user's applications can now present this certificate to other applications and by means of established protocols, and the other applications can verify the user's identity from the certificate. Additional functions exist which prevent the certificate being used fraudulently by a hacker. Many such protocols have been developed to meet different needs, but in an enterprise environment, the most widely accepted is the Kerberos protocol developed during the Athena project at MIT (Steiner et al., 1988). But on the Internet, the simple but effective protocols of Phil Zimmerman's Pretty Good Privacy (PGP, 1996) are very popular.

Lotus Notes is an application which has a very thorough security system. Access to a Notes server requires the client application to verification the user's identity using a password system that is considerably more secure than that of a typical operating system, and also requires the user to have been certified for access to the server. Notes databases then provide a sophisticated and relatively easy to manage set of access controls down to the level of individual documents. A key phrase here is "easy to manage." Most business users are quite unable to deal with the complexities of, say, UNIX file system access controls. One way to be sure of getting access wherever you want is to always work as the system manager—this is why you may get email from "root"—but it means in effect that you have thrown away the access control system. So "easy to manage" is an important concept; indeed, an excellent application for a *highly trusted* agent would be to manage access controls for business users.

By itself, the use of public-key cryptography does not guarantee a high level of security; rather it provides part of the basis on which to construct highly secure systems when used in conjunction with operating systems and languages that provide other essential parts of the basis. To be really useful more is needed than a certification protocol. Secure protocols for application-to-application interaction are required and many forms of these exist. A secure remote procedure call (Secure RPC) was introduced by the OSF Distributed Computing Environment (DCE), and has spread to many UNIX-derivatives; this provides authentication, privacy, and integrity in RPC sessions. The Secure Sockets Library (SSL) is a recent standard for IP-based networked applications; it provides a secure socket channel between two applications and was designed for use in the public Internet. Secure HTTP (SHTTP) is a recent development by Netscape and the Web Forum, and enables secure interaction based on HTTP.

In a small to medium-sized enterprise, it may be sufficient to have a single certification server. Generally, this level of security is used only to establish a session between two applications, as the overhead of attaching, transmitting, and processing a certificate on every message exchanged may be too high (or not, depending on the importance of the interaction). In large enterprises, multiple certification servers are needed to avoid certification itself becoming a bottleneck. These servers can mutually authenticate one another to form a federation and are then able to perform proxy certification. For example, a user certified by server A interacts with an application which trusts server B. The application passes the user's certificate to server B for authentication, and B authenticates it on behalf of server A.

When the interaction extends outside the boundaries of the enterprise, for example, in electronic commerce, additional steps are required. Clearly it is impossible, and probably undesirable, to perform mutual authentication with every potential external domain. The solution to this is the creation of certification hierarchies. Company A's certification server authenticates itself with a public certification authority, which is a publicly accessible server trusted by third parties. When a user application at company A performs a transaction with an application at company B, it tells company B that it is certified by one or more public certification authorities. B's certification server can then contact one of these public authorities to authenticate company A's user. To make the system scaleable, the public certification service is also implemented as a federation of distributed servers. Public systems of this kind are being introduced, for example, by credit card companies as they begin to deploy electronic transaction services.

Higher-level protocols such as SET (Secure Electronic Transactions), which are based on certification, implement secure electronic commerce. It is quite likely that your enterprise should be considering some form of electronic commerce, even if it is only for intraenterprise commerce. Many of the security needs of agent-based systems will be met by introducing security services for electronic commerce.

Figure 9.1 illustrates how an Internet-based service provides basic security services for itself. The publicly accessible servers are isolated from the company's development environment by a firewall, which is a router that will only forward packets for authenticated users. Dial-up access to the company's development facilities is also controlled through a gateway that requires authentication of the calling party before it will establish a PPP session. Users of the public service may also be checked by passing certificates that they present to a public certification server. Thus there is a very clear distinction between "inside" the company and "outside." Most of the threats are assumed to be on the outside. For internal security, the company has its own security server, which can perform certification of the users, and manages their public keys.

Figure 9.1   Placement of security functions in an Internet agent-based service.

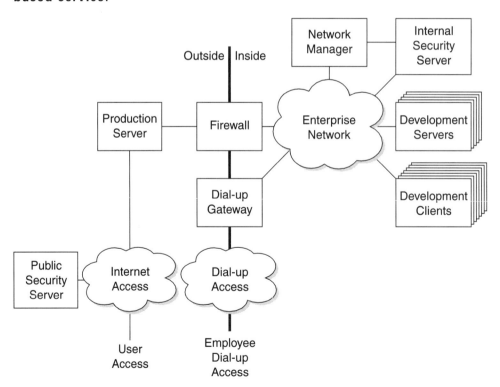

Security is thus more than just a set of protocols; it is an enterprisewide service that must be integrated into every application. While many companies have been content to rely on simpler methods for intraenterprise security, the advent of widespread access from enterprises to the Internet and of electronic commerce on the Internet demand the application of more sophisticated methods, such as those outlined here. As enterprises begin to migrate their new and existing applications onto Internet-based platforms, these security services are being bundled into those platforms by the manufacturers (Andresson et al., 1996). With few exceptions—which we will consider below—the security services provided by these new platforms for electronic commerce on the public Internet will meet the security needs of agent-based systems. These exceptions are:

- Delegation

- Mobility

- Trust

The following sections will address these areas.

Delegation for Agents

The purpose of an agent is to perform some tasks that would otherwise be performed by its user. To achieve this, the agent will need many, if not all, of the access rights of its user. In a security environment of the type outlined above, this is readily achieved by passing to the agent a copy of the user's certificate. In this regard, the agent is indistinguishable from any other application employed by the user. The agent can now perform operations on file systems, applications, and other machinery, just as if it were the user himself or herself. One little point to watch is that certificates are valid for finite periods, which are defined by the security administrators. These may be as short as 24 hours or as long as 30 days. For a real user, this may not be noticeable, as the certificate is reissued whenever the user logs in to the system; but for an autonomous agent (or any disconnected application), possibly a long way from home, whose certificate suddenly expires, this may cause obscure failures.

Controlled Delegation

So performing the delegation is not a big problem. The real problem is that the user has now given away the keys to the family jewels to an autonomous, invisible lump of software. As users we sit at the keyboard with the potential to do great damage to our computing environment, but we are restrained from this by our knowledge of the implications of our actions (although we all still manage to accidentally delete a file or an email message from time to time). An agent may have no such restraint. For example, what prevents the agent (in UNIX systems) from executing the shell command: `rm *.*` ? Well, you say, no one would be so dumb as to write an agent containing that command. But suppose you had a simple desktop agent which could perform background operations for you. You might well want an interface that would allow you to pass it shell command strings, and since it's your agent, you might not think to protect those messages. So a determined hacker might be able to intercept one of those messages, change it to `rm *.*` and there you are. You might propose including checks for all such potentially harmful commands, but suppose the hacker were capable of introducing a new shell program called `save` or `foo`, so that `foo *.*` has the effect of `rm *.*`? It is hard to foresee all such dangers.

In this respect, an agent is different from an application program. We know—or at least we believe we know—what an application program will do, and we generally do not expect it to delete the file system. Agents by intent are much more flexible than an application program, and much harder to predict. This problem is particularly acute with mobile agent systems, where an unknown program may arrive and want to execute on one of your processors. There are a number of approaches to this problem.

One is to give the agent a separate identity from its user. This separate proxy identity can be given greatly restricted rights compared to the user. For example, it may have only read access to most of the file system and write or execute access only to specific files. The disadvantage of this approach is the high administrative costs. It is hard enough to get the access permissions right for a human user; finding just the right subset to meet the minimal needs of an agent can be very difficult. This is particularly true when one comes to consider fine-grained access control rights on objects (Richardson et al., 1992; OMG, 1994), where rights must be defined at the level of individual methods. It is often very hard to determine what methods the proxy will need and what kind of access is required.

A second method is to execute the agent in a "padded cell," an isolated environment, where the agent has a limited access to critical resources such as the file system. This is an approach employed for mobile agents, and we will discuss it separately below.

A third method is to allow the agent to interact with the system environment only in a language with limited expressiveness, for example, an agent communication language (Chapter 7). In essence this moves the level of interaction of the agent up above the operating system command shell to a level which can only be executed by the agent framework. We saw in Chapter 7 that agent communication languages provide expression at the level of: `achieve`, `ask`, `deny`, `evaluate`, `forward`, `monitor`, `reply`, `subscribe`, `tell`, and so forth. These agent commands, you will recall, are passed from agents to execution front-ends which translate them in turn into database queries or transactions. By limiting the expressiveness of the agent in this way, its ability to use its delegated authority to cause damage is greatly limited. However, language developers traditionally find it hard to resist the desire to add access to system services to every language, bringing the problem back again. Microsoft's ActiveX is already accused of this failing, and Java may be headed down the same path. Watch out for this.

Limiting Resource Consumption

Another aspect of this delegation problem is the amount of each resource that the agent is permitted to consume. As users we are constantly making assessments of how much resource to allocate to a task. We will wait so many seconds for a Web server to respond. We will prune email folders after they exceed a certain size. We will spend so many dollars to buy a document. The agent has no understanding of the principles behind these kinds of decisions and needs to be given explicit budgets for these resources. This is an aspect of training. Initially you will want to be very limiting in the resources you allow your agents to spend, until you gain confidence in their decisionmaking, and until you get some idea of how rapidly they will want to consume each resource. Insufficient resources to complete a task should cause the agent to raise an error message to its user; the user can then decide whether to allocate additional resource or abandon the task.

General Magic's Telescript language expresses resource budgets and costs in terms of script currency units called Teleclicks (GMI, 1995). Teleclicks may be spent on computational resources or on purchasing services or goods. A Telescript agent is dispatched with a ticket which authenticates the user[1] and authorizes it to spend up to some maximum number of Teleclicks in accomplishing its task. Whenever the agent requests entry to a Telescript Engine, the Engine verifies that the agent has sufficient Teleclicks left to reasonably execute itself in the Engine. If the agent runs out of Teleclicks during execution, it dies. As a safety mechanism, an agent close to its spending limit will be placed in a special execution place (called "Purgatory") whose sole purpose is to permit a recovery action, such as returning an exception to its originating Telescript Engine, saying, in effect, "Send money!"

Security Issues for Mobile Agents

Mobile agents introduce their set of security concerns. Recall from Chapter 8 that by mobile agents we mean any agent that moves from one host to one other host and executes there.

Delegation and Authentication

As with static or nonmobile agents, the primary security requirement is a method of delegating authority to the mobile agent. The most fundamental security building block for this is *digital signature*. The dispatching application uses its certificate and an encoding of the agent's content to generate this signature, which is a token which can be decoded by the receiving server and used to verify both the authority of the agent and the integrity of the content. Two additional problems with mobile agents are the authentication of the executing server and the privacy of their own contents. While it is good for the executing server to be able to authenticate the authority of the incoming agent, the agent too ought to be able to authenticate where it has arrived. The agent should be entitled to protect itself against being executed on a spoofing host. In the case of a mobile agent which only visits a single server, this problem can be solved by encrypting the agent with the server's public key. However, this cannot be extended to mobile agents which may visit multiple hosts, unless the set of hosts to be visited can arrange to have a common public key.

---

[1]Strictly speaking, the Telescript ticket authenticates the Telescript Engine from which the agent originated. We can consider the Telescript Engine to be a proxy for the user.

There is no obvious answer to this problem, unless the agent execution is performed in a highly trusted environment, such as a special hardware processor.

Agent Privacy

A mobile agent which has previously visited other servers may contain private information, such as their prices for a good or service. Or it might contain a negotiating algorithm which it uses to determine which is the best offer it has received from the set of servers it visits. There is no obvious method to protect all of this information unless the agent execution is performed in a highly trusted environment, such as a special hardware processor, although tampering may be detectable in specific cases (see below). General Magic's response to this problem is that a Telescript agent can protect such information by keeping private the methods which access it. Telescript rigorously encapsulates all methods and instance data and has a very thorough approach to protecting the privacy of agents in a Telescript Engine (White, 1995).

Is This a Virus I See Before Me?[2]

If you admit an unknown program into your server, will it do damage? Damage in this context might include infinite loops (denial of service attack) or destruction of data (rm *.*). Worse, will it take up residence in the server, infecting it, or will it infect other visiting agents, and thus propagate itself to other servers? Is there some way to examine an incoming program and determine whether it has malicious intent? This is not a new problem. Existing PC viruses are only detected when they execute, although research continues on a priori detection of viruses. But PC viruses only propagate with human assistance: downloading shareware, copying diskettes, buying infected products; so we are already exposed to malicious programs. The difference with agents is the method of propagation; it is conceivable, although not necessarily feasible in any real environment, to write a mobile agent which can infect a host, replicate itself, and propagate the replicates via a network. What makes this more serious—and intellectually more fascinating—is that the speed of propagation of such a virus could be far higher than today's PC viruses.

It is impossible in principle to verify with complete certainty that an arbitrary program (such as an incoming agent) is not a virus (Cohen, 1987). In practice, the

---

[2]Portions of this section were contributed by David Chess.

problem of writing a program that can verify the correct (or even simply non-malicious) behavior of another program is unsolved. (This is Alan Turing's famous Halting Problem: it is impossible to determine whether a program written in a general, "Turing-complete" programming language will ever terminate, let alone what its effects on the host will be.) Analysis of the agent itself, to determine whether it is likely to exhibit viruslike behavior, is a difficult problem. It is difficult to define necessary and sufficient tests that the agent must pass in order to determine whether its intentions are benign or whether it intends to infect or otherwise corrupt the host system. Furthermore, clever virus writers may encrypt parts of the virus to prevent detection.

It is not the case that virus detection is undecidable in (and only in) Turing-complete programming languages. Nor is it the case that it is possible to write a virus in any Turing-complete language. Turing completeness is really a red herring when thinking about viruses, because:

- It is easy to design a non-Turing-complete language in which a virus can be written (just include an "infect" verb somewhere in the set of primitives).

- It is easy to design a Turing-complete language in which no virus can be written (and in which, therefore, the virus-detection problem is easy; the answer is always: "No, that is not a virus"). Consider, for instance, a language with the full programming power of C++, but able to do input only from the keyboard, output only to the screen, and with no access to any underlying operating system commands or functions. One could write arbitrarily complex games or Eliza programs in it, but since programs written in it cannot read or write other programs, they cannot be viral.[3]

- Turing completeness only comes in very slightly: If one has a language that includes ability to implement the "spread" operation, and the language is Turing-complete, then Cohen (Cohen, 1987) has shown that perfect virus detection is impossible. But his result does not say anything one way or the other about systems that are not Turing-complete, or that do not make the "spread" operation possible. This is important for the mobile agent question in at least one very large way: it means that one could design a mobile

---

[3]In theory, you could write an entire virtual operating system, including a file system, in this language, and there could be virtual viruses within that system, but that is not of practical relevance.

agent system in which agents are written in a Turing-complete language, and as long as the "spread" operation cannot be implemented (as long, that is, as agents cannot alter other programs), we can still avoid having viruses.

A simple example of this would be an agent language with the syntax of BASIC (say), but with only a very limited set of powers:

- To alter its own internal state variables
- To make database queries in the current server
- To move to another server
- To send text messages back to its owner

Despite being Turing-complete, there is no way to write a virus in this system. One can even allow such agents to add and update database entries (under proper access controls, of course), and as long as nothing ever interprets the contents of a database entry as a program, there are still no virus problems.

The techniques developed to detect and remove conventional viruses will be extended to agent viruses. If the language in which the mobile agent is written is moderately safe, and the agent execution environment is reasonably well-isolated from the critical system resources, it is actually quite difficult to write a virus that can propagate itself. The weakly used security services of UNIX systems can take some of the credit for the very small number of UNIX viruses. Even in the defenseless PC world, the vast majority of the thousands of documented PC viruses are in fact harmless; many contain bugs which prevent them even from executing. It is not a major burden to perform scanning of an incoming agent to see whether it contains a known (and hazardous) virus. The real concern about viruses in mobile agent systems is that if a successful—that is, self-propagating—virus were created, then it might be able to spread sufficiently fast that containing the resulting epidemic might be very difficult.

This is perhaps an area of exaggerated concern. Reasonable hygiene will contain this problem. The only successful virus spread by network transmission has been the *RTM* virus, which exploited three loopholes in the UNIX operating system; even the wave of imitators who immediately followed Robert T. Morris' "success" were unable to duplicate it. It is rather like the alleged dangers of transmitting a credit card number over the Internet. Despite the very real risk, there has been no documented case of anyone actually being defrauded in this way. Mobile agents are not the only method by which viruses might be propagated in network services, although the use of mobile agents may greatly facilitate their propagation. Nor are viruses the only epidemic threat to network services; other effects such as mail broadcast storms are at least as likely and equally hard to deal with.

Security-minded Languages for Agents

As indicated above, one of the methods to protect the server against potentially hostile agents is to isolate the agent execution environment from direct access to the underlying operating system. This is likely to have the incidental effect of creating a highly portable language, which is, of course, another desirable feature. With more effort one can create a "safe" language—one that prevents direct memory references and guards against common programming errors such as referencing an uninitialized pointer, overrunning a buffer, and so forth. A few languages have been developed in recent years with this goal in mind. These include Sun's Java (Java, 1996), General Magic's Telescript (GMI, 1995), Safe-Tcl (Ousterhout, 1996), and KQML (see Chapter 7). In all these cases, the language definition isolates the executing program or agent from the "dangerous" functions of the agent execution environment or host operating system.

Tcl (Ousterhout, 1994; 1995), an older script language with a strong user community, has been extended to produce Safe-Tcl. As a general-purpose programming language, Tcl contains a variety of verbs that are potentially dangerous when executed by unknown programs. Safe-Tcl addresses this problem by removing the execution of these "dangerous" commands to subclasses ("padded cells") of the Tcl interpreter (Borenstein, 1995; Safe-Tcl, 1996). Thus there is a primary or master interpreter, where all commands can be executed, and this is used for trusted applications. But if the program is untrusted, the master interpreter can relegate the program to a slave interpreter or padded cell, which does not have direct access to critical resources. If the untrusted program needs to execute a command which requires access to a critical resource, the slave interpreter can make a "safe call" to the master. This is very similar to the conventional relationship between user space and kernel space in a modem operating system.

Figure 9.2 shows a padded cell arrangement in which an incoming agent program is screened by a "Concierge" function to determine whether it is to be trusted.

If so, it is admitted to a trusted execution environment; if not, it might be rejected or it might be permitted to execute in the "untrusted execution environment," where it is isolated from system resources. If it performs safely in that environment, it may be trusted in the future.

Much attention was focused in making Java a "safe" language; however, it also incorporates security mechanisms (Java, 1996b) similar to Safe-Tcl, which permit a Java-enabled Web browser to isolate untrusted applets to "sandboxes"—Java-execution environments with reduced access to operating system resource—where they may

Figure 9.2 A padded cell for executing untrusted agents. Both execution environments can execute the full agent programming language, but requests for access to system resources for agents executing in the untrusted environment are passed back to the trusted execution environment for screening and possible rejection. The Concierge function screens incoming agents and determines whether a given agent is to be trusted or not.

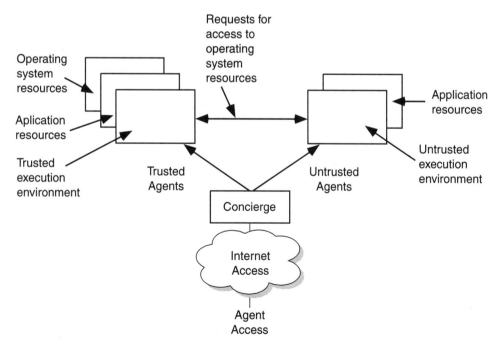

only communicate with the host which sent them. Signed applets, on the other hand, are allowed to communicate with any host, and may also access the file system.

The third of these "security-minded" languages, Telescript, which has been discussed above and in Chapter 8, has perhaps the most extensive overall approach to providing secure environments for agents (whether mobile or not). Telescript has its own proprietary certification and higher-level security protocols, and while these appear to be well-designed, they prevent Telescript-based applications from participating in emerging public standards such as the Secure Electronic Transaction (SET) standard. With Internet-based electronic commerce now almost upon us and destined to grow in the coming years, it is certainly worth your time to become familiar with one or more of these security-minded languages.

While KQML is not commercially available with security features, the Knowledge Sharing Effort community is aware of the practical necessity of such features and Thirunavukkarasu et al. (1995) describe a security architecture for KQML, which adds to the language a basic set of security features.

Security for Mobile Agents

In general, the more an agent travels from environment to environment, the more opportunities there will be for tampering; trusting an agent means trusting every program that ever had write access to it, and (therefore) every program that ever had write access to any of them, and so on transitively. Well-designed access controls and hierarchical authentication services will reduce the danger, but these issues of trust will have to be addressed in designing execution environment controls and agent abilities. Even though the above is somewhat disheartening, certain security goals are, nonetheless, attainable:

- *Origin authentication.* The origin of the agent can be unambiguously established. This can be accomplished by including the public key certificate of the originator as part of the agent. (In practice, this is not enough since data integrity goes hand in hand with origin authentication. In other words, the entire agent must be signed and integrity-protected.)

- *Data integrity.* The body (executable code) of the agent can be integrity-protected, thus allowing for after-the-fact detection of tampering. For example, a malicious execution environment receives a shopping agent that specifies a ceiling of $400 for an airline ticket. The execution environment cheats and ups the ceiling to $500. However, since it cannot produce a corresponding agent integrity check (computed with the aid of digital signatures), the originator can subsequently refuse to pay.

- *Access/itinerary control.* The number and the identity of the execution environments or servers to be visited can be restricted. The user can explicitly specify (or otherwise restrict) the execution environments allowed to execute his or her agent. This is, of course, meaningful only if the agent is protected from tampering (if the agent includes a strong integrity-checking mechanism). Also, access control by explicit naming is not very effective, since this severely handicaps the notion of a free-roaming agent. Consequently, it is more likely that access control (or policy) will be managed at a coarser level, based on attributes such as computing power available, existing level of occupancy of the agent engine, the agent's origins, and its willingness to pay.

- *Agent's privacy.* As alluded to above, it is impossible to keep an agent private unless it visits only a single server. Since one of the intellectually appealing features of mobile agents is precisely the freedom of movement, this is an unrealistic expectation. The bottom line is the fundamental trade-off between the security advantages of fixed itineraries and the flexibility of free roaming.

- *Privacy and integrity of gathered information.* A mobile agent's foremost task is most likely to be to gather information and the privacy of this information is perhaps of greater concern than the privacy of the agent's code. We identify two modes of information gathering: stateless and stateful. The former means that an agent intermittently sends parcels of acquired information home to its user. In the extreme case, the agent sends the information home at every hop. In the stateful mode, the gathered information is attached in some way to the agent (the amount of information that the agent carries grows), but it is only delivered to the originator upon the agent's eventual return. Protecting information in the stateless mode is not difficult; the execution environment currently executing the agent can take care of encrypting/ signing and delivering the information to the agent's originator (or someone designated by the originator). Multiple execution environments executing the same agent cannot interfere with one another unless a malicious execution environment unduly "terminates" an agent, thus preventing it from migrating to other execution environments.

Trusting Your Agents

We have used the word "trust" several times in this chapter, and that may seem an odd word in the context of software technology. It appeals once again to the tendency to anthropomorphism that surrounds agents. We have seen, though, that agents have a number of properties related to security that make this an appropriate term:

1. *Agents are delegated authority by their user.* They act with many of the rights of that user, and for many purposes cannot be distinguished from their user.

2. *Agents have a potential for causing damage.* Because they take on some of the actions of a user and have a much less rigid set of capabilities than a typical application program, they may be able—perhaps inadvertently—to perform actions that would normally be restrained by the observation and judgment of a user.

3. *Their behavior may not be predictable.* While this is true of almost any application program, application programs usually have very well-defined domains of action and can be thoroughly tested over those domains—though even here in practice it is impossible to test all possible combinations of all parameters of even a moderately complex application.

So "trust" begins to seem like an appropriate word. Trust is, after all, a concomitant of delegation. We do not delegate our authority to people we cannot trust. But where does trust come from? How do we arrive at being able to trust our colleagues or our agents? There are several possible sources:

- *Testing and training.* Before I let the agent perform real actions, I run it in a safe mode in which it proposes actions, but does not actually execute them.

- *Limited delegation.* Although the agent acts with my authority, I impose limits on its capabilities.

- *Verification.* The agent must leave an audit trail of its actions, so that I can determine post facto whether it is trustworthy.

- *Reputation.* If I receive a request from an agent client that can prove its user to be a known colleague, I am more inclined to trust it than if it comes from an unknown source. Likewise, if my agent reports information from a server operated by a well-known enterprise or one that was recommended by a friend, then I am inclined to trust it.

In short, it's like trusting people. If you are a trusting type, you will give everyone the benefit of the doubt—at least the first time. If you are not a trusting type, you will demand assurances from third parties. Let's look briefly at these aspects of trust.

Testing and Training

Testing methodologies for conventional applications are well-established, and IS managers should be well experienced in monitoring the incremental testing performed during development and then performing a system validation test before real-world deployment. Testing conventional applications is a costly business, frequently requiring more code development than the application itself. There is no reason to suppose that testing an agent-based application will cost any less. You should be prepared to perform the same stages of incremental testing on the components of an agent-based system as you would for any application.

System validation is a harder problem with agents. For example, if the agent system has a learning capability, its behavior may well be nondeterministic: Outcomes will depend on accumulated knowledge and may vary depending on the order in which the knowledge is acquired (if learning and actions proceed simultaneously). As with conventional applications, system validation should be done in an isolated environment, where accidents will not cause serious harm; but this may be difficult for an agent system that requires access to a very rich set of sources. In conventional testing, one knows a priori the boundaries of the parameter space in which the application must operate; this is much more difficult with agent-based systems.

Defining characteristics of agents include their autonomy and their ability to deal with imprecisely defined situations at the boundaries of their competence or awareness—exactly the combination that can get them, or users, into trouble. One approach, as always, is to establish a separate environment with historical data and to replay that environment against the agent while monitoring the outcomes. But just as it is often not possible to explore all combinations of parameters for a conventional application, so it is likely to be impossible with an agent-based application, and there is no substitute for "real-world" testing or training.

For training, your agents should be designed to be configurable:

- With knowledge of realistic bounds on every kind of action it can take
- With the ability to request confirmation of every kind of action it can take

■ With the ability to log every action performed and the basis of the decision to take that action

Testing will then be able to merge into a limited deployment or training phase, in which the agents have full access to their environment, but are constrained in the actions they can perform without human intervention. As training progresses and your level of trust rises, these "training wheels" can be progressively removed.

System validation would then have the following structure:

1. *Validate component and overall behavior with extensive parametric testing.* Test especially at boundaries of competence. If the agent can learn, start it off with a validated knowledge base, and disable learning until everything else works.

2. *Run live with actions disabled, and monitor proposed actions.* Yes, it takes a lot of time; so does training an assistant, or cleaning up a mess.

3. *Run live with limited authority, and monitor proposed actions.* Gradually increase the scope of the agent's authority, and decrease human monitoring and intervention.

4. *Trust, but verify.*

Training Human Agents

It may be helpful to think of training intelligent agents by analogy to training human agents. We have all had experience of training human agents: colleagues, subordinates, secretaries, and children. Training human agents consists of a number of steps:

1. *Identifying the goal:* "You need to get ready for the school bus."

2. *Identifying the process:* wash, collect, pack, dress; *and the content:* face, hands; books, projects, sports equipment, lunch; backpack, sports bag, lunch pail; shoes, jacket, gloves.

3. *Explaining the environment:* "Your books are on the desk. I will make your lunch."

4. *Identifying the limits of the trainee's authority:* "Do not wear torn clothing. Do not call a taxi if you miss the bus."

5. *Verifying the results:* "Let me look in your backpack."

The training (development) phase of these experiences is very input-oriented (children have a hard time understanding goals as opposed to actions). Over time children are able to recognize the goal itself and to adapt the inputs to meet the goal, so that when the world changes (*winter turns to spring*) they adapt the process to meet the new circumstances (*delete the jacket and gloves*). In a rule-based system, we would say that the agent had created a new rule: *If not winter then delete jacket and gloves*. In reality there is another, implicit goal active here: *keep warm*; agent applications are not today sufficiency sophisticated to deal with implicit goals.

The training phase also requires extensive verification, until the trainer believes that the trainee has understood the process (if not yet the goal); the trainer begins to trust the trainee. Early on, the trainer actively monitors the process execution and corrects errors. Subsequently, the trainer may perform spot checks. Finally, the trainer disengages from the process and gets involved only when problems arise because of errors in the process execution: "Don't blame me if you forgot your homework." In human situations, such problems tend to produce automatic learning on the part of the agent. In agent applications, the error should at least be flagged for human intervention, and may suggest to the trainer the need for additional training (rules).

Verification

Our goal is trusted, autonomous, but auditable behavior. While testing builds confidence, there is no substitute for verifying what is going on. Expect to spend a lot of time in the early phases of system validation trying to understand why the agent did what it did—just like an application, but with potentially many more variables. If the scale and complexity of your system are anything but trivial, you should invest in tools to analyze the agent's log to determine what is going on. You will always be glad to have them in the future, and you will learn much more by being able to run many more test cases than if you have to do it all by hand. Having such tools will make it worthwhile for you to collect extensive logs of the agent's reasoning and decision making. Collect lots; storage is cheap!

Reputation

We have seen above that there is no current technology to prove whether an agent or server is trustworthy, although there are software techniques that improve safety and improve privacy (see Table 9.2). Picking a reputable technology

Table 9.2   Dangers and Precautions in Agent Security

Security Failure	Consequence	Security Measures
Undocumented userids, guessable userids. Userids not requiring a password, guessable passwords. Userid and password information not treated securely.	Unauthorized system access by employees.	Routine and random audits of all hosts and all network management systems. Enforced userid and password policies.
User access to root/system operator privileges. Default resource access too liberal.	Unauthorized resource access; lack of use of access control tools.	Define specific employees with root/system operator privilege. Enforce access control policies.
Physical access to hosts. Physical access to removable media (tape drives, diskette drives).	Unauthorized system access by employees/ public. Loss of private data.	Physically isolate mission-critical hosts and data. Enforce access control policies. Disable diskette drives (very hard to enforce).
Public network access to private hosts. Lack of password attack defenses.	Unauthorized system access by employees/ public.	Remove dial-up access direct to hosts. Install secure dial-up getaway. Reject access after three failed attempts. Install a firewall. Put public servers outside the firewall.
Lack of certification of agents.	Lack of accountability for resource consumption; lack of audit trail; inability to distinguish friend from foe. Unauthorized access to and consumption of resources.	Enforce access controls. Define and enforce a certification policy for employee and public access.

continued

Table 9.2 *Continued*

Security Failure	Consequence	Security Measures
Lack of resource controls.	Unauthorized consumption of resources. Runaway resource consumption by agents. Denial of service attacks.	Enfore access control. Place limits on resource consumption. Test!
Virus admitted.	Servers infected. Other users' clients infected.	Put servers outside firewall. Screen incoming agents for known viruses. Reject unsigned/certified agents. Restrict access to system resources. Scan server files for known viruses. Shut down infected server and regenerate from clean source.
Lack of agent data integrity mechanism.	Agent data tampered with by server.	Visit only trusted servers. Use digital signatures for protecting agent integrity.

base for your agents is a good first step. If you are going to send your agent off to scour the world's Web sites for mission-critical information, stop to think for a moment how much of that information you can trust. The Internet is a free world; anyone can put up a Web site claiming absolute knowledge about trends in stock prices. Don't expect your agent to know the difference between Standard & Poor's and your neighbor's teenage son. You have to decide for yourself which servers you are going to trust; the servers themselves will not tell you. You will either have to manually validate each server to be visited or you will have to collect information about their reputations from colleagues or consultants. Be aware that even the major search engines (AltaVista, Lycos, Yahoo!) perform little quality control on the entries in their databases; they are after volume, not quality. Perhaps one day there will be reputation services for public servers and agent clients will come with an Underwriters Laboratory certificate of their safety. In the meantime, *caveat agent et caveat server!*

Table 9.3   Intelligent Agent Products

Intelligent Agent Product	Source
iKP	http://www.secureway.ibm.com/
Java	http://www.javasoft.com and dozens of other software houses
Kerberos	Implementations from DEC, HP, IBM, OSF, Sun, and many others
Safe-Tcl	ftp://ftp.smli.com/pub/tcl/stc10.2.tar.gz
Telescript	General Magic, Inc., 420 Mary Avenue, Sunnyvale, CA 94086. http://www.genmagic.com/

Summary

Like users or employees, agents can be malicious and they can be incompetent, especially at the boundaries of their training. Good technologies (shown in Table 9.3) exist today for imposing basic security on systems; use them and train your users to use them wisely. Technologies are emerging that include support for these security techniques, offer safer programming techniques, and attempt to prevent dangerous agents from doing damage; learn about them and introduce them. To date, agent software has not greatly worried about security. The two exceptions to this are Telescript, which has put a major effort into this area, and the standards for Web robots (Koster, 1995), which are most etiquette-than security-focused. Expect to spend at least as much effort in training as you would for a conventional application, and probably significantly more. Invest also in an extended training phase, so that you really understand what your agents are doing and are likely to do; you will sleep much better at night.

Technology cannot solve security problems.

Developing and Deploying Intelligent Agents

Developing Agent
Applications

In this chapter we show how the basic components of intelligent agents—
content, machinery, access, and security covered in the last four chapters—can
be put together to build an agent. We use the learning interface agent Open
Sesame! to illustrate the development approach. Since we believe that agents
will get into mainstream computing not as standalone entities but as features
of vertical applications, our particular emphasis will be on how the intelligence
and machinery of such an agent can be integrated into existing applications.

A Learning Interface Agent

Open Sesame! 1.0—released in 1993—was the world's first commercial user
interface (UI) learning agent (Caglayan, Snorrason, Jacoby, Mazzu, and Jones,
1996). What is a learning interface agent? A learning agent sits in the background and observes user interaction with an application, finds repetitive
patterns, and automates them upon approval. The learning agent paradigm
uses the metaphor of a personal assistant because it is responsible for
facilitating user tasks (such as opening and closing documents, performing
desktop maintenance, creating aliases, etc.).

Table 10.1   Open Sesame! UI Elements

Term	Definition
Instruction	A set of directions to the agent on how to carry out a task
Confirmation	A request for user's approval before the agent carries out an instruction
Observation	A behavioral pattern learned by the agent
Suggestion	An agent recommendation to the user

Open Sesame! acquires its knowledge from the user by employing a learning expert system architecture where machine learning techniques perform knowledge acquisition and conventional expert system techniques perform inference and knowledge maintenance. Table 10.1 defines the terms required to discuss the interaction between the user and Open Sesame! without ambiguity.

Open Sesame! watches for two kinds of tasks: *time-based* and *event-based.* A time-based task is something that the user does at a particular time. For example, opening electronic mail every day at nine-o'clock is a time-based task. An event-based task is something that the user does in relation to another task. For example, opening the clock desk accessory before logging into an on-line database is an event-based task. Open Sesame! is based on the learning expert architecture shown in Figure 10.1.

Open Sesame! compares the high-level events (such as opening a folder or quitting an application) generated by the user's mouse clicks and keystrokes with information stored in its learning engine *in the background* and with information stored in its inference engine *in real time.* The learning engine looks for repetitive patterns

Figure 10.1   Open Sesame! architecture.

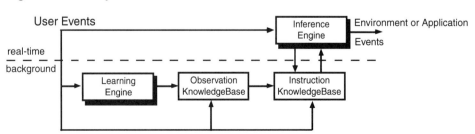

Figure 10.2   Observation dialog box.

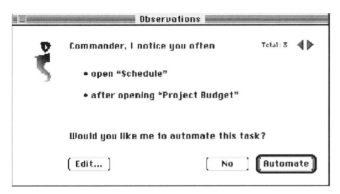

that haven't been automated. If it finds one, then Open Sesame! creates an *observation,* such as the one shown in Figure 10.2.

If the user gives her or his approval, then Open Sesame! creates an *instruction* to automate the task that it observed. The inference engine compares monitored user event patterns with patterns for existing instructions. When it finds a match, the interface engine automatically sends a set of events to the operating system to perform the instruction.

The user can either directly give instructions to the agent or accept the agent's offer of automation for an observed user work pattern. When the agent informs the user of an observation, the user has the following options:

- Accept the observation and have the agent create an instruction.

- Decline the observation.

- Edit the observation to fine-tune the instruction.

- Postpone a decision until later.

The pattern recognition in Open Sesame! 1.0 is based on a neural network paradigm called GEN-ART (Snorrason and Caglayan, 1994; Caglayan and Snorrason, 1993), based on Adaptive Resonance Theory (Carpenter, Grossberg, and Rosen, 1991) to categorize the high-level events it monitors. One advantage of ART type networks is their provision for self-organized learning, which does not require prior knowledge of event-pattern categories. This is accomplished via bottom-up competitive filtering of patterns for finding the "best match" category, combined with top-down template matching for determining if the best match is "good enough." GEN-ART allows the use of customized distance metrics to handle input patterns with qualitative variables. In Open Sesame! 2.0, the neural algorithm has been replaced by the Smarts engine that is based on an event model language due to the lack of scalable performance of neural algorithms on serial machines (Kumar, 1996).

As discussed earlier, there are other possible architectures for agent implementation other than the learning expert system employed in Open Sesame! For instance, case-based reasoning (CBR), based on situation-action pairs, and belief networks, based on casual influence hierarchies, result in architectures where there are no explicit rules. A learning expert system architecture has the advantage of incorporating the *a priori* knowledge directly into the agent application. In contrast, such *a priori* knowledge can only be indirectly incorporated as the behavior of experts in a CBR-based agent architecture.

The learning algorithm in Open Sesame! and other such agents with learning capability can be thought of as the generalization of statistical clustering algorithms onto data structures. What makes these algorithms computationally intelligent is that the results of these learning algorithms are interpreted in contrast to conventional statistical algorithms in which results must be interpreted by human analysts.

In the next couple of sections, we discuss each of the components of this learning agent.

Learning Agent Functional Architecture

Figure 10.2 shows a more detailed functional architecture of the Open Sesame! interface agent. In Open Sesame, the basic construct is an event. The event monitor extracts the high-level events of relevance, such as opening a document, from low-level data monitored, such as mouse clicks. The high-level events inferred from the monitored low-level events are stored in an event database for background processing.

The learning engine finds the facts in the events database. A fact is a logical expression stating a common set of properties shared by event clusters. For instance, a fact can describe an event sequence signifying a repetitive user behavior, or it can describe a set of events with common attribute values signifying the similar behavior of a group of users. The facts are interpreted by a domain-specific interpreter to generate if-then rules to be presented to the user as an observation. The primary function of the fact interpreter is to filter out trivial and inappropriate facts for a particular domain.

Observation database stores the interpreted facts that are presented to the user. If the user approves an automation suggestion, then the fact is turned into a rule to be stored in the instruction database. The instruction database also holds rules for predefined content. The predefined content is critical in the development of practical agent applications as most users do not have the patience to wait for agents to start acting intelligently. Essentially, the predefined content assures an acceptable out-of-the-box user experience until the agent collects a statistically significant amount of data to analyze.

The inference engine works in real time to perform the tasks in the then part of an if-then rule for which the if part matches the current monitored event in the instruction database. In Open Sesame!, the learning agent sends an appropriate event to the operating system such as open a document to execute an instruction.

The computational blocks in the learning agent architecture in Figure 10.3 map to the machinery, content, access, and security components of the agent model considered in the previous chapters as follows:

Figure 10.3   Learning agent functional architecture.

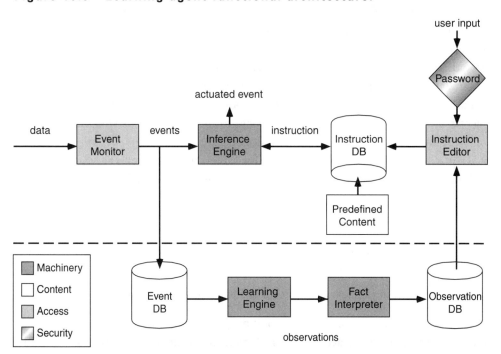

- *Machinery:* learning engine, fact interpreter, inference engine

- *Content:* event database, observation database, predefined content, instruction database

- *Access:* event monitor, instruction editor, event actuation

- *Security:* password protection of learning initiation, observation and instruction databases, encryption of email messages to agent

The learning agent architecture in Figure 10.3 can be easily adapted to an existing application. In this case, the event monitor would record the user's interaction with the application. The interpreted facts would be directly provided to an application program interface (API), unless it makes sense to use the personal assistant metaphor in the application. For instance, the facts can directly update a customer database table for a Web application running on an HTTP server.

Event Modeling

The development of an event monitor requires the cooperation of the third-party application in providing monitoring and actuation support to a learning agent. After more than a decade of personal computing, it is worth noting that the mainstream PC operating systems do not yet incorporate operating system services that would enable personalization such as user preferences, user model, or user work organization style. Monitoring at the operating system level typically involves patching the operating system. Most high-volume applications such as HTTP servers provide APIs suitable for monitoring. In the case of an existing in-house application, monitor development is analogous to factoring an application to make it scriptable or recordable. Whether it is for integrating a learning agent into an in-house application or third-party application with a published API, the process involves:

- Identifying an event dictionary for the application

- Determining an object model encapsulating the user action, application state, and environment of significance for each event

- Implementing the event object model and notification code

In general, the event dictionary is an appropriate subset of the user actions that the application user interface allows, such as menu commands, dialog buttons and controls, and so on. In Open Sesame! the domain is first modeled as a collection of objects, attributes, and events. An object represents a real-world entity such as a document on the desktop or an HTML page on a Web server. Attributes specify the structure and properties of an object. An event is modeled by the change in the value of an object attribute. We discuss each of these concepts briefly below.

An object type definition defines a category of modeled objects for the domain. This definition specifies the possible attributes of the object and establishes the criteria for distinguishing between distinct objects of the given object type. For example, the following defines a document type:

```
Object Type Document

{

Attributes:

    DocumentName: TypeName;

    DocumentCreator: TypeApplication;

    DocumentSize: TypeFloat

    CreationDate: TypeDate;

Forms:

    FormName: {DocumentCreator};

}
```

A form is defined as a named subset of the possible attributes of a given object type that is used in controlling the comparability of objects in the domain. Forms enable multiple views of the same object for clustering purposes. Essentially, object types define which objects can be compared, and object forms define the criteria for object similarity. An object instance represents a snapshot of an object in the domain. Every object instance has a unique object type and form identifier associated with it and defines a value for each of the attribute names in that form. Two object instances are said to have the same *identity* if they have the same object type and form identifier and agree on the values of all the attributes in the form.

Occurrences in the domain that affect domain objects are called events. An event has zero or more targets, each of which is an object instance, and one or more named attributes called the parameters of the event. The target of an event specifies an object whose attribute value changes due to this event. An event type defines a category of related events. For example, the following defines the print document event in Open Sesame:

```
EventType PrintDocument

{

TargetTypes:

    Document;

Parameters:

    Application: TypeApplication;

  Printer: TypePrinter;

};
```

The definition above sets up an event type whose targets are of type *Document,* defined earlier, and that has two parameters—the application, an attribute of type *TypeApplication,* and the printer, an attribute of *TypePrinter.*

Learning Engine

The learning engine processes the stream of events to find recurrent patterns. The event model described in the previous section is used to define the meaning of comparability, similarity, and proximity of events in the application domain. Comparability is defined by object type, similarity is defined by object form, and proximity is defined by the attribute metrics dependent on the domain. The learning engine uses this model to identify clusters of events, analyze the clusters, and generate facts describing the similarity found between the clusters. In general, the clusters can be composed of event sequences, in which case the engine finds recurrent sequential patterns such as repetitive navigation patterns of a user at a Web site. When specialized to the case of sequences of length one, the engine can find events with common attribute values such as the set of users with common information interests at a Web site.

For each new event (e.g., print Excel document; click on link Products on the home page of a Web site), the engine forms sequences by concatenating the event to existing subsequences in the event history. The maximum and minimum lengths of sequences constructed are configurable parameters of the engine.

For each new sequence, the engine identifies the unique collection of sequences with the same identity as the sequence and inserts the new sequence into this collection to form clusters (e.g., all Excel documents printed in printer Money; all users who clicked on Products from .edu domain). The unique collection of sequences that have the same identity as a given sequence is called the primary cluster for the sequence.

So a primary cluster is the set of all sequences derived from the event history that share the same identity. The use of the term *cluster* in this context is consistent with traditional statistical clustering, where a cluster usually denotes a set of vectors in a metric space that are close to each other according to a distance metric.

The clustering in the learning engine incorporates both bottom-up and top-down techniques in the formation and analysis of clusters. The primary clusters are produced from the bottom up by grouping all sequences with several attributes in common by virtue of their identity (e.g., all Word documents created this year; all users who clicked on a particular page from a .com domain). The engine then groups primary clusters according to a configurable set of criteria into a hierarchy of clusters called secondary clusters (e.g., all documents created this year; all users from any domain who clicked on a particular page in a Web site) as shown in Figure 10.4. Secondary clusters are formed by taking the union of primary clusters or other secondary clusters.

The criteria for the formation of primary and secondary clusters are structural—the primary level groups sequences together by identity, and secondary clusters group sequences together by the object and event types in a sequence. The form construct enables a measurement of proximity between events. For example, if a floating point value appears as the value of a parameter of an event, the model designer could "force" events with different values for this attribute to belong to the same primary cluster as an attribute of an object with a null form. Then, sequences containing event instances with *any* value for this parameter will be forced into the same primary cluster. Similarly, when primary clusters are grouped together into secondary clusters the criteria used are typically the types of the

Figure 10.4   Event processing in the learning engine.

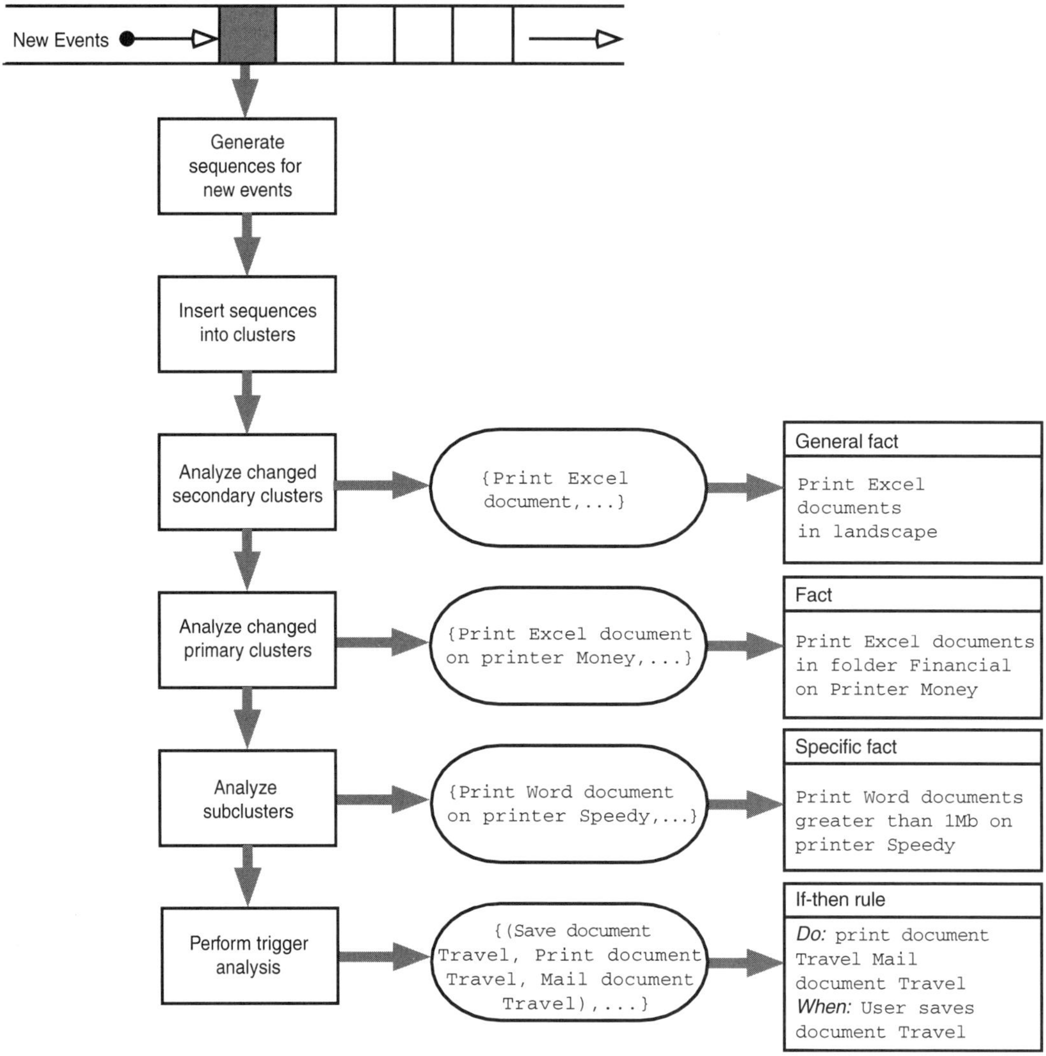

events, and the presence or absence of attributes rather than the proximity of attribute values.

Figure 10.5 shows the event processing in the engine. When a cluster (e.g., all Word documents with size ≥ 1MB; all Word documents with size <1MB), whether

Figure 10.5   Primary and secondary clusters.

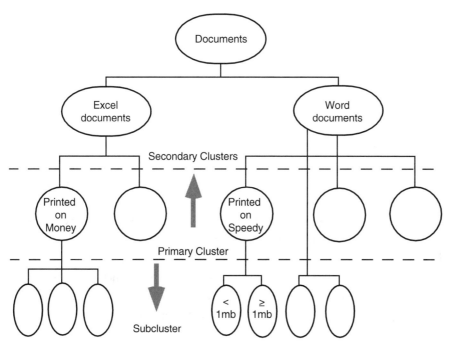

primary or secondary, is analyzed, it may be broken down into subclusters based on the proximity of events according to the type-dependent metric defined in the domain model. In general, the facts produced by analyzing the subclusters are more specific than those obtained by analyzing different clusters.

The output of the learning engine is a fact. A fact is a logical expression that states a common set of properties shared by sequences in a cluster. For example, a fact could signify that the identities of the targets of two events are the same, which implies that the values of the target form attributes agree. On the other hand, not all the attributes need to be in agreement. The nonform attributes on targets and object-valued parameters may vary quite widely between the sequences. The properties shared in common by the sequence are described by a sequence pattern, which may be viewed as a Boolean expression on the event attributes of events in the sequence.

In the cluster analysis phase, a cluster with a given base pattern is analyzed to produce a fact. The base pattern is guaranteed to satisfy the property that every sequence in the cluster satisfies the pattern. The fact output of the analysis will consist of the following:

- A sequence pattern is satisfied by a predetermined percentage of sequences in the cluster.

- A trigger (if one exists).

Figure 10.6 shows the cluster analysis steps. Triggers are used to convert a fact derived from a cluster into an if-then rule. The trigger (e.g., Select All event in a Word application) of a cluster (e.g., the set of sequences—Select All, Copy—in a Word application) is determined by considering a complementary cluster. A *complementary cluster* consists of all possible sequences in the event history which do *not* belong to the given cluster but also satisfy this prefix of the pattern in the analyzed cluster (e.g., the set of all other sequences that start with the Select All event: {(Select All, Cut), (Select All, Clear)}). If the ratio of the complementary cluster size divided by the analyzed cluster size is smaller than a predetermined fixed percentage, and is unique according to a predetermined criterion, then the prefix is used as

Figure 10.6   Cluster analysis steps.

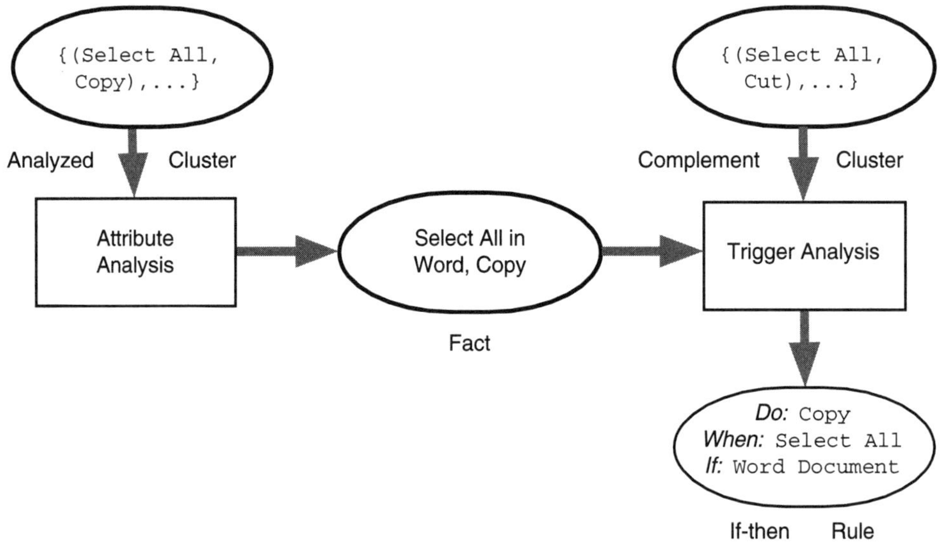

a predictive trigger for the reset of the sequence pattern. Thus, the trigger is used to convert the fact into an if-then form where the if part is the set of conditions in the prefix and the then part is the set of conditions in the rest of the pattern. Depending upon the domain, the part can then be interpreted as an action to be taken or a conclusion to be made, or can be used as a rule in a rule-based system.

During attribute analysis the learning engine examines the sequences in a cluster on an attribute-by-attribute basis. The values of a given attribute are compared to determine if a suitable attribute template can be generated for the attribute type definition. User-defined distance functions and comparison operators are used during this process. The order in which the engine learns the values for the attribute is summarized below.

- Learn an exact value for the attribute:
    - If the attribute behavior is *crisp,* then an attribute template is learned if a predetermined percentage of the attributes have the same value.
    - If the attribute behavior is *fuzzy,* the distance and comparison functions are used for learning. A fuzzy value is learned if, for a predetermined percentage of the attributes, the distance to the medium value is less than a fixed threshold.
- If an exact value cannot be learned, then the engine tries to learn a range using the specified distance functions and range widths.
- If an exact value or range for an attribute cannot be learned, then the engine tries to learn an object template such that a fixed percentage of the object values satisfy the template. This process recursively tries to learn the values of the attributes of the objects, on an attribute-by-attribute basis.

Fact Interpretation

The facts generated by the learning engine are interpreted by predefined domain-dependent rules. The main objective of fact interpretation is to validate, maintain, and decide on the course of action for facts. The validation typically involves filtering out trivial facts (similar to ignoring "the," "a," etc. in document filtering) and those determined inappropriate for the domain (e.g., repeated user mistakes such as `{(copy document A, delete copy of document A),...}`). In addition, the fact

Table 10.2 Knowledge Maintenance

Relationships	Description
Redundant	Candidate rule tasks are included in an existing rule
Reduction	Existing rule tasks are included in candidate rule tasks
Conflict	Candidate rule tasks conflict with the tasks of an existing rule
SelfConflict	A candidate rule conflicts with the other tasks of the same candidate rule
Abstraction	A candidate rule that generalizes one or more existing rules
Specialization	A candidate rule that is a special case of an existing rule
Equivalent	Two identical rules

interpretation involves knowledge maintenance functions. Table 10.2 outlines the possible set of assertions that can result when a candidate rule is compared against the list of known rules (rules in the instruction database and observations in the observation database). Here, the rule tasks are user actions performed after the trigger event.

Fact interpretation also handles special cases arising from learning of repetitive patterns in the user-agent interaction. These cases typically include the following:

- The user turns down agent offer to automate a specific kind of task.
- The user repeatedly undoes the action of an automation performed by the agent.
- The user repeatedly undoes the action of an automation performed by the agent under certain conditions.
- The user repeatedly disapproves the launch of a scheduled agent task.
- The user disapproves the launch of a scheduled agent task under certain conditions.
- The user's agent interaction preferences do not match the user's actual interaction with the agent.

Domain-specific rules are needed to interpret the learning agent's identification of the repetitive patterns in the user-agent interaction described above. Table 10.3

Table 10.3   Fact Interpretation for Agent-User Interaction

Behavior	Agent Interpretation Rule
User declines agent offer to automate	Offer only less general observations for this kind of behavior
User repeatedly undoes agent action	Offer to turn off the existing rule
User undoes agent action under some conditions	Offer to make the rule more specific to match the learned conditions
User repeatedly disapproves the start of a scheduled agent task	Offer to turn off the existing rule
User disapproves the start of a scheduled agent task under certain conditions	Offer to make the rule more specific to match the learned conditions
Agent interaction preference does not match user behavior	Offer to change the agent interaction preference to match user behavior

lists a possible set of interpretation rules for the generic kinds of repetitive patterns for user-agent interaction.

Let's consider some examples for the generic cases considered in Table 10.3. For instance, suppose that the user declines the agent's offer to set the sound Control Panel volume to high when the user inserts an audio CD. From then on, the agent would offer only a more specific observation such as setting the sound volume to high when the user inserts an audio CD in the evenings.

Suppose now that the user already has already given an instruction to the agent to set the sound volume high when the user inserts an audio CD, and suppose further that the user undoes the agent's action during the office hours. In this case, the agent would offer to change the instruction so that it would be in effect only during the evening hours.

As an example of an agent interaction preference, suppose the user has indicated a preference to have the agent immediately notify any new observations, and suppose further that the user dismisses the agent without reading any of these observations. In this case, the agent would offer to change agent notification to an interaction style that lets the user read observations at his or her leisure.

Observations

The facts from the fact interpreter are stored in an observation database. Depending on the application metaphor, these facts can trigger various courses of agent behavior. For instance, if a personal assistant metaphor is used, then the facts can be used to present the following:

- In-context tips
- Coaching when the user needs help
- Proactive assistance
- Shortcuts for a sequence of steps
- Customized offer based on learned user preferences
- Automation offer for repetitive user tasks
- Automation suggestions based on what the user is not doing
- Notification of significant events

Here are some examples for the generic class of observations listed above.

Tips: Figure 10.7 shows an example of an in-context tip. Here, the agent offers a tip when it observes that the user is shift-clicking a large number of items in a

Figure 10.7   In-context agent tip.

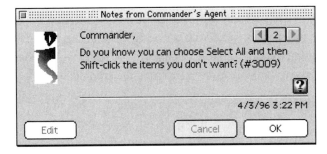

list one by one. Such functionality can be used to replace tip-of-the-day functionality found in most desktop applications. Alternatively, these tips can be seamlessly integrated into a dynamically generated HTML page for Web site personalization.

Coaching: Figure 10.8 shows a coaching suggestion when the user needs help. Here, the agent offers to bring the relevant system help to the user when the user needs it. In this example, the agent would notice that the user is capturing the screen in order to print the contents of a folder. Do you think that Internet search engines would benefit from an on-line coach?

Proactive assistance: Figure 10.9 shows an example of proactive assistance by a learning agent. In this example, the agent observes that the user is having a hard time in changing the name of a sharable disk and offers to do this task on behalf of the user. Don't you wish your Web browser could notice that you are having a hard time in guessing the correct URL address of an organization, and offer to help? So the agent can give you the correct URL for Fidelity Investments instead of the message in Figure 10.10.

Figure 10.8   Agent coaching when the user needs help.

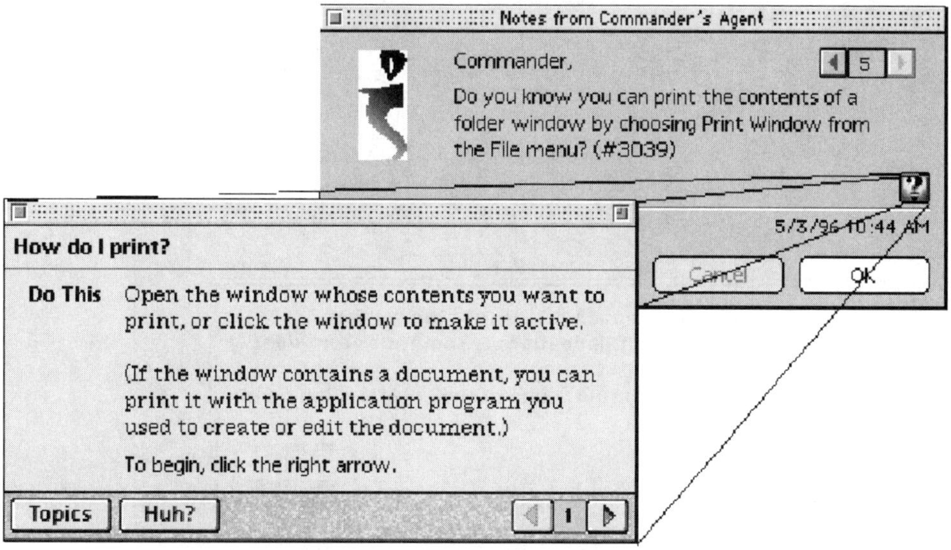

Figure 10.9   Proactive agent assistance.

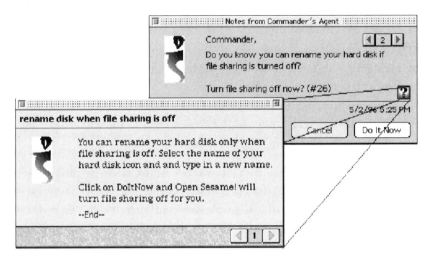

Figure 10.10   Need for proactive assistance.

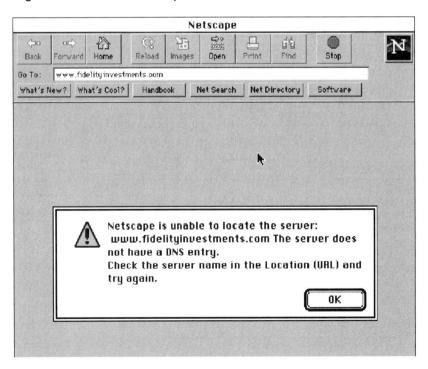

Shortcuts: Figure 10.11 shows an agent recommendation for a shortcut. Here the agent observes that the user repeatedly opens one application document with another application without taking advantage of the drag-and-drop feature, and suggests this shortcut to the user.

Customization: Figure 10.12 shows an agent offer to customize the user's Control Panel settings according to the learned user preferences. Here, the agent notices the user's preference to have her or his desktop icons aligned and

Figure 10.11 Agent shortcut recommendation.

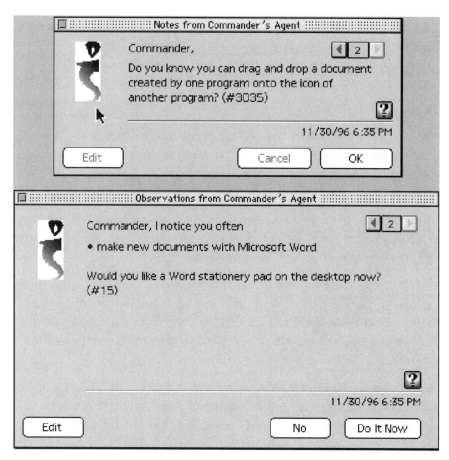

Figure 10.12   Agent customization.

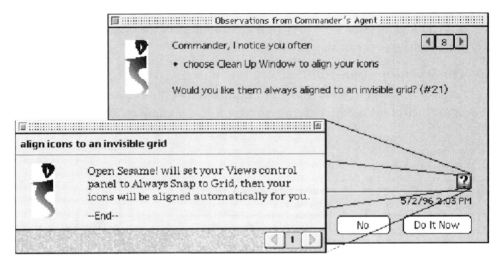

offers to customize the Views Control Panel to automatically accomplish this task for the user. When was the last time you changed the preferences in your Web browser or mail program to suit your workstyle?

Automation: Figure 10.13 shows an example of an agent offer to automate a repetitive user task. Here the agent learns that the user spell checks Word documents before printing them, and offers to automate this task for the user. In this example, the trigger is printing a Word document.

Suggestions: Figure 10.14 shows an agent suggestion. These agent suggestions are typically triggered by the user not performing desirable repetitive behavior. In this example, the agent notices that the user has not changed passwords for over a month, and offers to remind the user to change passwords every month.

Notification: Figure 10.15 shows an example of an agent notification for a significant event. This message is the result of an earlier user instruction to the agent to notify the user when a user connects to his or her machine.

Figure 10.13   Agent task automation.

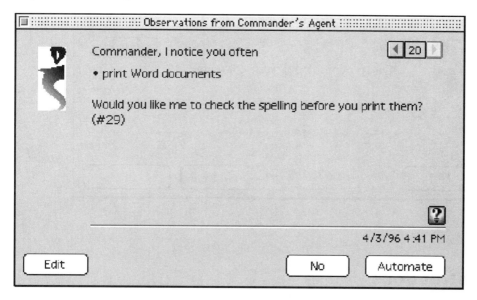

Figure 10.14   Agent suggestion for what the user is not doing.

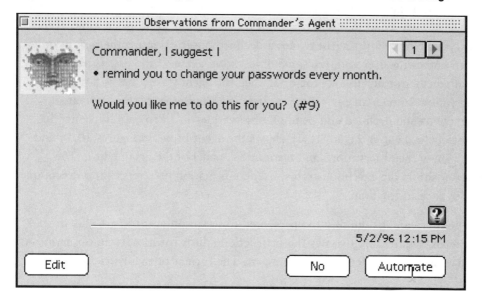

Figure 10.15   Agent event notification.

Instructions

In the last section, we covered a number of observations that the agent can present
to the user. If the user clicks Automate in any of these observations, then the agent
creates an instruction that will carry out the task at the appropriate time. If the
user clicks No, then the agent makes a declined observation for the task in order
not to bother the user with the same observation again. If the user is not sure
about whether or not to take the offer, then the agent leaves this as a pending
observation. In such an environment, there is a need to store the automated
instructions and declined and pending observations in a browser conveniently
accessible to the user. Figure 10.16 shows the agent browser. Figures 10.16 and
10.17 show the observations and instructions panel of the agent editor. The
browser shows the execution status, user confirmation preference, and execution
log for each instruction.

The user can also modify the presented observation according to his or
her needs. Figure 10.18 shows the instruction editor for modifying observations
or making new instructions for the agent. The format of the instructions is
given by:

Figure 10.16   Agent observations.

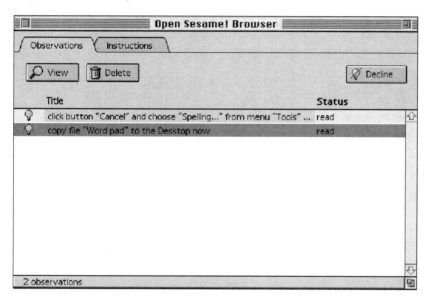

Figure 10.17   Agent instructions.

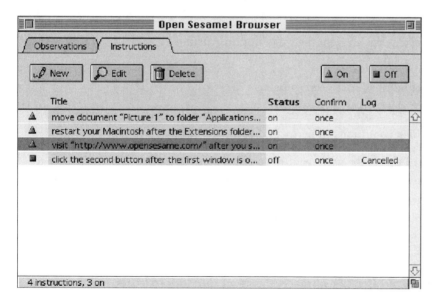

Figure 10.18   Agent instruction editor.

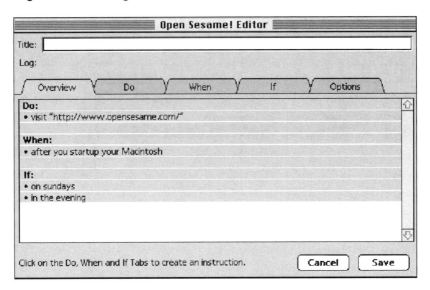

Do:

- A sequence of tasks to be performed by the agent

When:

- The event that triggers the execution instruction

If:

- The conditions that need to be true for execution

In summary, the editor enables the user to instruct the agent as to what, when, and under which conditions to perform a sequence of related tasks.

Figure 10.19 shows the user agent interaction preferences that enable the user to specify the user's desired communication style with the agent. Here, the user can specify the agent's interaction frequency (from time to time, once a day, rarely), and announcement options for new observations.

The instruction database also contains predefined content that defines the out-of-the-box experience of the agent. Typically, these instructions highlight the agent's functionality to the user. For instance, the agent can offer to let the user know

Figure 10.19   User agent interaction preference specification.

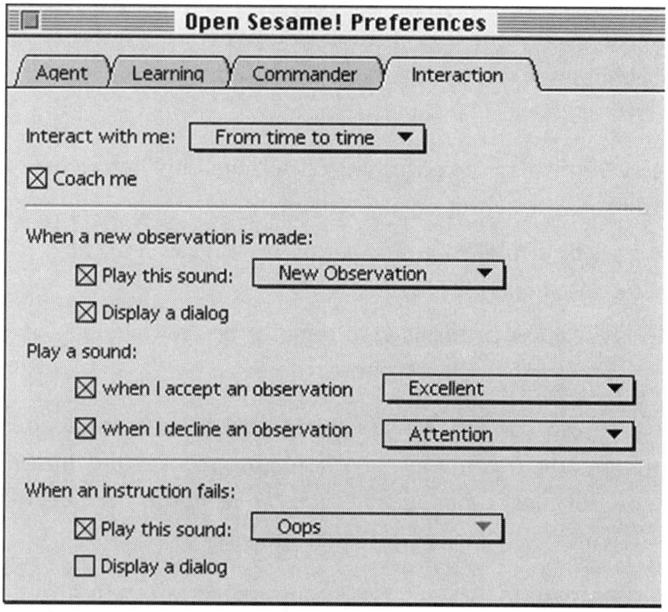

whenever someone connects or disconnects from his or her machine after the first occurrence of such an event.

User access to the instruction editor is password protected in order to guard the privacy of learned observations and user instructions. At startup the agent asks the user for his or her password. If someone else doesn't supply the correct password, then the agent won't run, so it won't learn anyone else's work patterns, and no one else will see the user's instructions. In addition, the user can send the agent instructions via an email message. In this case, the email message needs to be encrypted for security.

Inference

The agent inference engine compares the incoming user event patterns in real time to the trigger events of instructions that have already been automated. If the agent finds such an instruction, and if the "if" conditions of that instruction are also satisfied, then the agent performs the tasks specified under "Do" in the instruction. The user can instruct the agent to confirm with the user before carrying out the instruction in a number of different ways; by clicking on the "Edit" button in Figure 10.20.

- *Confirm Once:* The agent displays a confirmation message only before the first time it carries out the instruction.

- *Confirm Always:* The agent displays a confirmation message every time before it carries out the instruction.

- *Don't Confirm:* The agent never confirms with the user before carrying out the instruction.

It's a good design practice to use Confirm Always as the default for agent actions that are undoable (e.g., emptying the trash). On the other hand, the use of Confirm Once as a default makes sense for most other agent actions so as not to needlessly bother the user.

Figure 10.21 shows the confirmation message for an automated instruction. If the user clicks OK, then the agent performs the task. If the user clicks Cancel, then the agent does not perform the automated task for this specific occurrence.

Figure 10.20   Agent notification request.

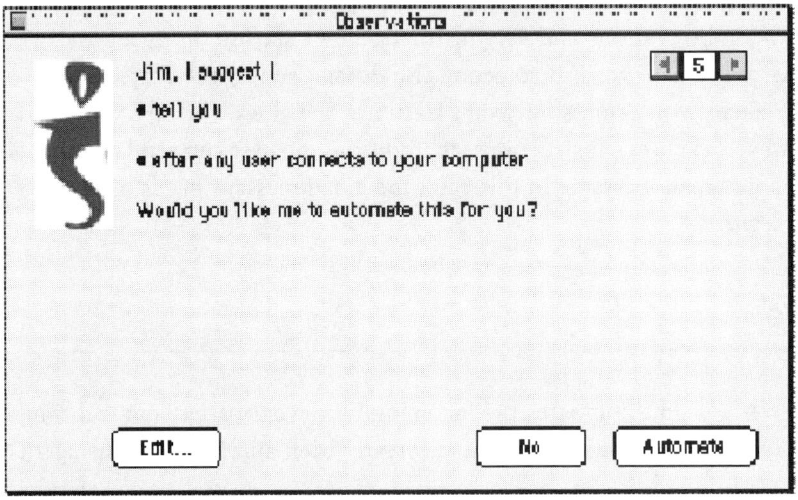

Figure 10.21   Agent confirmation message.

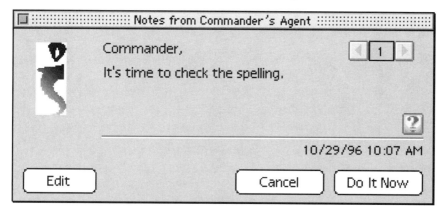

The inference engine then sends an appropriate message to the environment to carry out the task to be performed. For instance, this would involve sending an Apple Event in MacOS, a system message in Windows, an HTTP command for a Web application.

Summary

In this chapter we discussed how the basic components of intelligent agents—content, machinery, access, and security, discussed in chapters 5 through 9—can be put together to build an agent. In particular, we used a learning interface agent to show how the intelligence and machinery of such an agent can be integrated into existing applications.

The development methodology includes developing an object model for the application events, processing the modeled events with a learning engine to discover facts in data, and interpreting the generated facts by domain-dependent rules to produce agent tips, proactive assistance, shortcuts, recommendations, customization, and automation suggestions for the user.

Deploying an
Intelligent Agent
for a Web Site

In the last chapter, we showed how the basic components of intelligent agents—content, machinery, access, and security—can be put together to build an agent. In this chapter, we show how to personalize a Web site using the learning engine described in the previous chapter and other similar tools.

Web Site Personalization

Web site personalization can be broadly defined as the customized delivery of Web site content according to the unique individual preferences of each user visiting a site. That is, Web site personalization enables a business to establish a one-to-one communication channel with its customers. Many kinds of applications are possible with Web site personalization. Here are some examples:

- *Personalized newspaper.* A publisher can deliver personalized news to each of its subscribers.

- *Personalized store fronts.* An on-line merchant (book, music, computer retailer) can make customized recommendations based on user preferences and transaction history.

■ *Customized service providers.* An on-line service provider can make personalized recommendations (videos, advertisements, chatrooms, etc.) based on individual user preferences, and preferences of similar users.

In order to discuss the issues involved incorporating personalization into a Web site, we describe a concrete example—a personalized entertainment agent at http://www.opensesame.com. Figure 11.1 explains the operation of such a site. Here, the agent collects new content from content providers including book retailers and publishers, event listing services, music publishers and retailers, movie studios and ticket outlets, and TV studios and listing services. Users register with the site by completing a quick personal information and entertainment interest profile. The agent then serves a customized version of the available content according to the initial user profile. In this case, the customized information would be new books, concerts, CDs, movies, and TV programs that would interest the user. The agent then learns the user's special interests by watching what the user does with the recommended information. Based on the learned preferences, the agent makes recommendations and learns user interests further from the agent-user interaction. Each successive visit, the agent presents a more personalized package of the content matching the user's interests.

Before we discuss how such a personalized agent can be developed into a Web site, let's consider the design decisions involved in building such an application.

Personalization Content

Which content needs to drive the personalization, and what content will be customized through personalization? In general, user data drives the personalized delivery of the Web site content:

■ *User data.* User data drives the personalization process. For instance, persistent demographic information (e.g., age, gender), dynamic user interests (music, travel), user environment (e.g., location, browser, connection speed), user transaction history (e.g., seasonal purchases), user behavior at the site (e.g., hyperlinks clicked, followed, skipped) can all be used for personalization. Hence, it's necessary to develop and maintain a user content database for personalization. The choice of user information for personalization would imply the development of constructs ranging from a simple user profile form to a monitor for tracking user behavior at the site.

Figure 11.1   Personalized web site operation.

Read a book review

Listen to a CD clip

Buy concert tickets

1 Content

Agent collects new content directly from the Web or other content databases.

2 User Profile

Users register their interest preferences with the agent, choosing from lists of interests and interest profiles.

3 Customized Content

Agent serves new information to users according to their preferences, organized for clarity and hyperlinked for further action.

4 Learning at Work

Using machine learning, agent learns more about its users' preferences from what they click on and where they go.

5 User Interaction

Agent suggests changes to the user's profile and learns from user feedback.

6 Personalized Content

Each successive visit, agent gives new information and ideas matching user's interests, tastes and preferences.

Level of Personalization

What level of personalization does your application require? There are three options:

- *Customization.* The user fills out a profile, and the agent delivers content according to this profile without learning from user behavior. Currently, most personalized newspapers deliver using such a model. Unfortunately, such an approach requires the user to explicitly change his or her profile in order to change the delivered customized content. When was the last time you changed the preferences in your Web browser?

- *Learning user interests.* The agent monitors user behavior to learn individual user interests by watching what a user clicks does with a particular recommendation, and how much time he or she spends on a given page to learn repetitive behavior. Such an approach has the advantage of adapting to changing user preferences automatically.

- *Learning community behavior.* The agent compares user preferences to those of other users with similar interests. Such an approach usually requires that the user explicitly rate a particular topic, and is usually more applicable to domains involving a subjective rating. This approach has the advantage of encouraging user exploration.

Personalization Tasks

Once the level of personalization is selected, then the personalization tasks to be implemented need to be decided. These are mostly domain dependent and include:

- *Information filtering.* The domain problem usually dictates the kinds of information filtering, new product or service announcements, and product or service recommendations based on user preferences.

- *Presentation customization.* Content delivery (e.g., email, personal Web pages, etc.) and presentation format (e.g., based on user domain, Web browser, etc.) can be customized based on user preferences.

- *Customized communication.* The presentation of content about a company's products, services, and advertisements can be customized based on the learned history of user interaction with the company.

User Experience

The user experience decisions that need to be addressed include:

- *Explicit vs. implicit rankings.* Some collaborative filtering tools require that the user explicitly rate a minimum number of recommendations in order to determine his or her likes and dislikes. Some tools do not require the explicit user rankings as they rely on implicitly determining user likes and dislikes by watching user behavior. As explicit rankings impose an additional workload on users, the user experience design requires a decision as to whether such a ranking system makes sense for your Web site customers.

- *User identification.* Since HTTP is essentially a stateless protocol, a personalized site usually requires that the user specify a user name and password for revisits. The user can be identified by using cookies during revisits. However, the use of session ID is usually required to support users with older Web browsers that do not support cookies.

Architecture

The incorporation of personalization into a Web site involves making decisions about the following:

- *Client/server.* One of the issues to be decided is whether to require your users to have a client plug-in. Some personalization tools support a server-only personalization without requiring any client plug-in. With the emergence of Java-enabled browsers, such Web browser plug-ins will mostly fade away.

- *Content database.* A content database stores the information that is personalized for presentation to the user. The content database can cover Web site content, enterprise intranet content, content databases from service providers, and the Web. Because personalization requires the matching of individual user interests against the metadata, this content needs to be indexed. If the site incorporates a content database, then the database tables supply most of the needed indexing. If the site is a collection of HTML pages, then an indexing engine such as the Verity Search 97 is needed to generate the metadata via keywords. If the content is to be harvested from the Web, then a Web crawler is needed.

Business and Ethical Issues

The collection of user interaction data raises both business and ethical issues:

- *Business Issues.* Some personalization tools require a business model where the user interaction data belongs to the tool publisher, whereas some tools are licensed according to a conventional fixed-fee or royalty-based license model. The up-front acquisition costs are usually lower for the licensing models where the tool maker participates in the value generated by the personalized application, not unlike the royalty-based licensing model for high-end OEM databases and scripting environments. In the Web arena, there will be other models where your site may participate as part of a network that stores the user interaction data. Obviously, these are business decisions to be made depending on the particular application.

- *Ethics.* The introduction of learning user behavior brings about ethical issues as well. It would serve your company best if your personalized Web site protected the privacy of the personal data collected. Similarly, Web nettiquette suggests that the user should be made aware of the data collection for personalization so that he or she can make an active choice to participate in such a personalized site. Similarly, common courtesy would require that your site disclose the intended use of the collected data. In summary, we suggest that your company treat the collected user interaction data as jointly owned by your company and users.

Personalized Web Site Development

Here, we present the key backend development in building a personalized Web site such as http://www.opensesame.com, described in the previous section.

User Identification

Table 11.1 shows the SQL statements embedded in the HTML document that is responsible for identifying the user when the user logs in at http://www.opensesame. com. At this site, the user is assigned the session ID number 721704494, and the user ID 1428648848888411 is identified from the browser cookie on the user's client machine. The user ID number, time spent, and the page visited (whatsnew.cfm) is entered into the user database using the SQL statement INSERT INTO.

Table 11.1   SQL Statements for User Identification

WHOAMI (Records=1, Time=16ms)

SQL =

SELECT * FROM session WHERE sessionid = 721704494

USER (Records=1, Time=16ms)

SQL =

SELECT * FROM user WHERE id=1428648848888411

(Records=0, Time=0ms)

SQL =

UPDATE user SET lasthit='97-01-15 22:03' WHERE id==1428648848888411

(Records=0, Time=0ms)

SQL =

UPDATE session SET lasthit='97-01-15 22:03' WHERE sessionid=='721704494'

(Records=0, Time=0ms)

SQL =

INSERT INTO sessionlog (userid,timestamp,pagedef) VALUES

    ('1428648848888411','97-01-15 22:03:05','whatsnew.cfm')

User Behavior

The personalization agent uses the learning engine described in the previous chapter to learn the information interests of each user. The input for the engine comes
from user interaction data compiled using the technique in Table 11.1. The personalization goal is to identify topic categories and keywords of interest to specific
users of the Web site based upon the pages that they have visited at your site and
to present the Web site content according to the interests of each user.

To accomplish this task requires a mechanism that associates each URL on the
Web site with a set of keywords and a category for the URL. Such a mechanism is

available on this Web site built over a collection of databases. If this is not available then an indexing engine can be used. The categories are assumed to be organized in a hierarchy which is also specified within the domain knowledge, and the learning engine described in the previous chapter is used to determine the most specific category that matches the predominant number of the pages that the user visits.

Table 11.2 shows a sample of user interaction data (the pages visited by users) that lists a set of URLs requested by users. From this data we would like to obtain a description of the most specific category that matches the interests of each user based upon the pages visited as well as set of keywords that characterize the interests of each user. Figure 11.2 illustrates a sample category for this example.

Event Diagram

The learning engine (Caglayan et al., 1997) provides a framework for modeling a dynamic environment in which the states of domain *objects* undergo changes as a result of actions by other domain entities. The client application (in this case the Web server) presents the engine with a continuous stream of time-stamped snapshots called *events*, that describe occurrences in this environment and the states of the objects affected by these occurrences. The engine analyzes this event stream, and incrementally identifies recurrent sequential patterns in the event stream, called *facts*. These facts are then passed back to the client for application-specific interpretation.

Table 11.2   User Interaction Data

URL	URL
\music\brahms.htm	krishna@brain.com
\music\coltrane.htm	joe@aol.com
\music\mozart.htm	krishna@brain.com
\music\haydn.htm	krishna@brain.com
\music\miles.htm	joe@aol.com
\music\wynton.htm	joe@aol.com
\music\wynton.htm	krishna@brain.com

Figure 11.2   Music interest categories.

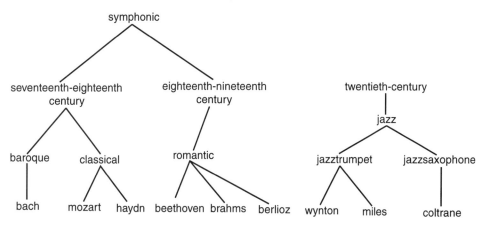

The learning engine includes a language that provides a structured vocabulary in which clients describe the domain objects and events. This language is used to construct a domain model that encodes client-specific notions of comparability, similarity, and proximity of objects and events. Using this model, the client converts application-specific data into an event stream, and interprets the facts output by the engine. The engine uses the model to identify *clusters* of similar sequences of events in the event stream, to analyze the clusters, and to construct facts describing the similarities found between the sequences in the clusters.

The engine used is a C++ toolkit which consists of a class library and header files that encapsulate the learning functionality described above, as well as a utility that compiles models written in the domain *model definition language* (MDL). The MDL compiler constructs the relevant tables needed by the engine. It also automatically generates certain header files that are needed to incorporate identifiers defined in the domain model into the C++ code used to construct events and interpret facts.

Figure 11.3 shows the visual representation of an object where an event is represented by a rectangular node. Each event has two parameters, a URL object and a network agent object indicating the user and the URL requested. For each URL, the event factory in the learning engine constructs the category and keyword objects and attaches the information to the URL object.

Figure 11.3   Visual representation of a user event.

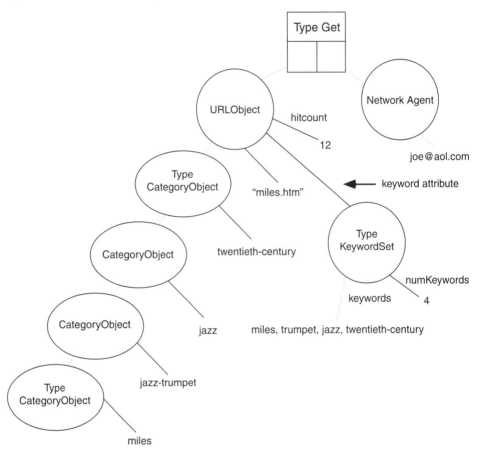

Target(s) are represented by objects attached to a double line emanating from the sides of the rectangle, while parameters are shown by edges emanating from the bottom. The type, ID, and version of the event are indicated within the rectangle.

The URL categories shown are used to map each URL to the most specific category that describes its contents, as shown in Table 11.3. Also each URL is also associated with a set of keywords, as shown in Table 11.4.

Table 11.3   URL Category Mapping

URL	Category
\music\beethoven.htm	beethoven
\music\mozart.htm	mozart
\music\haydn.htm	haydn
\music\berlioz.htm	berlioz
\music\coltrane.htm	coltrane
\music\bach.htm	bach
\music\brahms.htm	brahms
\music\bartok.htm	bartok
\music\miles.htm	miles
\music\wynton.htm	wynton
\music\branford.htm	branford
\music\ellis.htm	ellis
\music\ella.htm	ella

Domain Model

The following example shows the domain model for this application which was used to construct events such as in Figure 11.3. MDL particular to this learning engine is used for the machine representation of the visual notation in Figure 11.3. Tables 11.3 and 11.4 specify the domain knowledge, consisting of URL-keyword associations and URL-category associations.

Table 11.4   URL Keyword Mapping

URL	Keywords
\music\beethoven.htm	beethoven,romantic,piano,classical,composer,
\music\mozart.htm	mozart,classical,composer,symphony,piano, seventeenth-century,

continued

Table 11.4 *Continued*

URL	Keywords
\music\haydn.htm	haydn,piano,seventeenth-century,symphony,classical,
\music\berlioz.htm	berlioz,romantic,symphony,french,
\music\coltrane.htm	coltrane,saxophone,jazz,twentieth-century,
\music\bach.htm	bach,baroque,sixteenth-century,classical,
\music\brahms.htm	brahms,romantic,symphony,piano,classical, nineteenth-century,
\music\bartok.htm	bartok,twentieth-century,classical,
\music\miles.htm	miles,trumpet,jazz,twentieth-century,
\music\wynton.htm	wynton,trumpet,jazz,twentieth-century,marsalis,
\music\branford.htm	branford,marsalis,saxophone,jazz,twentieth-century,
\music\ellis.htm	ellis,marsalis,piano,jazz,twentieth-century,
\music\ella.htm	ella,vocal,jazz,twentieth-century,

In this sample MDL code, objects of type URL are attached to events and objects through this attribute type. This attribute type defines a distance metric for URL attributes which will be used in clustering URLs. The distance between two URLs is defined as the distance (in links) between the categories in the category hierarchy. Two URLs are considered close if they are within three links of each other. The URL DistanceFunction is implemented in the Class Factory.

```
//======================================================
//World model for the HTTP server world (WebWorld.mod)
//======================================================
AttributeType TypeString
{
BaseType: Text;
}
AttributeType TypeLocator
```

```
{

BaseType: Text;

}

AttributeType TypeUnsigned

{

BaseType: Unsigned;

Behavior: Fuzzy;

FuzzyNeighborhood:20;

RangeWidth: 50;

}

//Objects of type category will be attached to events and objects

through this attribute type.

AttributeType TypeCategory

{

BaseType: Object;

}

AttributeType TypeBinary

{

BaseType: Binary;

}

//Objects of type keyword set will be attached to events and

objects through this attribute type.

AttributeType TypeKeywordSet

{

BaseType: Object;

}
```

```
AttributeType TypeURL

{

BaseType: Object;

Behavior: Fuzzy;

FuzzyNeighborhood : 3;

DistanceFunction: URLsDistanceFunction;

}

//Objects of type Agent will be attached to events and objects

through this attribute type.

AttributeType TypeAgent

{

BaseType: Object

}

//======================================================

//OBJECT TYPES

//======================================================

ObjectType URLObject

{

Attributes:

    Locator: TypeLocator;

    Category: TypeCategory;

    HitCount: TypeUnsigned;

    URLKeywords: TypeKeywordSet;

Forms:

    FormLocator:{Locator};

}
```

```
//Each category has a name and a pointer to its super-category

object.

ObjectType CategoryObject

{

Attributes:

    Name: TypeString;

    Super: TypeCategory;

Forms:

    FormNameSuper: {Name,Super};

}

ObjectType NetworkAgentObject

{

Attributes:

    IPAddress: TypeString;

    UserName: TypeString;

    UserAddress: TypeString;

    UserDomain: TypeString;

Forms:

    FormAddress: {IPAddress};

    FormNameDomain: {UserName,UserAddress,UserDomain};

}

ObjectType KeywordSet

{

Attributes:

    Keywords: TypeString;

    NumberOfKeywords: TypeUnsigned;
```

```
Forms:

    FormKeywords: {Keywords};

}

//==================================================

//EVENT TYPE

//==================================================

EventType Get

{

Parameters:

    GetURL: TypeURL;

    RequestingAgent: TypeAgent;

}
```

The learning engine determines the types of clusters from the domain model. For the domain model above, there is only one event type GET. For simplicity, we consider only sequences of length one.

Clustering

The learning engine determines the primary clusters formed by events, allocating one primary cluster for each distinct event identity. Table 11.5 shows how identity is determined for the event objects.

Secondary clustering uses the default clustering which drops all the attributes and retains only the types of the events and objects. This implies that there is only one secondary cluster formed for the entire set of data for this example.

Table 11.5   Event Object Identity

Identity	Determined by
GET	URL Object and requesting agent
URL	Locator attribute of URL object
User Agent Object	User ID

The distance between two URLs is defined as the number of links between them in the category hierarchy. The distance is infinite if there is no path between the categories associated with the URLs. The engine is configured to subcluster the secondary clusters, and so the analysis of the secondary clusters groups together URLs that are close to each other and were visited by the same user. In fact, it is this group of secondary clusters that typically yields information about the general interests of a specific user based upon the URLs visited by the user.

Learned User Interests

The sample data shows that the user krishna@brain.com looks at the pages brahms.html, mozart.html, and haydn.html. The most specific category that covers this set of pages is the category *symphonic*. Similarly, the user joe@aol.com looks at the wynton.htm, miles.htm, and coltrane.htm pages and the most specific category that covers this set of pages is *jazz*.

From the given data there are seven unique URL-user pairs, which each have a primary cluster and one secondary cluster corresponding to the event type GET. Subclusters of the secondary cluster contain information about the general interests of each user.

The more interesting results come from the analysis of the subclusters in the single secondary cluster. The subcluster consisting of the URLs requested by joe@aol.com yields the following fact, shown visually in Figure 11.4.

```
-------------------FACT-------------------

Source: Secondary Cluster (Id=2)

Trigger Prefix: [0..0]

Pattern length = 1

-----------

Get

{

  GetURL

  {
```

```
URLObject()

{

 Category

 {

  CategoryObject(FormNameSuper)

  {

   Name==twentieth-century

   Super

   {

    CategoryObject(FormNameSuper)

    {

      Name==jazz

      Super

      {

       CategoryObject()

       {

        Super

        {

         CategoryObject()

         {

         }

        }

       }

      }

     }

    }
```

```
      }

       }

      }

   HitCount==4

   URLKeywords

   {

    KeywordSet()

     {

    Keywords==jazz

     }

    }

   }

  }

 RequestingAgent

 {

  NetworkAgentObject()

   {

    IPAddress==joe@aol.com

   }

  }

 }

Proxies

 {

 }
```

Figure 11.4   Learned fact—jazz interest.

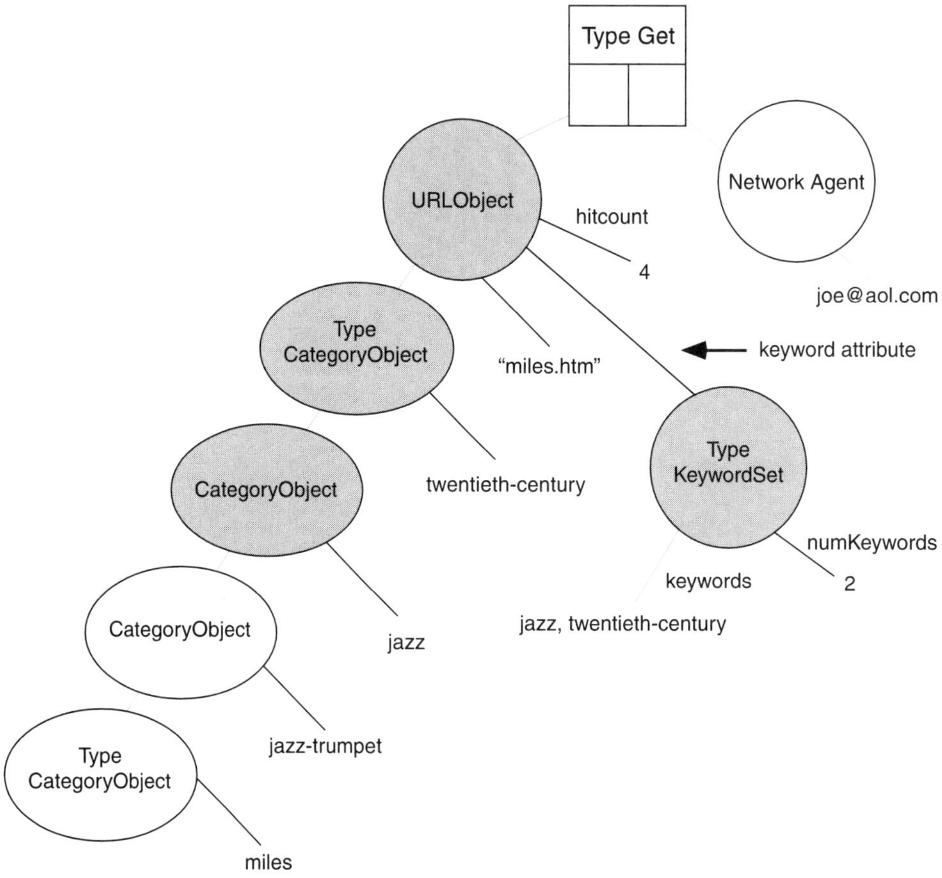

The fact shows that *jazz* is the most specific category that describes the interest of joe@aol.com. Because category information for an URL is represented as a path from a root to the category associated with the URL, the category covering a number of URLs is represented by an object template in which only the categories learned for a predominant number of URLs in a cluster appears with values learned. For all categories below this level no attribute could be learned. Contrast this with the fact generated from the primary cluster shown earlier to see how a learned category would be represented if an attribute could be learned at every level.

Similarly, another subcluster of the secondary cluster generates the fact shown in Figure 11.5, which shows the general interests of the user krishna@brain.com.

Figure 11.5   Learned fact—classical interest.

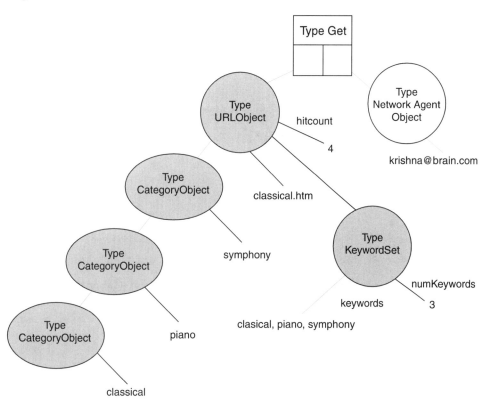

The fact that the cluster ID is the same indicates that the facts arose as sub-clusters of the same secondary cluster. Again, this fact indicates that the interests of krishna@brain.com are covered by the category *symphonic*. And the set of key-words that characterizes the interests of this user are "classical, piano, symphony."

Personalized Delivery

The learned user interests are used to create dynamic pages for each individual user. The sample code below performs this personalized delivery. This code is written for the Allaire Corporation's Cold Fusion tool for Web servers.[1] Netscape LiveWire and other such environments can similarly be used. In this example, if the music purchase link is not empty, then the music purchase link is displayed to the user.

---

[1]Thanks to Robert Hewlett for this example.

This example shows how the rule-based inferencing required for an agent implementation can be bound to dynamic HTML pages.

```
<CFOUTPUT>

<!--- Purchase Link --->

<CFIF #music.purchlink# GT "">

        <IMG SRC="images/general/all_pagegr_bul.gif" ALT="*">

        <A HREF="#music.purchlink#" target="LINK">Purchase this

CD</A><BR>

</CFIF>

<!--- Description Link --->

<CFIF #music.desclink# GT"">

        <IMG SRC="images/general/all_pagegr_bul.gif" ALT="*">

        <A HREF="#music.desclink#" target="LINK">More about

#music.title#</A><BR>

</CFIF>

<!--- Review Link --->

<CFIF #music.reviewlink# GT"">

        <IMG SRC="images/general/all_pagegr_bul.gif" ALT="*">

        <A HREF="#music.reviewlink#" target="LINK">Read a

review</A><BR>

</CFIF>

<!--- Sample Link --->

<CFIF #music.samplelink#GT "">

        <IMG SRC="images/general/all_pagegr_bul.gif" ALT="*">

        <A HREF="#music.samplelink#" target="LINK">Listen to a

sample</A><BR>

</CFIF>

</CFOUTPUT>
```

Figure 11.6 shows the presentation of personalized content to the user. In this example, the agent recommends the addition of the keywords Stephens, Astronomy, and Zen to the user's book interests. If the user were to click on Astronomy, then the agent would start bringing more books on astronomy to the user, and start ranking astronomy books higher in presenting books to the user.

Figure 11.6   Personalized Web site.

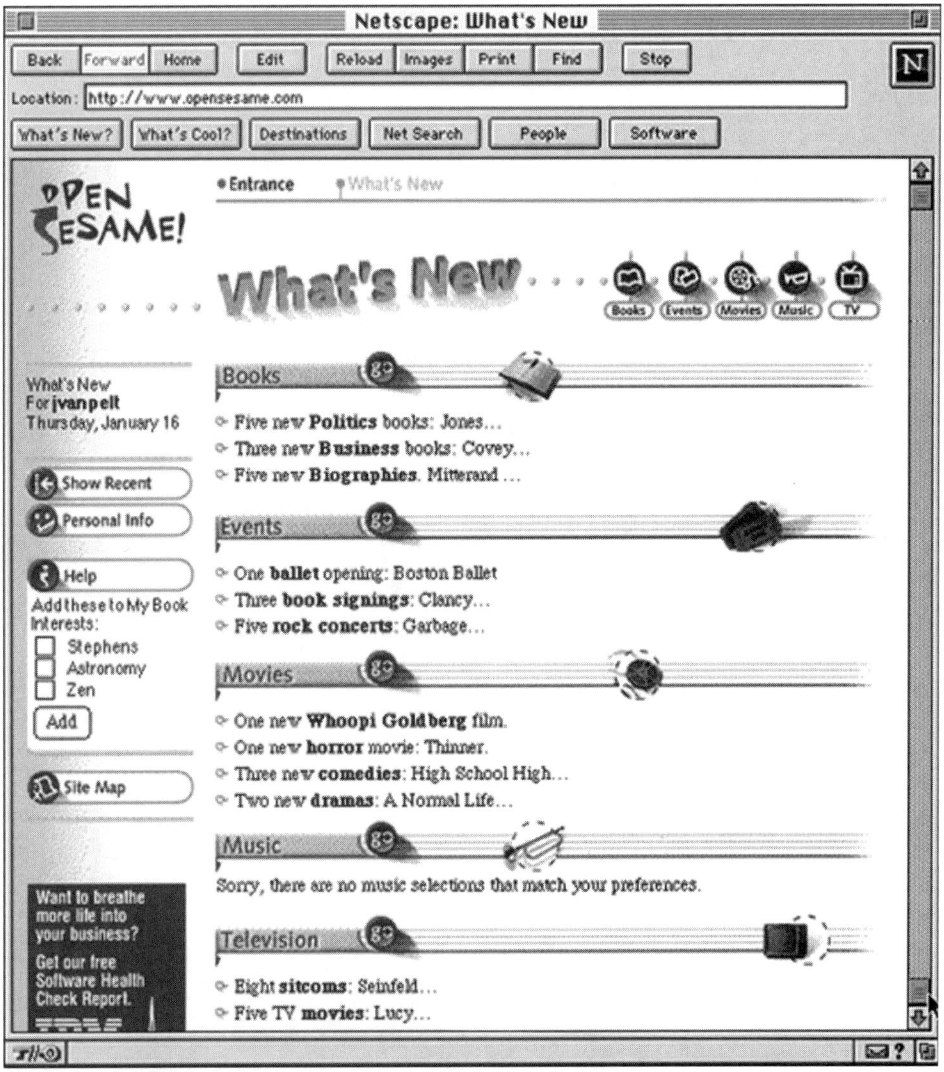

Summary

In this chapter, we would have liked to show you how to develop every possible kind of agent you could think of. As you will have realized by now, that is roughly equivalent to saying we would have liked to show you how to develop every kind of intelligent application! Instead, we showed you how to go about developing and deploying a practical intelligent agent for Web site personalization. The deployment process for this example shows how agent toolkits can be embedded into conventional software engineering development applications.

12

Summing Up

This book puts forward a recipe for incorporating agent technology into an organization. Before we summarize what our recipe does call for, let's discuss what it doesn't call for:

- *Agents do not need to be humanlike to be useful.* The level of human-like behavior appropriate for agents is still an open research question. Therefore, it makes sense to allow other organizations such as on-line service providers that have a vested interest in this agent feature to experiment with this technology first.

- *Agents do not need to be mobile to be useful.* While the creation of a pervasive agent framework would bring about a large number of com-mercial applications, such an approach does not seem to be taking over the public networks. In fact, it is possible that mobile agents will be confined to wireless networks where agents are ideally suited to serve the interaction between wireless clients and corporate servers.

- *Agents do not need massive support from artificial intelligence to be useful.* A little intelligence will go a long way in adding richness and value to an application. A key part of our thesis is that there is no magic in agents, just the straightforward application of some well-established technologies.

Our recipe calls for the incorporation of agent-enabled features into IS solutions in contrast to the deployment of standalone agents. This recommended approach while being incremental can nevertheless have a revolutionary impact on your business. We have enumerated the end-user benefits of software agents throughout the book. You can expect the following significant business benefits in your organization:

- Agents will turn self-service into room-service[1] by enabling your business to offer a 24-hour self-service interaction as a convenience for your employees, customers, and suppliers. Self-service operation will be run in the background by tireless software agents, thus reducing the personnel requirements to support customer interaction with resultant cost savings. Such agent automation will enable your organization to make optimal use of the most important asset of your organization—people—in servicing the task exceptions while software agents automate the repetitive tasks performed by your personnel. Given globalization trends, such a 24-hour self-service customer interaction will be a requirement for most businesses.

- Software agents will enable your business to create a personal one-to-one relationship between your business and the employees, customers, and suppliers of your business. That is, software agents will personalize your self-service operation by treating your customers as individuals. Such personalization will require agents that remember and analyze customers' previous interactions with your business, and narrowcast the presentation of your business to the dynamic personal interests of your customer. The business benefits of such an interaction include retaining existing customers, building a loyal customer base, and cultivating evangelists in your customer base to help support marketing.

- Agents will enable your business to institute a proactive dialogue with your employees, customers, and suppliers. Currently, most businesses rely on a reactive model where the various functional units of a business respond to customer-initiated queries. Software agents can initiate dialogues with your customers to inform them of information regarding new as well as existing products and services from your business and the status of pending customer-specified tasks from your business. Such proactivity will improve

---

[1]Thanks to Herb Bethoney of *PC Week Labs* for the metaphor.

customer service while reducing costs. In fact, such a superior service will enable your business to increase customer loyalty.

- Software agents will enable your business to form virtual communities among your employees, customers, and suppliers, and to provide product and service recommendations by making use of the shared experiences of similar groups in these communities. Such collaboration will require agents that analyze customer interaction data and find groups made up of individuals with similar preferences. The business benefits of such collaborative agents include building a loyal customer base and targeting your products and services to narrow segments.

- Software agents will substantially increase the speed at which your business interacts with its employees, customers and suppliers. What now takes days and weeks in collecting and analyzing the data capturing the interaction between your business and its customers in order to develop tactical corrections to your business operations will be done almost real-time in the future. Such an operation will require upgrading the current batch-oriented IS systems into a real-time operation that can support online interaction with customers.

- Software agents will enable your business to mass produce customized products and services. These kinds products with intelligence will customize themselves according to customer preferences learned during customer usage. Such customization can be a significant differentiator of your product and services in the market place, which, in turn, would improve the profit margin of these products or services.

- Agents will be your enterprise's face to the world. The Internet and intranets will increasingly change and expand the number and types of users on your information systems. The largest number of new users will be your customers, accessing your IS to retrieve account and product information, to submit or modify orders, and to view order status. Increasingly, the IS will be the "visiting card" of the enterprise, and factors such as ease of use, personalization, and proactiveness will be key differentiators for your enterprise.

- Agents allow the computer to do more of the work. A final element of our recipe is that the developer exports some of his or her judgment into the agent-based application. This delegated judgment is then used to drive tools that were formerly driven directly by the user. We often think of end-users driving individual applications—spreadsheets, text processors, inventory systems. In reality, the user (an agent of some business process) applies his or her knowledge and judgment to achieving some goal which he or she knows, but which may not be explicit in any one of the tools: *A result observed in a spreadsheet causes the employee to schedule a meeting with a manager.* This judgment is based on procedures established by the employer, or the employee's own preferences. Agent techniques allow these associations to be observed and acted upon by the agents, resulting in reduced effort for human users.

If you're still not convinced, let's look at one last example illustrating the business benefits of intelligent agents—a hypothetical package delivery service. First, such a service company can offer 24-hour self-service by allowing Internet access to permit users to track the status of a specific package. Such an interaction can be accomplished using process agents. Second, such a service can proactively notify a customer about the delivery status of a package.[2]

The example above shows the glimmer of agent functionality that can be built into a service application. Here is the potential of such applications. The shipping service provider Web site can present the status of all outstanding packages whenever the user visits the shipper's Web site after customer authentication. Notification features can be expanded to cover packages sent to the user as well. Would a potential customer be impressed with your company if that customer routinely got email notification of pending delivery by your company? Similarly, such a service can let users specify their notification preferences as well for further personalization. What if your service monitored customer behavior to select default delivery options based on the attributes of the recipient, date, package, and so on? What if your marketing department could offer a customized plan automatically when the customer's use exceeds a certain threshold before your competitor makes such an offer?

The adoption of agent-enabled features into the IS solutions of your company requires, first, the collection of data—capturing a customer's interaction with your organization along with the values for environment attributes enabling agent functionality. So if you are in the package delivery business, then you can start by collecting the sender's email address, the recipient's email address, and the sender's

---

[2]FedEx provides customers with package delivery tracking via email. That is nice, but why not let customers specify their tracking notification preferences (e.g., email, pager, fax) in the airbill as long as they need to fill in the forms?

and recipient's notification preferences. Next you can start transacting your business with your customer electronically in order to keep track of customer interactions in realtime, and to build the content on which the agent machinery needs to work.

Final Process Checklist

Developing an agent-based application requires you to answer a series of questions.

- *What benefit are we trying to create?* This could range from reducing the level of effort to provide customer information to trying to detect fraud in securities trading. Agent technology can help with a wide range of problems, but it requires a solid base of existing processes and data with which to work.

- *What are the desired outcomes?* These could range from an absence of spelling mistakes in documents to the ability to set up meetings of a dozen people. It is essential to choose a realistic goal. Automated spelling checking is a feasible goal. Multiparty negotiation may not be.

- *What are the inputs that lead to these outcomes?* These could range from keyboard input to an individual's calendar entries. Are these inputs accessible? Are they sufficiently formalized to form the basis for an automated process?

- *What are the factors that relate inputs to outcomes?* Here we have to consider both content (a dictionary, hierarchical employee/manager relationships) and machinery (string comparison, multiparty negotiation). Do we understand these factors adequately to express them and execute them?

- *How can we ensure that we get the right outcome?* Does the application do what I want, not what I said? How does it behave under extreme conditions? Most "intelligent" applications are extremely fragile at the boundaries of their capabilities; we need to provide safety mechanisms that can detect failures of reasoning or negotiation.

- *What is the best user interface for the agent-based tasks?* What is the best way to present or explain these new applications to the current users? Do the applications reduce the required skill level for the users? Do the applications eliminate the work of a class of users?

In some sense we all have considerable experience in developing agents: We have all trained another human being to do a task. In some cases, we are training our children to get themselves ready for school in the morning. Or we are training a subordinate to perform a process we have developed. We train administrative assistants in the ways we want to run our office lives. Applying agents to business processes is fundamentally equivalent to developing an employee to perform a delegated task. What makes this new, is that the process is being implemented in software by the IS developers, rather than by an operational manager. The application of intelligent agents to business processes is one more step along the road of eliminating human intermediaries in running a business.

In conclusion, agents are poised to enable businesses to add significant value to the interaction between a business and its employees, customers, and its suppliers. If your company does not have an agent strategy, then we advise you to develop a corporate strategy, identify key areas for development, and start incorporating agent features into your IS solutions. Your employees, customers, suppliers, and (most importantly) your shareholders will be glad you did.

Commercial
Agent Software*

Academic Resources

UMBC Intelligent Software Agents Resources: http://www.cs.umbc.edu/
agents/. One of the most comprehensive Web resources about intelligent information agents, intentional agents, software agents, softbots,
knowbots, and infobots; maintained by Tim Finin of the University of
Maryland. Also includes the AgentNews WebLetter published monthly.

Software Agents Group at the MIT Media Lab: http://agents.www.media.
mit.edu/groups/agents/. Publications on research performed by Pattie
Maes' software agents group at the Media Lab on collaborating multiple
agents that learn from experience.

Softbot Research at University of Washington: http://www.cs.washington.
edu/research/projects/softbots/www/softbots.htm1. Research on goal-
directed software robots by Oren Etzioni and his colleagues.

Transportable Agents at Dartmouth College: http://www.cs.dartmouth.
edu/~agent/ Mobile agent research using Tcl.

---

*An on-line version of this appendix will be maintained at http://www.opensesame.com/agents.

Interface Agent Info: http://www.cs.bham.ac.uk/~amw/agents/. Interface agent resource maintained by Andy Wood of the University of Birmingham in UK.

Distributed AI Research Unit at Queen Mary and Westfield College in UK: http://www.elec.qmw.ac.uk/dai/ Research on agents for business process management directed by Nick Jennings.

Nobotics Group at Stanford University: http://robotics.stanford.edu/groups/ nobotics. Research on formal framework for software agents headed by Yoav Shoham.

Oz Project at CMU: http://www.cs.cmu.edu/afs/cs.cmu.edu/project/oz. Research on believable social and emotional agents.

Agent Languages

Most commercial agent toolkits are available as C libraries and C++ class frameworks. C++ would be the language of choice for commercial agent application development where performance is critical. The following languages can be used for specific niches as well.

Smalltalk: Smalltalk, developed at Xerox Parc, dates back to the birth of AI. Particularly popular in the telecommunications industry for developing object-oriented distributed client/server solutions. Commercially available from a number of vendors including IBM, ParcPlace, Quasar, and others. http://www.oti. com/jeffspg/smaltalk.htm is a good Smalltalk resource on the Web.

Tcl/Tk: A machine-independent interpreted scripting language, implemented as a library of C procedures so that it can be embedded in applications. Freely distributed on the Internet, Tcl/Tk is suitable for small-scale commercial applications and prototyping. Tk is a Motif-style X toolkit for Tcl, supporting widgets such as buttons, scrollbars, menus, and so on. http://www.cs.curtin.edu.au/ ~jules/www-tcl.html and http://cuiwww.unige.ch/eao/www/TclTk.html contain pointers to a host of Tcl/Tk support sites including downloadable software.

Safe-Tcl: A variation of Tcl for intelligent mail application that ensure safety.

Perl: An interpreted scripting language with C-like syntax with faster performance than Tcl/Tk. Suitable for medium-scale commercial applications. http:// www.metronet.com/perlinfo/per15.html contains pointers to Perl resources.

KQML: A language developed through ARPA knowledge sharing effort aimed at developing sharable large-scale knowledge bases to enable agent-to-agent communication and knowledge sharing. KQML is a message passing protocol to support runtime knowledge sharing among agents. Suitable for development agent prototypes for integration into existing applications. http://retriever.cs. umbc.edu/kqml/ is a Web resource containing pointers to KQML documents and software.

Telescript: An object-oriented, remote programming language for building mobile agents. Suitable for commercial applications in wireless network environment. Available from General Magic, http://www.genmagic.com. The company also announced Tabriz AgentWare—a set of Web class libraries for accessing a Telescript engine on a Web server environment.

Java: http://www.javasoft.com. The leading contender for agent application language on the Web. Java is an interpreted, multithreaded, and secure cross-platform language. The Java interpreter can execute Java bytecodes directly on any machine to which the interpreter and runtime system have been ported. The multithreading and built-in security features give Java an edge in the implementation of interactive electronic commerce applications.

ActiveX from Microsoft: http://www.microsoft.com. Microsoft's answer to Java embracing both Java and Microsoft's Component Object Model (COM) based on OLE.

Search Engines

Fulcrum SearchServer: http://www.fulcrum.com. A multiplatform engine for information solutions based on an SQL-based query language supporting Open Database Connectivity (ODBC). The company offers products based on this engine such as Surfboard, which can be used to build intranet search agents.

SEARCH '97 Agent Server: http://www.verity.com. A toolkit for building personal retrieval agents to proactively search, filter, categorize, and deliver information to users from heterogeneous sources. Built over Verity's SEARCH '97 information server information retrieval platform. Used in personal newspapers such as IBM infoSAGE. Netscape recently announced a catalog server based on the Verity engine.

PLWeb from Personal Library Software: http://www.pls.com. A retrieval engine that supports building multiple views of support multiple interfaces quickly. An optional module Personal. Agent enables users to make permanent queries to PL Web indexed documents.

Excalibur RetrievalWare: http://www.excalib.com. An information retrieval tool using neural and semantic networks with self-organizing pattern indexes and fuzzy searches. Berry incorporated into Informix database management solutions.

Dataware NetAnswer: http://www.dataware.com. A search and retrieval tool for Web Servers based on the company's BSR/Search text-management and retrieval software. Suitable for large-scale multiple database environments.

Web User Monitoring

Interse Market Forcus: http://www.interse.com. A statistical and temporal analysis of Web site activity. Produces reports in popular formats.

WebTrends by e.g. Software: http://www.egsoftware.com. A statistical marketing and traffic analysis tool for Web servers. In particular, tracks user sessions across different elements of the Web site to evaluate referral efficiency and other tasks.

net.Analysis Pro by net.Genesis: http://www.netgen.com. A Web site traffic analysis tool with an RDBMS backend. Generates interactive reports.

Dynamo by ART Technology Group: http.atg-dynamo.com. A toolkit for Web site development that supports user tracking. Enables dynamic page generation with Java code embedded into HTML files.

Web Site Personalization Tools

Allaire Cold Fusion: http://www.allaire.com. Development tool for building dynamic Web applications. Uses the Cold Fusion Markup Language extension to HTML for customized SQL query to ODBC databases.

Broadvision One-to-One: http://www.broadvision.com. Development tool for building Web services with personalized content, advertising, and incentive programs. The backend engine supports Common Object Request Broker Architecture (CORBA) standards.

ManageIT by Imperative!: http://www.imperative.com. A set of Perl scripts to develop personalized content matching user demographics. Supports session and user profile management.

ParcPlace VisualWare: http://www.parcplace.com. A client/server development tool for dynamic Web applications. Supports session management for each individual user.

WebObjects by Next Software: http://www.next.com. A commerce application development environment supporting, in particular, user state management.

Web Learning Agent Tools

Digital Each-To-Each: http://www.each.com Automated recommendation system using collaborative filtering technology. Used in the movie recommendation service EachMovie http://www.eachmovie.com.

Firefly: http://www.firefly.com. A collaborative filtering tool for building a Web site that makes recommendations based on the communities of users with similar interests. Used in the Firefly music agent site, and in My Yahoo!

Learn Sesame: http://www.opensesame.com. A software toolkit for building personalized Web sites that makes recommendations by learning the personal behavior of each user and user communities with similar interests. Used in the personalized entertainment site Open Sesame and in iVillage chatrooms.

LikeMinds by Songline: http://www.songline.com. A collaborative filtering tool that makes recommendations based on the communities of users with similar interests. Used in the Movie Critic site http://www.moviecritic.com.

Net Perceptions GroupLens: http://www.netperceptions.com. Collaborative filtering toolkit based on research on Usenet news filtering.

Off-line Delivery Tools

BackWeb: http://www.backweb.com. Server software enabling companies to develop personalized broadcast channels. Information is downloaded during the idle time in Internet connections using client plug-ins.

Intermind Communicator: http://www.intermind.com. Communications software enabling publishers to form direct channels with interested subscribers.

WebCrawler by ForeFront: http://www.ffg.com. A desktop tool for download-ing entire Web sites to view them off-line.

Freeloader Individual: http://www.freeloader.com. An advertising-supported desktop tool that downloads entire Web sites with a specified level of hierarchy according to a user-defined schedule.

Open Market Express: http://www.openmarket.com. Desktop software for retrieving Web information for accelerated viewing; independent of a particular browser.

PointCast Network: http://www.pointcast.com. An advertising-supported desk-top tool for delivery of personalized information from Web. Works as a screen saver on continuously updated information.

WebEx by Traveling Software: http://www.travsoft.com. Formerly known as MilkTruck, another off-line delivery desktop tool particularly focusing on the mobile market.

Electronic Money

ecash by DigiCash: http://www.digicash.com. With ecash, the user withdraws a digital form of money from a bank to store on a client machine for later use in electronic payments.

CyberCash: http://www.cybercash.com. An Internet-secure payment system that preserves the metaphor of the physical credit payment system.

VeriFone: http://www.verifone.com. Markets the vPOS virtual point of sale pay-ment applications. Included in the Microsoft Merchant Server.

Security

Netscape SSL: http://home.netscape.com. Secure Socket Layer (SSL) in Netscape's security protocol for server and client authentication.

Secure Electronic Transactions (SET): http://www.mastercard.com. An industry standard for secure on-line transactions supported by Mastercard and SET partners.

RSA: http://www.rsa.com. Markets the public key encryption software underlying most secure communications solutions including the secure Multipurpose Internet Mail Extension used for email.

PGP: http://www.pgp.com. Pretty Good Privacy (PGP) software uses a decentralized approach to security. Used predominantly in email encryption.

Chat Rooms

iChat ROOMS: http://www.ichat.com ROOMS is a server application that chat-enables any Web page. Based on Internet Relay Chat (IRC).

Worlds Chat: http://www.worlds.net. A software toolkit for building interactive chatrooms with avatars.

Virtual Places: http://www.vplaces.com. Software for building interactive Web sites using avatars.

Newsgroups

Robots Mailing List: http://info.webcrawler.com/mailing-lists/robots/info.html. A popular technical forum for Web robot authors, maintainers, and administrators. Check http://info.webcrawler.com/mailing-lists/robots/index.html for list archive.

Software Agents Mailing Lists: http://www.cs.umbc.edu/agenlist/archive. Software agent mailing list managed by UMBC. Discussions confined to software agent research. See http://www.cs.umbc.edu/agentslist/ for subscription details.

Intranet Agent Software

Edify Electronic Workforce: http://www.edify.com. Software tool for building process agent automating back-office systems.

DSS Agent: http://www.strategy.com. Software tool for incorporating intelligent agents into relational OLAP environments.

PointCast I-Server: http://www.pointcast.com. Server version of the PointCast Network software for developing a corporate communication channel.

Verity SEARCH '97 Agent Server: http:www.verity.com. A software toolkit for building retrieval agents on corporate intranets.

Bibliography

Agrawal, R (1993). "Database Mining: A Performance Perspective," *IEEE Transactions on Knowledge and Data Engineering,* vol. 5, no. 6, pp. 914–925 (December).

Alan, K. (1984). "Computer Software," *Scientific American* (March).

Allen, J. F. (1983). "Notes From The Editor," *American Journal of Computational Linguistics, Special Issue on Ill-Formed Input,* pp. 3–4.

Andresson, M. et al. (1996). "The Netscape Intranet Vision and Product Roadmap." http://www.netscape.com/comprod/at_work/white_paper/intranet/vison.html.

Bacon, J., Bates, J., Hayton, R, and Moody, K. (1995). "Using Events to Build Distributed Applications," Whistler, BC, Canada: *Second International Workshop on Services in Distributed and Networked Environments,* pp. 148–155 (June).

Bachant, J., and Soloway, E. (1989). "The Engineering of XCON," *Communications of the Association for Computing Machinery,* vol. 32, no. 3.

Bayer, D. (1995). "A Learning Agent for Resource Discovery on the World Wide Web," MSC Project Dissertation, University of Aberdeen.

Bhandari, I., Colet, E., Parker, J., Pines, Z., Pratap, R, and Ramanujam, K. (1996). "Advanced Scout: Data Mining and Knowledge Discovery in NBA Data," IBM Research Report RC20443 (April).

Blustein, W. J. (1993). "Evaluation of Tools for Converting Text to Hypertext," MSC Project Dissertation, University of Western Ontario.

Boggs, J. K. (1973). "IBM Remote Job Entry Facility: Generalized Subsystem Remote Job Entry Facility," *IBM Technical Disclosure Bulletin,* vol. 752 (August).

Borenstein, N. S. (1995). "E-mail with a Mind of Its Own: The Safe-Tcl Language for Enabled Mail." ftp://ftp.fv.com/pub/code/other/safe-tcl.tar.

Bowman, C. M., Danzig, P. B., Hardy, D. R, Manber, U., Schwartz, M. F., and Wessels, D. P. (1995). "Harvest: A Scalable, Customizable Discovery and Access System," (Technical Report CU-CS-732-94), University of Colorado, Boulder (March).

Brustoloni, J. C. (1991). "Autonomous Agents: Characterization and Requirements," (Carnegie Mellon Technical Report CMU-CS-91-204), Pittsburgh, Carnegie Mellon University.

Burkhard, H. D. (1994). "Agent-Oriented Programming for Open Systems," Berlin, Springer-Verlag: *Proceedings of the ECAI-94 Workshop on Agent Theories, Architectures, and Languages,"* pp. 291–306.

Caglayan, A., and Snorrason, M. (1993). "On the Relationship Between the Generalized Equality Classification and ART2 Neural Networks." Portland, OR: *World Congress on Neural Networks '93.*

Caglayan, A., Snorrason, M., Jacoby, J., Mazzu, J., and Jones, R. (1996). "Lessons from Open Sesame!" London, UK: *First International Conference on the Practical Application of Intelligent Agents and Multi-Agent Technology.*

Caglayan, A., Snorrason, M., Jacoby, J., Mazzu, J., Jones, R, and Kumar, K. (1997). "Learn Sesame–A Learning Agent Engine" Vienna, Austria: *International Journal of Applied Artificial Intelligence Special Issue, Best of PAAM 96.*

Carpenter, G. A., Grossberg, S., and Rosen, D. B. (1991). "ART2-A: An Adaptive Resonance Algorithm for Rapid Category Learning and Recognition." *Neural Networks,* pp. 493–504.

Chess, D. (1996). "Security Considerations in Agent-based Systems," Portland, Oregon: *1st Annual Conference on Emerging Technologies and Applications in Communications* (etaCOM'96), May 7–10.

Chess, D., Grosof, B., Harrison, C., Levine, D., Parris, C., and Tsudik, G. (1995). "Itinerant Agents for Mobile Computing," *IEEE Personal Communications Magazine,* pp. 34–49, vol. 2, no. 3 (October).

Chess, D., Harrison, C., and Kershenbaum, A. (1995). *Mobile Agents: Are They a Good Idea?* Research Report RC 1987 (88465): IBM (December).

Cohen, F. (1987). "Computer Viruses: Theory and Experiment," *Computers and Security,* pp. 22–35, vol. 6.

Crowley-Milling, M. C. and Shering, G. C. (1978). "The Nodal System for the SPS," Geneva: CERN Report 78–07 (September).

CRA (1996). "Open Sesame!" Cambridge, MA: Charles River Analytics, Inc. http://www.opensesame.com/products/sesame/sesame.html.

Dreilinger, D. (1995). "Integrating Heterogeneous WWW Search Engines," (May). ftp://132.239.54.5/savvy/report.ps.gz.

Etzioni, O., and Weld, D. (1994). "A Softbot-Based Interface to the Internet," *Communications of the Association for Computing Machinery* (July).

Fass, D. C. and Cercone, N. J. (1992). "Research in Natural Language Processing at Simon Fraser University." *Canadian Artificial Intelligence Magazine* pp. 11–20 (summer).

FTP Software, Inc. (1996). Andover, MA. http:/www.ftp.com/cyberagent.

Finin, T., Fritzson, R, McKay, D., and McEntire, R (1994). "KQML as an Agent Communication Language," *Proceedings of the Third International Conference on Information and Knowledge Management* (CIKM), pp. 456–63.

Firefly (1996). Cambridge, MA: Firefly Network, Inc. http://www.agents-inc.com/.

Foner, L., and Maes, P. (1994). "Paying Attention to What's Important: Using Focus of Attention to Improve Unsupervised Learning." Brighton, UK: *The Third International Conference on the Simulation of Adaptive Behavior.*

Franklin, S. (1995). "Artificial Minds," Cambridge, MA: MIT Press.

Gao, Y. (1997). "Cyberagent: An Integrated Mobile Agent System Based on Java," Marina del Rey, CA: *Proceedings of the First International Conference on Autonomous Agents,* February.

Gasser, L. and Briot, J. P. (1992). "Object-based Concurrent Programming and Distributed Artificial Intelligence." Kluwer Academic Publishers: *Distributed Artificial Intelligence: Theory and Praxis,* pp. 81–108.

Genesereth, M. R and Ketchpel, S. P. (1994). *Communications of the Association for Computing Machinery,* pp. 48–53, vol. 37, no. 7 (July).

Genesereth, M. R and Fikes, R E. (1992). "Knowledge Interchange Format, Version 3.0 Reference Manual," Stanford University: Technical Report Logic-92-1 (June). http:logic.stanford.edu/knowledge-sharing/papers/README.html#kif.

Genesereth, M. R (1995). "Interoperability: An Agent-Based Framework." *AI Expert,* pp. 34–40 (March).

GMI (1995). Sunnyvale, CA, General Magic, Inc.: *General Magic White Papers,* nos. 1–4.

GMITS (1995). Sunnyvale, CA, General Magic, Inc.: *Telescript Language Reference,* p. 78 (October).

Gosling, and McGilton, M. (1995). "The Java Language Environment: A White Paper," Mountain View, CA, Sun Microsystems.

Gray, R (1995). Gray (1995) *Agent Tcl: Alpha Release 1.1* (AFOSR contract F49620-93-1-0266 and ONR contract N00014-95-1-1204). http://www.cs.dartmouth.edu/~rgray/transportable.html.

Grosof, B. and Foulger, D., (1995a). "Globenet and RAISE: Intelligent Agents for Networked Newsgroups and Customer Service Support," *Proceedings of the 1995 AAAI Fall Symposium on AI Applications in Knowledge Navigation and Retrieval.*

Grosof, B. (1995b). "Conflict Resolution in Advice Taking and Instruction for Learning Agents," Tahoe City, CA: *Proceedings of the ML-95 Workshop on Agents that Learn from other Agents, Twelfth International Conference on Machine Learning* (July).

Gruber, T. R (1992). "Ontolingua: A Mechanism to Support Portable Ontologies," Stanford University: Technical Report KSL-91-66, March. http://www-ksl-svc.stanford.edu/knowledge-sharing/papers/README.html#kif.

Guha, R V. and Lenat, D. B. (1994). "CYC: Enabling Agents to Work Together," *Communications of the Association for Computing Machinery*, pp. 127–142, vol. 37, no. 7 (July).

Guilfoyle, C., and Warner, E. (1994). London: Ovum Ltd.: *Intelligent Agents: The New Revolution in Software.*

Guralmile, D. (.ed) (1970). *Webster's New World Dictionary of the American Language, Second College Edition.* New York: The World Publishing Company.

GVU (1996). "GVU's 6th WWW User Survey," http://www.ccgatech.edu/gru/user-surveys/.

Halfhill, T. R (1996). "Agents and Avatars," Byte, pp. 69–72, vol. 21, no. 2 (February).

"High-Tech Hangup" (1995), *The Boston Globe,* p. 22 (November).

Hohl, F. (1995). "Konzeption eines einfachen Agentensystems und Implementation eines Prototyps," Universitat Stuttgart: Diplomarbeit Nr. 1267, 1995. http://www.informatik.unistuttgart.de/cgi-bin/ncstr_rep_view.pl?/inf/ftp/library/ncstrl.ustuttgart_fi/DIP-1267-DIP1267.bib.

Janca, P. C. (1995). "Pragmatic Application of Information Agents," *BIS Strategic Decisions* (May).

Java (1996a). "Java: The Language." http://java.sun.com/doc/language.html.

Java (1996b). "Java: The Security FAQ." http://www.javasoft.com/sun.com/sfaq.

Jennings, N. R, Wooldridge, M. (1995). *Applied Artificial Intelligence (USA),* pp. 357–369, vol. 9, no. 4 (July–August).

Jennings, N. R, Faratin, P., Johnson, M. J., Norman T. J., O'Brien, P., and Wiegand, M. E. (1996). "Agent-Based Business Process Management," London, UK: *First International Conference on the Practical Application of Intelligent Agents and Multi-Agent Technology.*

Kallski, Jr., B. S. (1993). "An Overview of the PKCS Public-Key Cryptography Standards," RSA Data Security, Inc. (November). http://www.rsa.com/pub/pkcs.

Kaufman, C., Perlman, R, and Speciner, M. (1995). Englewood Cliffs, NJ, Prentice-Hall: *Network Security: Private Communication in a Public World.*

Koster, M. (1995). "List of Robots." http://web.nexor.co.uk/mak/doc/robots/active.html.

Krulwich, B. (1995). "Learning User Interests in Heterogeneous Document Databases." Stanford University: *Proceedings of the AAAI Spry Symposium on Information Gathering.*

Kumar, K. (1996). *Smarts Learning Engine: Conceptual Overview,* Charles River Analytics (June).

Lashkari, Y., Metral, M., and Maes, P. (1994). "Collaborative Interface Agents," Seattle, WA: *12th National Conference on AI* (AAA90), pp. 444–449, vol. 1 (July–August).

Lieberman, H. (1995). "Letizia: An Agent that Assists Web Browsing," Montreal, *International Joint Conference on AI.*

Lin, J. and Vitter, J. (1994). "A Theory for Memory-Based Learning," *Machine Learning,* p. 143, vol. l7, no. 2/3 (November).

Maes, P. (1994). *Communications of the Association for Computing Machinery*, pp. 31–40, vol. 37, no. 7 (July).

Mayfield, J., Labrou, Y. and Finin, T.; "Desiderata for Agent Communication Languages."

McDermott, J. (1982). "R1: A Rule-Based Configurer of Computer Systems," *Artificial Intelligence* pp. 39–88, vol. 19, no. 1.

McDermott, J. (1993). "R1 (XCON) at Age 12: Lessons from an Elementary School Achiever," *Artificial Intelligence* pp. 241–247, vol. 59, nos. 1–2 (February).

McKay, D., Finin, T., and O'Hare, A. (1990). "The Intelligent Database," *Proceedings of the 7th National Conference on Artificial Intelligence.*

Microsoft. (1995). "Microsoft Plus! for Windows '95: Guidelines for Independent Software Vendors." http://www.microsoft.com/win32dev/guidelns/sageapi.html.

Mitchel, T., Caruana, R, Freitag, D., McDermott, J. and Zabowski, D. (1994). "Experience with a Learning Personal Assistant," *Communications of the Association for Computing Machinery,* pp. 80–91, vol. 37, no. 7 (July).

Molva, R, Tsudik, G., Van Herreweghen, E., and Zatti, S. (1992). "KryptoKnight Authentication and Key Distribution System," Toulouse, France: *Computer Security—ESORICS 92, Second European Symposium on Research in Computer Security,* pp. 155–174 (November).

Munk, N. (1996). "Technology for Technology's Sake," *Forbes*, pp. 280–288 (October).

Mycin (1977). *Artificial Intelligence,* p. 15, vol. 8, no. 1.

Nass, C. I., Steuer, J. S., Tauber, E., and Reeder, H. (1993) "Anthropomorphism, Agency, and Ethopoeia: Computers as Social Actors," Amsterdam, Netherlands: *Proceedings of the International CHI Conference.*

Norman, D.A and Shallice, T. (1980) "Attention to Action: Willed and Automated Control of Behavior." La Jolla, CA, UCSD: *CHIPP 99.*

Norman D. (1983). "Some Observations on Mental Models," Hillsdale, NJ, LEA: Mental Models.

OMG (1992). *Common Object Request Broker Specification.* New York: Wiley.

OMG (1993). *Object Management Framework Specification.* http://www.omg.org/public-doclist.html.

OMG (1995). *Common Facilities Architecture Specification.* http://www.omg.org/public-doclist.html.

OMG (1994). "Security White Paper" (1994/94-04-16), http://www.omg.org/public-doclist.html.

Ordille, J. (1996). "When Agents Roam, Who Can you Trust?" Portland, Oregon: *1st Annual Conference on Emerging Technologies and Applications in Communications* (etaCOM'96) (May).

Orwant, J. (1991). "The Doppelgaenger User Modelling System," *IJCAI Workshop on Modelling for Intelligent Interaction.*

Orwant, J. (1993). "Doppelgaenger Goes to School: Machine Learning for User Modelling," M.S. thesis, MIT (September).

OSA (1995). Reading, MA, Addison-Wesley: *Inside Macintosh: Interapplication Communication.*

Ousterhout, J. K. (1994). Reading, MA, Addison-Wesley: *Tcl and the Tk Toolkit.*

Ousterhout, J. K. (1995). "Tcl: A Universal Scripting Language," http://www.smli.com/research/tcl.

Ousterhout, J. K. (1996). "Scripts and Agents, the New Software High Ground," New Orleans, LA: *Winter USENIX Conference* http://www.smli.com/research/tcl.

Palmer, E. R (1994). "An Introduction to Citadel—A Secure Crypto Coprocessor for Workstations," Curacao, Netherlands Antilles: *IFIP SEC'94 Conference Proceedings* (May), and IBM Research Communication Report #18373 (September, 1992).

Patil, H. V. D., Fikes, R E., Patel-Schneider, P. F., McKay, D., Finin, T., Gruber, T., and Neches, R (1992). "The DARPA Knowledge Sharing Effort: Progress Report," in C. Rich, W. Swartou, and B. Nebel (eds.), *Proceedings of Knowledge Representation and Reasoning* (KR&R-92), pp. 777–788.

PGP (1996). "The International PGP Home Page." http://www.ifi.uio.no/pgp.

Piatetsky-Shapiro, G., and Frawley, W. J. (1991). Menlo Park, CA: AAAI Press: *Knowledge Discovery in Databases.*

Poggi, A. (1995). "DAISY—an Object-Oriented System for Distributed Artificial Intelligence," Berlin, Springer-Verlag: In Jennings and Wooldrige (eds.), *Intelligent Agents—Lecture Notes on Artificial Intelligence,* pp. 341–354, vol. 890.

Quarterman, J. (1995). Austin, TX, Matrix Information and Directory Services, Inc.: *Matrix News,* July.http://www.mids.org.

Reeves, B. and Nass, C. (1995). Cambridge University Press: The Media Equation: How People Treat Computers, Televisions and New Media as Real People and Places.

Rich, C. (1996). "Windows sharing with collaborative interface agents," *SIGCHI Bull.*, pp. 70–78, vol. 28, no. 1 (January).

Richardson, J., Schwarz, P., and Cabrera, L.F. (1992). "(CACL): Efficient Fine-Grained Protection for Objects," *ACM SIGPLAN Notices* 27.10.

Rivest, R., Shamir, A., and Adleman, L. (1978). "A Method for Obtaining Digital Signatures and Public Key Cryptosystems," *Communications of the Association for Computing Machinery* (February).

Rosenschein, J. S. and Zlotkin, G. (1994). MIT Press: *Rules of Encounter: Designing Conventions for Automated Negotiation among Computers.*

SafeTcl(1996). http://minsky.med.Virginia.EDU/sdm7g/Projects/Python/safe-tcl/.

Schneier, B. (1996). *Applied Cryptology: Protocols, Algorithms, and Source Code in C,* 2nd. ed., New York: Wiley.

Sculley, J. (1987). *Knowledge Navigator* (video), Cuperetino, CA, Apple Computers, Inc.

Selker, E. (1994a). "COACH," *Communications of the Association for Computing Machinery,* pp. 92–99, vol. 37, no .7 (July).

Selker, E. and Barrett, R. C. (1994b). "Finding What I am Looking For: An Information Retrieval Agent," IBM Research Report RJ 9816 (84879), May 16. http://www.research.ibm.com/.

Shneiderman, B. (1993). "Beyond Intelligent Machines: Just Do It," IEEE Software (USA), pp. 100–103, vol. 10, no. 1 (January).

Shoham, Y. (1993). "Agent Oriented Programming," Springer-Verlag: *Lecture Notes in Artificial Intelligence,* pp. 123–129.

Snorrason, M., and Caglayan, A. K. (1994). "Generalized ART2 Algorithms," San Diego, INNS Press: *World Congress on Neural Networks.*

Steiner, J. G., Neuman B. C. and Shiller, J. I. (1988). "Kerberos: An Authentication Service for Open Network Systems," *Proc. Winter USENIX,* pp. 191–202. ftp://athena-dist.mit.edu/pub/kerberos/doc/techplan.PS

Bibliography

Takeda, H., Iino, K. and Nishida, T. (1995). "Agent Organization and Communication with Multiple Ontologies," *International Journal of Cooperative Information Systems*, pp. 321–337, vol. 4, no. 4.

Tardo, J. and Valente, L. (1996). "Mobile Agent Security and Telescript," San Francisco, CA: Proceedings of IEEE CompCon (April).

Thirunavukkarasu, C., Finin, T., and Mayfield, J. (1995). "Secret Agents—A Security Architecture for the KQML Agent Communication Language," Baltimore, MD: *CIKM'95 Intelligent Information Agents Workshop*. http://www.cs.umbc.edu/~cikm/iia/submitted/viewing/chelliah.ps.

Turlock, R. (1993). *SIFT: A Simple Information Filtering Tool*, NJ: Bellcore.

UMBC (1996). http://www.cs.umbc.edu/agents/security.html.

Unisys (1996). "Unisys Natural Language Assistant: Natural Language Understanding Technology for Customer Service and Marketing," (June).

Virdhagriswaran, S. (1995). Crystaliz, Inc. http://www.crystaliz.com/.

Wayner, P., and Joch, A. (1995). "State of the Art: Agents of Change." *Byte* pp. 94–95 (March).

Weizenbaum, J. (1976). *Computer Power and Human Reason*. New York: W. H. Freeman.

White, J. E. (1995). "An Introduction to Safety and Security in Telescript," http://www.genmagic.com.

White, J. E. (1996). "Mobile Agents," Menlo Park, CA, AAAI Press/MIT Press, in Bradshaw, J.(ed.), *Software Agents*.

Whittaker, S., and Sidner, C. (1996). Vancouver: Lotus Corp: *Proceedings of CHI–96*.

Wildfire (1995). http://ww.wildfire.com.

Witten, I. H., Moffat, A., and Bell, T. C. (1994). New York, Van Nostrand Reinhold. *Managing Gigabytes*.

Wooldridge, M. J. and Jennings, N. R (eds.) (1995). *Intelligent Agents, Proceedings of the ECAI-94 Workshop on Agent Theories, Architectures, and Languages*, Berlin, Springer-Verlag, pp. 2–39.

Index

DATE DE RETOUR L.-Brault